Jack Morehouse
July 1991

THE GRAND DESIGN

THE GRAND DESIGN

Selected Masonic Addresses and Papers of Wallace McLeod

". . . I make no doubt but we shall all unite in the grand design of being happy and of communicating happiness."—
William Preston, *Illustrations of Masonry* (second edition, 1775), page 126.

Published by ANCHOR COMMUNICATIONS
Highland Springs, Virginia
for
Iowa Research Lodge No. 2. Des Moines, Iowa

Published by
Anchor Communications
Highland Springs, Virginia 23075-0070

Library of Congress Cataloging-in-Publication Data

McLeod, Wallace, 1931–
    The grand design : selected Masonic addresses and papers of
Wallace McLeod.
        p. cm.
    Includes bibliographical references and index.
    ISBN 0–935633–10–3 : $17.95
    1. Freemasonry. 2. Freemasonry—History. 3. Freemasonry—United
States—History. I. Freemasons. Iowa Research Lodge, No. 2 (Des
Moines, Iowa) II. Title.
HS397.M38   1991
366′.1—dc20   91-14958
                                                                      CIP

Printed in the United States of America

FOREWORD

This is a book that had to be published! It brings under one cover the decades-long philosophical words of an outstanding teacher. It brings to life a philosophy that will be found nowhere else.

Students of Freemasonry, whether or not they are members of the Craft, deserve the perspective non-Americans have to share. *The Grand Design* gives us that perspective, and far more. It incorporates a point of view with which we can readily agree. It takes us to the dramatic vastness that is Freemasonry. It shows us how we can all "unite in the Grand Design of being happy and communicating happiness."

Many years ago I learned that each person is a product of his environment. We all see life through restricted windows. How narrow these windows are depends on many things, not the least of which are our teachers. Professor Wallace McLeod is certainly aware of this. The impressive list of those whom he credits with his success proves this.

Few Freemasons impressed me as quickly as did Wallace. In those early days it was evident his talent belonged to all of Freemasonry, not merely to his native country. Fortunately for the Masonic world he agreed to share his knowledge with the Craft in general. His genius was rapidly recognized.

He joined The Philalethes Society, a Masonic organization dedicated to communicating and sharing Masonic knowledge. In a short time he was elected a Fellow of the Society, and then an international officer. In 1992 he will become its President. He was chosen a member of the Society of Blue Friars, an organization of Masonic authors. In 1991 he became its Grand Abbot (presiding officer).

He is the only North American to have served the prestigious Quatuor Coronati Lodge No. 2076, London, England, as a Master. And he was one of the rare individuals chosen to present a Prestonian Lecture. What he had to say on both occasions will be found within the pages of this book.

Wallace continues to serve his Canadian Brethren through the Grand Lodge of Canada in the Province of Ontario.

Each chapter in *The Grand Design* is full of interest. His chapter on anti-Masonry will be quoted for decades to come. His treatise on the origin of Freemasonry is among the best to be found anywhere. His account of the *Old Charges* could have been written only by a student of the history of the Craft.

The proof of the excellence of the "taste" will be found in the reading. Read the book; digest the teachings. Learn from the master. Then build on his foundation.

If you will, you'll join with him in uniting in the Grand Design of being happy and communicating happiness.

Allen E. Roberts
Past President, Executive Secretary
The Philalethes Society

PREFACE

I am deeply honored that Anchor Communications has decided to publish this collection of my Masonic papers and addresses. I am particularly grateful that my friend Allen E. Roberts consented to edit the collection, and to write an introduction to it. I also must thank the Master, Wardens, and Fellows of Iowa Research Lodge No 2 for their encouragement during the early stages of this project.

Several strong arguments might well have been a deterrent. In the first place, I am a Canadian, and my Masonry has an unfamiliar bias. Secondly, I am interested in history, and historical papers can be dull. Their determination to go ahead, despite these difficulties, has won my admiration and gratitude.

The selection includes both written and oral papers. There is no particular unifying theme, unless it be that they are all written from the standpoint of a Craft Mason. They deal with various matters: the practical problems of writing for a Masonic audience; journalistic summaries of what is known about a particular subject; popular biographies of brethren who are for one reason or another important; and progress reports on more serious research. In all of them but one, footnotes have been ruthlessly suppressed.

An effort has been made to cut down repetition from one paper to another, but even so certain topics are raised more than once, such as the Old Charges of the British Masons, the evolution of the ritual, the introduction of the Craft to America, and the nature and significance of Masonic benevolence. In some quotations from old documents the spelling has been modernized. A few small errors in papers that had previously been published have been tacitly corrected.

I express my gratitude to those brethren who have acted as my hosts during speaking engagements in Canada, Great Britain, the United States of America; and to those who have helped me by providing information, and by other encouragement; particularly to the late Harry Carr, Secretary of Quatuor Coronati Lodge and editor of its *Transactions*; John M. Hamill, Librarian and Curator at Freemasons' Hall in London; Terence O. Haunch, the former Librarian and Curator; but as well to Keith Arrington, William K. Bailey, Cyril N. Batham, Charles W. Booth, Allan Boudreau, David C. Bradley, Frederic R. Branscombe, Francis J. Bruce, Robert J. Burns, Frank Collins, T. Richard Davies, Robert E. Davies, William C. Durow, Colin Dyer, Jennie Hall, Roberta Hankamer, Tom Harpur, Barrie S. Hayne, June Hewitt, Jay Macpherson, Jerry Marsengill, William J. Powers, Jr., R. Anthony K. Richards, Allen E. Roberts, Lawrence Runnalls, David Stevenson, Edward

Stolper, and Wendell K. Walker; and to the editors of the various publications in which some of these pieces first appeared, for permission to reprint them: to William R. Pellow, Grand Master, Robert E. Davies, Grand Secretary, and Eric W. Nancekivell, President of Masonic Holdings, all of the Grand Lodge of Canada in the Province of Ontario; to Robin L. Carr, President of the Masonic Book Club; to Charles R. Crisman, Secretary of Walter F. Meier Lodge of Research; to Neville Barker Cryer, Secretary of Quatuor Coronati Lodge, London, England; to Jerry Marsengill, Editor of the *Philalethes* magazine; to Jacob Pos, Editor of the *Proceedings* of the Heritage Lodge, Ontario; to N. R. Richards, President of the Masonic Foundation of Ontario; to Allen E. Roberts, Editor of *Transactions* of Virginia Research Lodge; to the editors and publishers of the *Canadian Historical Review*; and above all to Elizabeth, without whose forbearance and encouragement none of this would have been possible.

We can hardly expect to profit from Masonic education unless we enjoy the educational process. Over the years Freemasonry has brought me much joy, and research into its background has been a source of satisfaction. I only hope that those who turn these pages may learn something new, and that in so doing they will be able in some measure to share my happiness. What more could any educator ask?

Festival of the Four Crowned Martyrs, 1990,
Toronto, Canada.

Wallace McLeod.

APPRECIATION TO REPRINT IS GRATEFULLY ACKNOWLEDGED TO THE FOLLOWING:

1. **HOW TO WRITE A SHORT TALK.** Reprinted, with permission, from the Report of the Committee on Masonic Education, in the *Proceedings of the Grand Lodge A.F. & A.M. of Canada in the Province of Ontario*, 1979, pages 101–104.

2. **PREPARING A PAPER FOR PRESENTATION IN A RESEARCH LODGE.** Delivered before The Heritage Lodge, Cambridge, Ontario, 21 September 1983. Reprinted, with permission, from the *Proceedings of The Heritage Lodge, A.F. & A.M., No 730, G.R.C.* , volume 7 (1983–84), pages 4–19.

3. **HOW TO PRODUCE A BOOK FOR GRAND LODGE.** Reprinted, with permission, from the Report of the Special Committee on the History, *Proceedings of the Grand Lodge A.F. & A.M. of Canada in the Province of Ontario*, 1980, pages 152–154.

4. **THE ORIGIN OF FREEMASONRY AND THE EARLY YEARS OF THE BRITISH GRAND LODGES.** Reprinted, with permission, from W. McLeod (editor), *Beyond the Pillars: More Light on Freemasonry*, Hamilton (Ontario): Grand Lodge A.F. & A.M. of Canada in the Province of Ontario, 1973, pages 21–33.

5. **THE OLD CHARGES.** The full lecture is printed as a separate pamphlet under the title,*The Old Charges, with an Appendix Reconstituting the Standard Original: The Prestonian Lecture for 1986*; also published in *AQC* 99 (1986) 120–143; and in (Neville Barker Cryer, editor,) *The Collected Prestonian Lectures*, Volume 3: 1975–1987, London, 1988, pages 260–290.

6. **WHY I STILL BELIEVE IN THE TRANSITION THEORY: OPERATIVE TO SPECULATIVE.** Expanded from notes and comments printed in *AQC* 94 (1981) 38–39, 95 (1982) 160–162, and 99 (1986) 148–149.

7. **EARLY MASONRY IN AMERICA.** Reprinted, with permission, from W. McLeod (editor), *Whence Come We? Freemasonry in Ontario 1764–1980*, Hamilton (Ontario): Grand Lodge A.F. & A.M. of Canada in the Province of Ontario, 1980, pages 3–6, 11–12.

don (England). An abbreviated form of a paper that was printed in full in *AQC* 96 (1983) 1–35.

19. **MacLEOD MOORE AND PIKE**. Presented before the Spring Assembly of the Moore Sovereign Consistory, S.P.R.S., 32° A.A.S.R., Hamilton, Ontario, Canada, 6 May 1988. Reprinted, with permission, from *The Philalethes* 41.5 (October 1988) 4–6, 19.

20. **HIRAMIC MONOLOGUE**. Reprinted, with permission, from *The Philalethes* 37.4 (August 1984) 7.

SELECTED ABBREVIATIONS

A.F. & A.M.	Ancient Free and Accepted Masons
AQC	*Ars Quatuor Coronatorum: Transactions* of Quatuor Coronati Lodge, No 2076, London
c.	about
DCB	*Dictionary of Canadian Biography*
E.A.	Entered Apprentice
F. & A.M.	Free and Accepted Masons
F.C.	Fellowcraft
G.M.	Grand Master
G.R.C.	Grand Register of Canada
H.M.	His Majesty
H.R.H.	His Royal Highness
(M)	(Moderns)
MS	manuscript
M.W. Bro.	Most Worshipful Brother
P.G.L.	Provincial Grand Lodge
P.G.M.	Provincial Grand Master
R.W. Bro.	Right Worshipful Brother
S.G.W.	Senior Grand Warden
V.O.S.L.	Volume of the Sacred Law

TABLE OF CONTENTS

THE GRAND DESIGN

HOW TO WRITE A SHORT TALK

*[A Grand Lodge Education Committee is sometimes asked to pro-
vide material that can be presented ready-made in the lodges. On
one occasion the Chairman of such a Committee offered some
advice that was intended to help anyone to make up short educational talks.]*

THE METHOD

A number of brethren have appealed to us for five-minute talks that might
be presented in lodge. Of course we want to do everything in our power to
help, but we are not in a position to supply speeches in large quantities. One
of the purposes of this report however is to give advice. So we are going to
tell you how to write a short talk on some Masonic symbol. It takes a little
time, but there's no magic involved; you simply follow certain rules.

(1) Look around the lodge-room until some particular object claims your attention.

(2) Refer to a copy of The Work, to see how this object fits into our ritual.

(3) Consult a few standard books, to find out the background and interpretation:
my favorites are a good dictionary; *Beyond the Pillars*; *Mackey's Encyclo-
paedia of Freemasonry* or *Coil's Masonic Encyclopedia*; Harry Carr's *The
Freemason at Work*; Jones, *Freemasons' Guide and Compendium*; Knoop-
Jones-Hamer, *Early Masonic Catechisms*; and Glick's *Treasury of Masonic
Thought*. (It would be useful if every lodge had its own copy of these
books. . . .) As you read, keep some small sheets of paper beside you, and
make notes of anything that seems interesting.

(4) Now you've got your raw material, and you must put it in order. Make a
brief plan of your talk, under three or four headings. (The same plan will
serve for different talks.)
   (a) The connection of this symbol with operative Masonry.
   (b) Its historical background in speculative Masonry.
   (c) What it stands for.
   (d) Its moral lesson.
      Take your notes, and classify them according to these headings. Put
   them in order, and see how they fit together. You may have to try several
   different arrangements before you find the one that works best.

(5) Then write out your talk. Remember to keep your sentences short and easy
to follow. Try to combine information with inspiration. Give your facts, and
then give your brethren something to think about.

1

(6) Read over what you have written, to see how it sounds. You may find you will have to rewrite parts of it more than once.

Just to show how the plan works out in practice, your committee has prepared a sample talk, by following the rules.

AN EXAMPLE: THE ASHLARS

In the Junior Warden's Lecture, we are told that "The immovable Jewels are the Tracing Board, Rough Ashlar, and the Perfect Ashlar. . . . They are called immovable Jewels because they lie open in the Lodge for the brethren to moralize on." Two questions come to mind. In the first place, isn't it nonsense to call these large stones "Jewels"? And secondly, what moral lessons can we possibly draw from them?

The word "ashlar" is part of our heritage from the operative stonemasons of long ago. An ashlar wall is one which is composed of rectangular blocks laid in courses. An ashlar is a squared stone. A "rough ashlar" is the stone as it comes from the quarry, roughly hewn to its intended shape but not dressed smooth. A "perfect ashlar" is "perfect" in the sense of the Latin *perfectus,* that is, "brought to completion, finished."

We first meet the jewels in an early Masonic catechism from Scotland, dated 1696—twenty-one years before the formation of the Premier Grand Lodge. One of the questions runs as follows (if we may venture to correct obvious mistakes):

Q.: Are there any jewels in your lodge?

A.: Yes, three: perpend ashlar, a square pavement, and a broached ornel.

Though the names have changed, here we have the three jewels; and they have been together ever since. Their operative functions are defined for us as early as 1727. The pavement is "for the Master to draw his design upon." The ashlar is "for the Fellow Craft to try their Jewels on." The broached ornel is "for the Entered Apprentice to Work upon." We note that each of them is associated with a different degree.

The name "broached ornel" looks very odd, and demands a moment of our time. "Ornel" is "a kind of soft white building stone;" "broached" means "roughly shaped by a broaching axe." So the name really means "roughly squared stone." Such an unfamiliar term was liable to corruption; surprisingly enough, it still survives in our ritual. "The ornaments of a M.M.'s Lodge are the Porch, the Dormer, and the Square Pavement." The porch and dormer are strangely out of place in eastern architecture; and in fact, we are told, "porch, dormer," arose from a misunderstanding of "broach dornel," itself a debased form of "broached ornel."

The jewels are first called "Immovable" in 1727. If you visit a lodge in the United States, you will find that they are called "Movable," and that the term "Immovable Jewels" is there applied to the Square, Level, and Plumb Rule, "which are permanently appropriated to the East, West, and South." This change was made at the Baltimore Masonic Convention in 1843.

The great William Preston provides some guidance as to how we should moralize upon the ashlars. In his lectures he explains that, in a metaphorical sense, they are jewels of inestimable value, because of the moral tendency they display. The rough ashlar, he says, symbolizes the human mind in its original state, rude and uncultivated. The perfect ashlar represents the mind improved by culture and civilization, enjoying all the advantages that can be derived from study, example, and education.

We see then that the ashlars when taken together set before us a lesson which is expressed several times in the E.A. Degree. They provide a further example of progress, from darkness to light, from ignorance to knowledge, from wickedness to virtue, from fallibility towards perfection. They prefigure the raising of a superstructure, perfect in its parts and honorable to the builder. They exhort us, without neglecting the ordinary duties of our station, to consider ourselves called on to make a daily advancement in Masonic knowledge. They remind us of our duty to improve ourselves, and thereby to improve the world in which we live.

Do you wish the world were better?
    Let me tell you what to do.
Set a watch upon your actions,
    Keep them always straight and true.
Rid your mind of selfish motives,
    Let your thoughts be clean and high.
You can make a little Eden
    Of the sphere you occupy.

Do you wish the world were wiser?
    Well, suppose you make a start,
By accumulating wisdom
    In the scrapbook of your heart;
Do not waste one page on folly;
    Live to learn, and learn to live.
If you want to give men knowledge,
    You must get it, ere you give.

THE GRAND DESIGN

Do you wish the world were happy?
    Then remember day by day
Just to scatter seeds of kindness
    As you pass along the way.
For the pleasures of the many
    May ofttimes be traced to one,
As the hand that plants an acorn
    Shelters armies from the sun.

PREPARING A PAPER
FOR PRESENTATION IN A
RESEARCH LODGE

[Sometimes a research lodge has trouble persuading its members to give a talk in front of the lodge. Often this is because they have no idea how to prepare one. The Master of one such lodge thought it might be useful to have a set of practical instructions, step-by-step, on how to go about it.]

INTRODUCTION

If you have been following the advance notices of papers scheduled for presentation in The Heritage Lodge, you will recall that at one time you were looking forward to hearing more this evening about "The Old Charges." In the Spring of this year however your Master was talking to me, and he happened to remark that not too many of the Brethren were coming forward and volunteering to present papers. This is a trifle disquieting, because one of our stated aims is "to encourage participation . . . in the activities of the . . . lodge."

Here, it seems, we have a problem. Is there a solution? After we'd discussed it for a while, your Master asked me to come and talk to you about it this evening. That accounts for the change of topic.

There may be several reasons why you are not participating. Maybe you're not interested. If so, we can't help you. Maybe you're interested, but you don't have time. There's not too much we can do there, either. Maybe you're interested and have a bit of time, but you just don't know how to start. **That** gives us something to work with.

Some of us, I'm afraid, are under the impression that there's a kind of **magic** involved in preparing a paper, or that it makes impossible demands on your time, or that it requires tremendous talent and intensive training. It can do all these things, but **it doesn't have to**. The main purpose in presenting a paper to The Heritage Lodge, or to any lodge, or to any group, is to tell your audience something they don't already know, and to make them think that they **want** to know it. That's all there is to it. It's a simple rule that's been known for centuries. "To please and to instruct" was the way the ancient Romans put it.

FINDING A TOPIC

How do you find a subject that your audience doesn't know about? Here again it's not as hard as we sometimes imagine. Every one of us has a store of specialized knowledge, or a particular skill, and can do something, or talk about something that the rest of us can't. Perhaps it has to do with our work, or maybe it arises out of our reading, or perhaps it's connected with a place we've seen, or a person we've met. The point is that we do not all have identical memory-banks, we have each had unique experiences, and we all have something to say to our fellows that will interest them. It's just a case of finding something that will be appropriate to talk about in a Masonic lodge; and for that, you may have to do some research.

And **there's** another word that frightens many people: "research." It shouldn't, you know. It's not very different from the word "search." If you are **researching**, you are really just **searching**, just **looking** for something to say. If you want, you can draw a distinction between "original" research, that is, looking at original sources and documents that shed light on a particular question, and "secondary" research, that is, looking at what **other** people have written and published about the subject.

Often we think that only the first kind, the original research, is worth doing; but that's not true at all. Secondary research, our Senior Warden has told us (*Newsletter* of the Committee on Masonic Education, volume 1, No 3 [October 1981], page 28), "is more common, and it is not to be despised. What you find will not be new, but it may be new to you"—and, we may add, new to your friends and brethren as well.

Well, now, the first stage in your research, in your **looking**, is to look for a topic. Since we are talking primarily about preparing a paper for a Research Lodge, your topic will undoubtedly concern Masonry, and it will probably deal with our Masonic Heritage—what we have inherited from our predecessors. It may focus on the Craft of today, but it will set it against the perspective of the past.

In some sense then it will be a **historical** paper. If it discusses Masonic symbolism, it will show **how** our symbols evolved into their present significance. That is what Bro. Timothy H. Barnes did in his paper on "The Great Lights of Masonry," that appeared in the Lodge *Proceedings*, volume 4, No 3 (March 1981). If it concerns our Constitution, it will show how the legislation gradually developed over the years. That is what M.W.Bro. W. K. Bailey did when he discussed "The Constitution of Grand Lodge 1855–1979" (*Proceedings*, volume 2, No 6 [September 1979]).

The range of possible Masonic historical topics is practically endless. You could talk about some symbol, or about the constitution, yes. But consider some of the other possibilities:

Masonic postage stamps (Did Britain really issue a stamp with the square and compasses at the end of World War II? What famous Masons have appeared on Canadian stamps?)

Masonic music (What does Mozart's *The Magic Flute* have to do with the Craft? What can we learn about Sibelius's Masonic music?)

Masonic poems (Tell us about Robbie Burns. Who was Rob Morris, and why is he an honorary Past Deputy Grand Master of our jurisdiction?)

Masonic stories ("The Man who would be King," by Kipling. Are there any traces of the Craft in the stories of Sir Arthur Conan Doyle or Mark Twain?)

Masonic artifacts (A discussion of some old Tracing Boards in Ontario. What is the significance of the Master Mason's certificate?. . . .)

Relations with other Grand Lodges (Why does the United Grand Lodge of England not recognize the Grand Lodge of Japan? What is the Universal League of Freemasons?)

The relationship with the Roman Catholic Church. . . .

Anti-Masonry (It's still with us. I have a pamphlet called *Freemasonry—A Way of Salvation?*, by John Lawrence, published in 1982 as part of a conservative Anglican Pastoral Series. . . .)

Women and Masonry. . . .

Blacks and Masonry (Who was Prince Hall anyway? Is it just racial prejudice that keeps us from recognizing Prince Hall Masonry?).

It's just a case of sitting down, and learning something interesting that your brethren don't know that you can persuade them they want to know.

TAKING NOTES

Once you have your topic, how do you proceed? Well, you have to gather your information. Whether you are dealing with original research or secondary research, the method is the same. Read, read, read! If you are reading a lot, it's practically impossible to retain all the details in your memory, and so you will have to take notes.

Keep a lot of small pieces of paper at your side as you read, 3 " x 5 "cards, or 5 " x 7 " cards, and take notes. "Why use cards or little pieces of paper?" I hear someone ask. Well, you **could** do it all on large sheets, but you're not just planning to copy out a whole book in order. You will want to select and rearrange the facts. You could perfectly well reorganize the material on large pieces of paper, copying it over each time; but it's far easier to manage with the little ones.

If you are not already thoroughly familiar with the topic, a lot of your notes will be background material; but be careful to record anything that strikes you as particularly interesting. In general use your own words.

If you do quote directly from your source, make sure that the quotation is accurate, and enclose it within quotation marks. You should put only one fact on each card. Your notes should not consist of long excerpts, but should be simply an abbreviated summary, together with a heading and a page reference. The summary will recall the details to your mind, or if it doesn't, your page reference will let you look it up again. If you were collecting information about Simon McGillivray, for example, a typical entry on one of your cards might look like this.

SIMON McGILLIVRAY

CHARACTER: GENEROUS

—contributed his own money to the relief of Bro. Chris. Danby (of whom he did not approve).

Robertson, vol. 1, p. 1121.

ARRANGING THE NOTES

Then, when you think that you have a fair grasp of the material, and have amassed a lot of cards, you can start to sort them. If you've gathered your information from more than one source, you will find when you come to look at your cards that they are all mixed up. Sort through them once or twice, to remind yourself of what's on them. You will usually find that several of them can now be placed together. For example, suppose that you found two other cards like these:

SIMON McGILLIVRAY

CHARACTER: GENEROUS

—contributed his own money to pay off the debts of his lodge in England.

Robertson, vol. 2, p. 164.

SIMON McGILLIVRAY

CHARACTER: GENEROUS

—advanced his own money to pay off the debts of the Provincial Grand Lodge of Upper Canada, and was never repaid.

Robertson, vol. 2, p. 109; also p. 143, p. 151.

You will see that those three cards can be put together as striking testimony to Bro. McGillivray's generosity with his money.

There will be more than one possible way of arranging your cards; try various combinations until you find the one that seems best to you. If you are putting together a biography, one possible arrangement would be:

(1) outline of his life;

(2) Masonic activities;

(3) character;

(4) significance.

In any event, before you start to write you should make out a plan of the whole paper, in order to make sure that it is clearly organized. You may have to try more than one plan before you can actually start writing. Ideally, a paper should have a "thesis." That is, it should not simply recite the facts; it should attempt to **prove** something. That makes it more interesting. The thesis can be quite simple. "To demonstrate that Simon McGillivray was important in the history of Canadian Masonry" would be one way of dealing with a biography.

WRITING

Once you have your facts, and your outline, you can start to write. This is really where the hard work you've done begins to pay off. If your notes are thorough enough and if your plan is logical, you'll find that the essay will almost write itself. Use your own words as much as possible, and try to keep your style brisk and readable. Of course you will probably still have to write out the whole thing several times, because as you re-read it you will see changes that must be made. It is a good idea to write your first draft using only every other line of the paper, or even every third line. That way you will have lots of room to make some of the alterations, and perhaps save yourself the labor of copying out at least one draft. As you go, put the page-references to your sources in the margin or at the foot of the page. That way you will always be in a position to check the facts as need arises. Don't try to include everything you have found out. You will not be able to use all your cards. Some of them provide information that just doesn't fit into your essay plan.

If you're not in the habit of writing, it will be useful to consult someone—your long-suffering wife, or your son or daughter, or a friend—about such things as sentences and paragraphs. In fact it's a good idea to get someone to read your whole paper and criticize it.

One of the hardest things in the world is to accept constructive criticism readily; but it is one of the surest ways to improve a paper. It's a very good idea to put your paper away for a few days so that you aren't so close to it, and then come back to it and try to read it with a fresh eye, as if it were someone else's work. That way, you'll have a better chance of making sure that it is clear, logical, and interesting.

Your final version should be typewritten, on standard 8½" x 11" white bond paper. It should be double-spaced, or even triple-spaced, with wide margins at the top and bottom and on both sides. That will make it much easier for the Editor to deal with, and it will also be easier to deliver in Lodge. This final version should include your footnotes, or endnotes.

You don't have to document every statement you make, because much of what you say will be common knowledge. The notes will serve to give your authority for a particular statement that may be controversial or less well known, or to tell the source of a direct quotation, or to refer to fuller discussions of certain topics that you mention in passing.

Once you have finished your paper, be sure to keep an extra copy of it in a safe place, so that your work will not all be wasted if the mail should somehow go astray, or some other calamity occur.

A written paper is not quite the same thing as an orally delivered paper, and you will want to make certain small adjustments before you come to speak in Lodge. For one thing, in the spoken version you won't include the notes and references to particular pages, though you may well want to mention in general terms where you found most of your material. Likewise, if there is some detailed technical point debated in the paper, it may be preferable to curtail that part of the discussion.

Remember that your function is "to please" as well as "to instruct." It would no doubt be useful to tell you how to present a paper orally before Lodge, but that question would want a whole evening to itself, and I do not propose to address it on this occasion. Let me say simply that it can be a terrifying experience the first time you have to do it. But it is much easier if you have a written text in front of you to read from; that way, it doesn't matter quite so much if you get stage-fright and your mind "goes blank."

TOPICS TO START WITH

There are, as we have said, an almost infinite number of topics. But for the Masonic researcher who is just beginning, it's easy to choose a subject that is too big. Once we start working on it, we find that we have to keep reading more and more books, and taking more and more notes, and we never seem to reach the end. It gets very discouraging, and we may feel tempted to give up altogether. Some very good subjects are like that; the study of a single Masonic symbol would make a good paper, but it would take a lot of work, and it would be better to cut your teeth on something else first.

There are two types of topic in particular that commend themselves as suitable for beginners. They are lodge histories and biographies. Let us dilate on each. In general, a lodge will have all the material that is needed for the writing of its own history; this will involve the reading and digesting of the secretary's minute book, and any other relevant papers that are available. That is, it is primary or original research. If the lodge is one of the older ones there may be an overpowering mass of material; and you will always have the problem of deciding what to include and what to leave out.

A lodge history can be a fascinating document, or it can be mind-numbingly dull. It's up to the writer. A lot depends on the selection of detail. But since R.W.Bro. Charles F. Grimwood has given us a number of practical pointers in the booklet "The Lodge Historian," printed as the First Special Publication of The Heritage Lodge, this topic need not detain us any longer.

MASONIC BIOGRAPHIES

But the type of essay that is the easiest to do, and one of the most interesting, is biography. There are hundreds of famous Masons; it may be that they were not all famous for their Masonic activity, but they were famous for some reason, and they happen to have been Masons. Often books have been written about them that did not even mention Masonry. It would be quite acceptable in a Research Lodge to give a paper that tied both halves of their lives together.

Let me give you some examples. *Whence Come We?* [the official history of the Grand Lodge of Canada in the Province of Ontario] tells us on page 258, "Bishop William C. White . . ., the missionary who amassed the great Chinese collection in the Royal Ontario Museum, was Grand Chaplain in 1937." But Lewis C. Walmsley published a life of this man, under the title *Bishop in Honan* (University of Toronto Press). It would make a great paper to summarize Walmsley's book and to find out about White's Masonic career, and see if he did anything for Masonry. We note that *Whence Come We?* says (page 204) that he was responsible for the memorial service we still use. Most of this would "only" be secondary research, but it would still be most valuable. Really, it would be just a glorified book review, but there's nothing wrong with that! There are lots of other examples.

Let me quote from the report to Grand Lodge of the Library Committee for 1976. "Mary Beacock Fryer, *Loyalist Spy* (Besancourt Publishers, Brockville), is the gripping story of Captain John Walden Meyers, British courier in the American Revolution, and first Worshipful Master of Moira Lodge, No 11, Belleville.

Marjorie Wilkins Campbell's *Northwest to the Sea* (Clarke, Irwin) relates the adventures of William McGillivray, head of the fur-trading Nor' West Company and founder of Fort William; he was Provincial Grand Master of Montreal and William Henry at the same time that his brother Simon was Provincial Grand Master of Upper Canada. . . .

In Desmond Morton's *The Canadian General* (Hakkert), we read of Sir William Otter, who fought in the North West Rebellion, and led the Canadians in the Boer War; he was appointed Grand Steward in 1923. . . .

Watson Kirkconnell, member of Faithful Brethren, No 77, Lindsay, and sometime President of Acadia University, has written his memoirs under the title *A Slice of Canada* (University of Toronto Press)". . . . The Lodge would welcome a paper on any of these men.

If you are more venturesome, you could try a life of somebody whose biography has not yet been written. This would entail a bit more work, perhaps looking up obituary notices in the newspapers, or the like. A number of our Past Grand Masters would amply repay further study. I think in particular of Daniel Fraser Macwatt and Frederick Weir Harcourt, but there are others. There is just one request that I should make. The man whose life you write you should have done something of lasting importance either in Masonry or in the outside world (or both). It would be a waste of the lodge's time to present a life of someone who had contributed nothing to the world or to Masonry.

In *Whence Come We?* you will find nine brief biographies, which (I can say modestly) are models of their type; each one explains clearly why the man was important. Chapter Eighteen of the same book names more than a hundred famous Masons; virtually every one of them might justly claim our attention, and could well be the subject of an address to the Lodge.

If it turns out that you don't find enough information about your man to make a full paper, you could perfectly well treat several of them together. One could imagine a fascinating talk dealing with two or three newspapermen, or architects, or physicians, or railwaymen.

Well, once again, my advice to beginners in Masonic research is to begin with Lodge histories, or, even better, lives of Masons. My judgment is confirmed as I look at the publications of certain other lodges of research. In the *Transactions* of the American Lodge of Research, volume 14, for 1980, we find "An Historic Account of Freemasonry on Staten Island, N.Y. from about 1776 to 1981" (all in 9 pages); and we also find an article on "Daniel E. Lemm, Master Mason." It turns out that he was the cause of a dispute in the years 1888–1891 between New Jersey and New York about territorial jurisdiction.

In the *Bulletin* of the Illinois Lodge of Research, volume 2, No 3 (for July 1981), there are short lives of the First President of the University of Chicago, of the founder of the service club Lions International, and of the two doctors who first made extensive use of the medical preparation later patented under the name of Murine. All four were Masons.

Or again, in the *Transactions* of the Texas Lodge of Research, volume 17 (1981–1982), there is "A History of Kerrville Lodge No 697, A.F. & A.M.: The First Fifty Years." And there are five Masonic biographies: one of a Texas Mason who was hanged as a spy in the American Civil War, one of the first Mason in El Paso to preside over a Craft Lodge and a Royal Arch Chapter and a Knights Templar Commandery, one of the second Grand Secretary of the Grand Lodge of Texas, one of a millionaire from the early days of Dallas, and one of an early Methodist minister (written by his grandson). . . .

CONCLUSION

In this paper, we have tried to do several things. We've said repeatedly that a biography is the easiest kind of paper to write; . . . and we have outlined the mechanical steps that you need to follow in composing a paper. They are, in order:

(1) Find a topic;

(2) Read about it;

(3) Take notes as you read;

(4) Review your notes;

(5) Draw up a plan, and establish a thesis;

(6) Write a first draft;

(7) Revise your draft, and have it criticized;

(8) Write your final version.

That looks like a long list; but if you take it a step at a time, it becomes quite manageable. So now, the secret is a secret no longer. You all know how to write a paper for The Heritage Lodge. Go out there and get to work. We shall be waiting impatiently to hear the results of your researches.

HOW TO PRODUCE A BOOK FOR GRAND LODGE

[Often people will say, "You can't have a book that's any good if it's written by a committee." Well, that's not true. You can. The Grand Lodge of Canada in the Province of Ontario produced three excellent books that way. I know because I was the editor. But in order to do it you need to follow a strict set of rules. Here they are.]

THE SUBJECT

The subject is assigned or approved by the Grand Master, or Grand Lodge, who delegates responsibility to an individual author or editor.

THE COMMITTEE

If the book is to be written by more than one author, a committee is useful in order to distribute **(a)** labor; **(b)** responsibility (or guilt). The committee should be chosen by the editor. Its first duty is to set policy. It determines:

(a) the audience for whom the book is written;

(b) the approach and emphasis;

(c) the general contents;

(d) the detailed contents, with an estimate of the space available;

(e) the policy to be followed with the contributors; for example, they should be warned if their work is not to appear over their names, or if their words are likely to be tampered with;

(f) a list of potential contributors;

(g) a tentative schedule of successive stages in production;

(h) a tentative estimate of costs.

CONTRIBUTORS

The editor contacts the potential contributors, soliciting their assistance. He tells them:

(a.) the specific topic allotted them;

(b.) the amount of space allowed;

(c.) the deadline for submissions;

(d.) the policy laid down by the committee.

Not every contributor will meet the deadline. Send one or more reminders, if necessary extending the deadline. Not every contributor will meet the extended deadline. Ensure that those parts not submitted are prepared by an alternate.

EDITING

As the contributions are submitted they are read and criticized by members of the committee or by other critics. They may in some instances be returned to the original writer for revision. If the book is to have any sense of unity, every contribution will have to be rewritten to some degree in order to bring it into conformity with a uniform standard and to prevent excessive overlapping.

Some portions will want extensive review. This presumably is the work of the editor. After the text is revised and essentially complete, it is well to have it criticized, as a whole, for content and style by one or two skilled brethren. Have the manuscript retyped, to provide clean copy for the printer. Then comes the copy-editing, that is, marking the manuscript for the instruction of the printer, telling him what to set in smaller type, and so on.

INDEXING

Decide whether or not to include an index, which is toilsome to compile, expensive to print, and in many books seldom consulted. Is there to be a single comprehensive listing, or one or more partial ones (names, places, lodges, topics)? The easiest way to compile the index is to re-read the complete book, making entries as you go on 3″ x 5″ cards, and including the page numbers from the typescript. The page numbers of the book will be different and must be inserted before the index can be printed. It follows that the index cannot go to the printer until the page proofs are available.

ILLUSTRATIONS

If illustrations are to be included, look for suitable ones. Have photographs specially taken, or drawings specially made. If the illustrations come from a book or a special collection, obtain permission from the copyright holder. If the maps are to be specially drawn, discuss with the artist the information to be included.

PRINTING

Obtain quotations from more than one printer. Discuss with the printer the size of the potential run, the type of paper, the type of binding, the schedule of production. Submit the quotations for approval to the Grand Master (through the Grand Secretary), together with the Committee's recommendation as to which printer should be used. Ensure that the contract is signed before the date at which the quotation expires. Decide, in consultation with the printer, the style and size of type to be used, the stock, color, and design of the cover. Read three or more sets of proofs (galley-proofs, page proofs, revised page proofs). The Grand Master will determine the size of the run (i.e., the number of copies to be printed), after consultation with the committee and the financial officers of Grand Lodge. If the contributors are to receive special commemorative copies, arrange to have presentation certificates printed and signed, and to have the recipients' names imprinted on the covers.

PUBLICITY

Prepare brief news releases from time to time for publication in the [Grand Lodge] *Bulletin* or elsewhere. Prepare a longer publicity release and an order-form, to be sent to every Mason in the jurisdiction. The order form will have to include a pre-publication price, which should be set in consultation with the Committee on Audit and Finance. Discuss the details of the order-form, and its mailing, with the Grand Secretary, since his office will probably have to assume responsibility for this. Try to persuade the officers of Grand Lodge and the Members of the Board of General Purposes to play an active role in promoting sales.

MAILING

Arrange for mailing containers for the books. The printer may be willing to package them and mail them under a special mailing permit for bulk rate. Discuss with the Grand Secretary the typing of mailing labels and their delivery to the printer.

[*And that's all there is to it! Of course I did neglect to mention that it is helpful if the designated editor has a nasty disposition, and is prepared to be officious and overbearing when it is necessary.*]

THE ORIGIN OF FREEMASONRY, AND THE EARLY YEARS OF THE BRITISH GRAND LODGES

[A few years ago the Grand Lodge of Canada in the Province of Ontario decided to prepare a book that would give the young Mason a reliable introduction to the Craft. It included a brief summary of the early history of Freemasonry. None of the contributors was allowed to sign his name to his work; but after so many years I am prepared to take credit for the following chapter.]

INTRODUCTION

[The book in which this chapter originally appeared was issued by the Grand Lodge A.F. & A.M. of Canada in the Province of Ontario.] The words represented by the initials may seem like a riddle. Why Ancient? Why Free? Why Accepted? Why Masons? A partial explanation is offered by one of the charges in the *B[ook] of C[onstitution]:* "ancient, as having existed from time immemorial," that is, "from a time we cannot remember." But memories are short, and the thoughtful Mason may still wonder where the fraternity springs from, and how it got its peculiar name.

If one consults older histories of Freemasonry, he may read that the modern Craft is like a mighty river produced by the confluence of two separate streams. The source of one is found in the Roman Colleges of Artisans (*Collegia Artificum*) established by Numa, King of Rome from 715 to 673 B.C. They had several grades of membership, and various officers not unlike our Master and Wardens. Besides their industrial functions, they carried out certain religious observances.

As the Roman legions conquered Europe, the College of Builders went with them. Then, when barbarian invasions shattered the empire in the fifth century of our era, the mystic art lingered on in the Lombard community of Como, Italy, where it was nursed through the Dark Ages by the famous Comacine masters. When order finally returned after centuries of turmoil, the masters ventured forth from Como with the Pope's blessing as "traveling masons," and proceeded to fill Europe with majestic Gothic cathedrals. They implanted Masonry in England, and engendered the craft guilds, the eventual parents of Freemasonry.

At some stage in its long career, the builders' craft absorbed the tenets and methods of the ancient mystery religions. The latter, no matter where they were established, had certain moral and philosophical truths which they communicated to their initiates by means of symbols. At the center of their ritual was often a legend recounting how some hero or divinity was raised from the dead.

Such, in bare outline, is the history that has often been taught in the past. Now the truth of the matter is that there have been stonemasons all over the world from the dawn of time, even before the great pyramids of Egypt.

In like manner, from an early period there have been innumerable fellowships which have inculcated lessons of morality by means of allegory. In some sense both can be called forebears of Masonry, but no conclusive link has been traced. Indeed, one could argue that both types of institution are merely recurrent responses to permanent human needs, and that their resemblances to Masonry are purely fortuitous.

We can say with certainty that modern speculative lodges descend in unbroken line from British craft masons of six hundred years ago. Earlier than that we cannot go. That descent we propose to trace in the following pages.

In the course of its evolution, Masonry has passed through several stages. The sequence is clearest in the London Masons' Company, which goes back to 1376, and which gave rise to a "lodge" including non-operatives in 1682; and in the Lodge at Edinburgh (Mary's Chapel), No 1 in the Scottish Constitution, which has an unbroken run of minutes going back to 1599.

MASONS' GUILDS

In the Middle Ages any skilled trade or craft was known as a "mystery." This is not our word "mystery," meaning "a secret that is not to be revealed," which is connected with the Greek *myo,* "to keep mum." It is an English corruption of a totally different word, the Old French *mestier* (modern French *métier),* "a trade or occupation."

The so-called craft guilds (or gilds) began in England soon after A.D. 1100. They were associations of men who worked at a common trade, and were designed to protect their interests and to administer their own affairs. They served the public by ensuring good material and adequate workmanship. They excluded competition from migratory unskilled laborers. They set rules for apprentices, journeymen, and masters, settled disputes, and so on. In many ways the craft guilds prefigured the modern trades unions.

As time passed, their influence grew, and they were eventually recognized by the civic authorities. In London by 1319 each craft ran a "closed shop." All men of that craft within city limits were compelled to belong to the guild. They could not obtain the "freedom" of the city—the full rights of trade and industry—without being endorsed by a company of their peers.

Because the masons had fewer craftsmen than did many trades, and because not a few of them lived and worked outside the cities, they were slow to organize their own guild. In fact we have proof positive that there was no trade organization of masons in London before 1356. In that year a dispute broke out between "mason hewers" and "mason layers or setters," in the matter of defining what work a specialist was permitted to do. Men of both parties came before the city fathers and drew up a code of trade regulations. The preamble asserts that the masons' trade "has not been regulated in due manner by the government of folks of their trade, in such form as other trades." One provision of the new code settled the demarcation dispute by ruling that every man of the trade could do any work connected with it, provided that he was fully skilled in it.

By twenty years later, in 1376, the masons had won recognition as one of forty-seven "mysteries" in London. They were to elect four men of the trade to serve on the Common Council. This is the earliest British Masonic craft guild of which we have record. Not many others are known. In England they are mentioned at Norwich and Lincoln. In Edinburgh the masons and wrights petitioned the city jointly in 1475, and were granted self-government as an incorporation.

MASONS' LODGES

The guilds and incorporations were town bodies. There were also jobs for masons outside the towns, building castles, churches, or fortifications. If the site was isolated, the builders would have to live on location, sometimes for years on end.

In time the name "lodge" came to be applied to such a group of masons, probably from the lodge or hut in which the craftsmen worked, kept their tools, and rested. "Lodges" of masons are mentioned at York Minster in 1352, at Canterbury Cathedral in 1429, at the Church of St Nicholas, Aberdeen, in 1483, and at St Giles, Edinburgh, in 1491. When in due course the task was finished, the lodge would be disbanded, and its members would have to seek work elsewhere.

One may readily imagine how they would have modes of recognition to attest their status when they came to another lodge where they were not known. From these temporary lodges are derived the *Manuscript Constitutions* or *Old Charges,* a series of documents which contain among other things the rules of the Craft. They also include, somewhat unexpectedly, moral regulations . . ., reminders of religious duties, and instructions in good manners.

The *Old Charges* further give a history of the Craft drawn largely from the V.O.S.L., the only book ever seen by most people in the Middle Ages.

The term "lodge," which was originally restricted to impermanent non-urban bodies of masons, ultimately was extended to include "territorial" lodges in the cities. Their earliest mention is in Edinburgh in 1598. By then the lodge had already assumed certain duties formerly assigned to the incorporation.

THE OPERATIVE MASON OF THE LATER MIDDLE AGES

In the fourteenth and fifteenth centuries the official in charge of the technical side of a large building project was known as the Master Mason or Master of the Works. Usually he was the architect who designed the edifice. For this he had a "tracing board," which served as a drafting table. Most of his workmen were journeymen masons, who had given proof of their skill and had been certified as fellows of the craft. On large jobs there would be a few apprentice masons, learning the trade by working with the fellows. Normally they were engaged by the Master or by the institution that employed him. The journeymen themselves had too little job security, and not enough money, to maintain an apprentice.

In Scotland by 1598 a new stage had come into being, probably to restrict the number of fully qualified masons on the pay roll. A journeyman who had completed his apprenticeship was to serve a further term of from two to seven years, according to location, before he was admitted a fellow of the craft. In the meantime he was called an "entered apprentice."

In most localities there would also be men who had learned to build walls or dikes without being apprenticed to the trade or being admitted to a lodge. In Scotland a "dry-diker" was known as a "cowan," which is defined as "a mason without the word." The Schaw Statutes of 1598 ordered "that no Master nor Fellow of the Craft receive any Cowans to work in his society or company, nor send none of his servants to work with cowans."

In a matter of bread and butter, however, expediency could take precedence over doctrinaire principle. Cowans could be employed by Master Masons for any kind of work, provided that no regular craftsman could be found within fifteen miles. Originally the word was not necessarily derogatory. Today it means an impostor or eavesdropper who has not been regularly admitted to lodge. A Masonic catechism of 1730 asks, "If a cowan (or listener) is catched, how is he to be punished?" Answer, "To be placed under the eaves of the houses (in rainy weather) till the water runs in at his shoulders and out at his shoes" (*Early Masonic Catechisms*, p. 163).

Many sets of regulations survive which were laid down for the governance of operative masons by craft guilds, by incorporations, and by both non-permanent and territorial lodges. Certain clauses recur repeatedly in these codes, above all those which maintained the quality of the work and protected the rights of the employer. The term of apprenticeship was fixed, usually at seven years.

The competence of apprentices or other applicants for admission was to be supervised, tested, and certified. Masters were to respect the integrity of other Masters, and not take work over their heads, nor employ nor entice their workmen. Disputes between Masters and workmen were to be settled. Some rules were appropriate only to municipalities: the provision for periodic "searches," that is, inspections of work already completed; and trade restrictions on those who were not full fellows of the craft.

One rule, from the *Old Charges*, was applicable only to the transitory lodges; a traveling mason who arrived was either to be given work or, if that was not possible, money enough to see him to the next lodge.

As well as regulating the trade some of the masonic bodies also filled religious functions and collected funds for pious uses and for benevolence.

Throughout the whole period from 1376 to 1650 or even later, operative masons were known sometimes as freemasons. There is no clear distinction between "mason" and "freemason," and at times they clearly mean the same thing. The latter came to have certain distinct connotations. Originally it was simply an abbreviation of "freestone-mason," a mason who worked in freestone (a kind of English limestone). Later, after the name became established it was misunderstood. A freemason was thought of as "free" because he had the "freedom" (membership) of a company, guild, or lodge. Still later it was taken to mean a mason who was free by birth, that is, who was not a bondsman. Gradually the word came to be associated with non-operative masons. About 1655 it was dropped from the title of the London Company of Masons.

DECLINE OF OPERATIVE MASONRY

As we have seen, medieval masons' organizations exercised a restrictive trade control, partly to protect the brethren, but largely to serve the bosses. In order to enforce regulations they needed exclusive supremacy over all masons within their reach. So long as access to the area under jurisdiction of a guild could be controlled, its authority was unchallenged. Once the monopoly was cracked, it could no longer police the trade. In Scotland at least, the downfall of operative masonry came as the cities expanded and work became available outside the old city walls. Cowans or alien masons could now enter and be hired without let or hindrance.

Perhaps the last straw came with the Great Fire of London in 1666, and with a disastrous series of fires in Edinburgh culminating in 1674. A vast amount of stone rebuilding was required, too much by far for the local masons to undertake. Masons from elsewhere were encouraged to contribute their skills.

In 1667 the freedom of London was granted for seven years to anyone who could hold a hammer and nail. To those who completed the seven years the grant was extended for life. These benefits had formerly been available to craftsmen only through the guilds.

The Masons' Company had lost the chief incentive it formerly offered for new members, and its domination of the trade was effectually smashed. It could no longer finance its activities by admission fees alone, and it reverted to the old custom of collecting a "quarterage," a levy of sixpence per member every three months. Quarterages were continued by the premier Grand Lodge; hence derives our practice of submitting an annual return of members to Grand Lodge, together with a *per capita* appropriation.

Now that their original objectives were unattainable, the lodges had to find other ways to justify their continued existence. At first they became to a large extent benevolent societies. A preoccupation with the relief of distressed brethren begins to appear in masonic documents of the 1670s and 1680s. Once the aims were changed it became possible to have more than one lodge in a city, or even to hold lodges where there had not previously been a stonemasons' guild.

ACCEPTION OF NON-OPERATIVES

This decline of the guilds heralded another important innovation. By 1621 the London Masons' Company was using the words "making of Masons" in connection with men who had already reached the highest ranks of operative masonry. The company apparently had within it a more exclusive body which one could enter by paying a required fee and "being made a Mason." By 1631 it was "making Masons," or **accepting**, men who had no connection with the building trade. "Accepting" is used as a technical term, meaning "receiving non-operatives into the Craft." This particular segment of the company was at first called The Acception. By 1683 it was The Lodge. It had no function in regulating trade.

Elsewhere too we find non-operatives being accepted or adopted as masons. Often they were members of the upper classes. For them the rule fixing the term of an E.A. was suspended, so that they could be advanced to F.C. immediately. Otherwise the nature of the lodge remained unchanged for them. The earliest certain example of a non-operative mason is on June 8, 1600, when John Boswell, Laird of Auchinleck, attended the Lodge at Edinburgh.

[*This statement was taken from old sources, and is probably incorrect. The meeting took place not in the lodge's regular meeting place, but at Holyrood House, in the presence of the King's Master of Work, who presided. It was not a lodge meeting, but a trial of the Warden for some unspecified offense, and Boswell was probably present either as counsel for one of the parties or as the guest of the Master.*]

In July, 1634, the same Lodge admitted Lord Alexander of Menstrie, Viscount Canada, and two other noblemen as F.C. In 1646 the diaries of the antiquarian Elias Ashmole record how he was made a Mason at Warrington, in Lancashire. Other names can be cited, later than these, in both England and Scotland.

The reasons that led the gentry to interest themselves in an artisans' craft are obscure. It seems likely that the lodges benefited financially.

In Scotland higher fees were charged to gentlemen masons than to operatives. Men of distinction were perhaps encouraged to enter in order to promote contributions to charity. They may have consented for antiquarian reasons—curiosity about the history and mystery of cathedral building; or perhaps "the meetings of the lodge provided a convenient opportunity for that compound of refreshment, smoking and conversation, in circumstances of ease rather than elegance, and undisturbed by the society of women, in which many men can take a rational pleasure" (Knoop-Jones, *Genesis of Freemasonry*, p. 141).

In due course there came to be lodges in which the number of non-operatives outweighed the operatives. This was already the case at Ashmole's lodge at Warrington in 1646, at Chester about 1673, at Dublin in 1688, at Chichester in 1695, and at several locations in London and Yorkshire between 1693 and 1717.

THE PREMIER GRAND LODGE AND ITS IMITATORS

The stage was now set. The craft lodges were in eclipse, or were eking out a precarious existence, with the support of non-operatives, as social and charitable clubs. Against this background the first Grand Lodge came into being. Whether it was a symptom of the turning tide, or whether it caused it to turn, we cannot say. All that is really known is told in the oldest version of the story. Late in 1716, "the few lodges at London, finding themselves neglected by Sir Christopher Wren, thought fit to cement under a Grand Master, as the center of Union and Harmony, viz.: the lodges that met:

1. At the Goose and Gridiron Ale-House, in St Paul's Churchyard. [This lodge is still working, under the name of Antiquity, No 2, E.R.]

2. At the Crown Ale-house, in Parker's Lane, near Drury Lane. [It lapsed in 1736].

3. At the Apple-tree Tavern, in Charles Street, Covent Garden [now Fortitude and Old Cumberland, No 12, E.R.]

4. At the Rummer and Grapes Tavern, in Channel Row, Westminster [now Royal Somerset House and Inverness, No 4, E.R.

They, and some old brothers, met at the said Apple-tree Tavern. [This was late in 1716 or early in 1717.] And, having put into the chair the oldest Master Mason (now the Master of a Lodge), they constituted themselves a Grand Lodge *pro tempore*, in due form, and forthwith revived the Quarterly Communication of the officers of Lodges (called the Grand Lodge), resolved to hold the Annual Assembly and Feast, and then to choose a Grand Master from among themselves, till they should have the honor of a noble brother at their head.

Accordingly, on St John the Baptist's Day [June 24], in the third year of King George I, A.D. 1717, the assembly and feast of the Free and Accepted Masons was held at the aforesaid Goose and Gridiron Ale-House. Before dinner the oldest Master Mason (now the Master of a Lodge) in the chair proposed a list of proper candidates; and the brethren by a majority of hands elected Mr Anthony Sayer [about 1672–1742], Gentleman, Grand Master of Masons."

This date marks the formal beginning of modern Freemasonry. From the first meeting we derive our traditions of a regular Annual Communication to choose the officers, and of the Grand Master's Banquet. At this time the most distinguished brother was the Rev. Dr John Theophilus Desaguliers (1683–1744), a noted scientist. It has been surmised that he engineered the preliminary meeting of 1716/17. In 1719 he became the third Grand Master.

In 1721 the Order got its first noble Grand Master, John Montagu, 2nd Duke of Montagu (1690–1749). His tenure made membership in the Masons more fashionable. Ever since, the premier Grand Lodge has been headed by none but peers of the realm or princes of the blood royal. During Montagu's year in office the task of perusing, correcting, and digesting the "Old Gothic Constitutions" was assigned to a Presbyterian clergyman, the Rev. Dr James Anderson (1679–1739). Two years later he published his *Constitutions*, which contained a fanciful history of the Craft, a series of charges which are reprinted basically unaltered to this day, and thirty-nine articles to regulate lodges and Grand Lodge.

Anderson is sometimes charged with wholesale innovation, but surely the members of Grand Lodge would not have consented to radical departure from existing practice, or betrayal of their collective wishes. Among the ancient customs which are endorsed is the practice of charity "for the relief of indigent and decayed brethren."

The Old Charges had enjoined staunch devotion to the established church, and even after 1717 the ritual was resolutely Trinitarian. Thus, in a Masonic exposure published in London in 1724, we read, "How many lights? Three. . . . What do they represent? The three persons, Father, Son, and Holy Ghost" (*Early Masonic Catechisms*, p. 78).

Here Anderson's *Constitutions* did break new ground in leaving Masons' particular opinions to themselves, "by whatever Denominations or Persuasions they may be distinguished." One effect of this was seen in 1732, when the Master of a London lodge was Daniel Delvalle or Dalvalle, "an eminent Jew snuff merchant."

Even though the number of lodges increased rapidly, the Grand Lodge was confined to London for several years. There were certainly old lodges meeting outside London which did not place themselves under it. As late as November, 1723, the fifty-two constituent lodges were all situated within ten miles of Charing Cross. But once expansion began it was dramatically swift; by 1725 there were lodges at Bath, Bristol, Norwich, Chichester, and Chester.

At the same time English Freemasonry began to spread throughout Europe (lodges at Paris, 1725; Madrid and Gibraltar, 1728; The Hague, 1731; Bordeaux and Valenciennes, 1732; Florence and Hamburg, 1733), and even beyond (Calcutta, 1728; Boston, 1733). In 1735 the Grand Lodge first claimed jurisdiction over the whole of England.

The notion of a grand lodge seems to have been contagious, for in 1725 an old lodge in the city of York—independent of course of the London Grand Lodge—constituted itself as the "Grand Lodge of All England." (It was never a missionary lodge, and eventually withered away in 1792.) About the same year the Grand Lodge of Ireland was instituted. And in 1736 the Scottish lodges organized the Grand Lodge of Scotland. Both bodies were active far beyond the homeland.

In 1756 the Grand Lodge of Scotland founded lodges at Boston, Massachusetts, and Blandford, Virginia. In the following year Colonel John Young was named Provincial Grand Master over all the lodges in America under the Scottish Constitution.

The Grand Lodge of Ireland was less prompt to institute lodges overseas. The first warrant issued for America seems to have been to a lodge at New York in 1763. Long before this however lodges under the Irish Constitution had been active all over the world. These were the military lodges— regiments of the British army with traveling warrants. They were a peculiarly Irish development; though the other Grand Lodges eventually followed suit, most military warrants continued to be Irish. The earliest was issued in 1732, to the First British Regiment of Foot.

Back in England, in 1738, a second much expanded edition of Anderson's *Constitutions* was published. It is the source of the story of the formation of Grand Lodge quoted in a modernized form above.

RELATIONSHIP WITH THE ROMAN CATHOLIC CHURCH

When the Pope proclaims an official ruling which is binding on all Roman Catholics, his edict is called a Papal bull (from the Late Latin *bulla*, "a lead seal"). On the subject of Freemasonry, Pope Clement XII in 1738 issued a bull which is usually called by the title *In eminenti apostolatus specula* ("In the lofty watch-tower of apostleship"), from the Latin words which begin it. Under pain of excommunication it forbade all Catholics to join Freemasonry, or to do anything to help or encourage it.

The following reasons are given. (1) In lodges, "men who are attached to any form at all of religion or sect are associated together." (2) "Whatever goes on at their meetings, they are bound by a strict oath taken on the Bible, and by the accumulation of heavy penalties, to veil in inviolable silence." (3) Because of this secrecy, "they have aroused suspicions in the minds of the faithful, . . . and won the name of wickedness and perversion; if they were not doing wrong, they would not be afraid of the light." (4) Lodges inflict very serious injuries "not only upon the tranquillity of the temporal state, but even on the spiritual health of souls. . . . They pervert the hearts of the simple." (5) "For other just and reasonable causes known to us."

Terms of this bull were renewed, amplified, and confirmed by a number of subsequent Popes. The fullest exposition is in the encyclical letter *Humanum Genus* ("The Human Race") of Leo XIII, in 1884. He charges that Masons "deny that anything has been taught by God;" that they accept into their ranks men who deny the very existence of God, and the immortality of the soul; that they work officially against the Catholic church; that they teach that citizens may despise the authority of their rulers; and that they favor the designs of the communists.

Whatever was the target of Pope Leo's thunderbolts, it was clearly not Freemasonry as we know it. Actually some of his accusations are deserved by "irregular" or "Latin" masonry, which is practiced in a number of grand lodges of the French, Italian, Spanish, and Portuguese tongues. The encyclical tars "regular" or "English" masonry with the same brush.

The ban is still in effect against Masons and "other associations of the same type, which plot against the church or the lawful civil power" (*Code of Canon Law* of 1917, No 2335). The authority of the church has naturally fostered a venomous hostility towards Freemasonry on the part of many Catholics.

The lack of substance in the accusations has roused sorrow in the hearts of many Masons. No doubt some have tired of turning the other cheek, and have lashed out with equal intolerance. English Masonry's official response has always been, "Let a man's religion, or mode of worship, be what it may, he is not excluded from the Order, provided he believe in the Architect of Heaven and Earth. . . ."

Since the Second Vatican Council of 1962–65, a new spirit of ecumenism has been abroad in the Roman Catholic Church. There are encouraging signs of a softening in the traditional attitude to Freemasonry. Most tangible, several books sympathetic to "regular" Masonry, and drawing a clear distinction between it and "irregular" Masonry, have been published with the doctrinal sanction (*nihil obstat* and *imprimatur*) of the church: one by a Parisian lawyer, Alec Mellor, *Our Separated Brethren: The Freemasons* (published in French 1961 and in English 1964); and another by a Jesuit priest, a specialist in canon law, Father José Antonio Ferrer Benimeli, *Masonry since the Council* (in Spanish 1968).

[*The foregoing words were written in 1973, when the future looked bright for a civilized relationship between Freemasonry and the Catholic Church. Alas, things have not turned out so well. While the new Code of Canon Law does not mention Freemasonry by name, the ecclesiastical authorities have made it quite clear that the ban is still in effect.*]

SPECULATIVE MASONRY

In the phrase "speculative Masonry," the word "speculative" probably means "contemplative, reflective, thoughtful." Freemasons are thoughtful masons rather than operative ones. They contemplate the W[orking] T[ools] rather than employing them. They apply these tools to themselves rather than to the rude mass. That is, "speculative Masonry" refers to Masonry as a "system of morality veiled in allegory and illustrated by symbols."

"Non-operative" does not automatically connote "speculative." The lodges of acceptance in the seventeenth century were non-operative, but their primary activities seem to have been convivial and charitable. In like manner, it can be established that the ritual used in 1717 was almost entirely non-speculative. The actual term "speculative Mason" is first found in 1757. It seems likely that the emphasis on the philosophical side was brought in about 1730, after the evolution of the Third Degree. . . . Naturally this aspect was much enhanced about 1770, with the work of the three great expounders of the ritual.

THE "ANTIENTS"

Between 1723 and 1730 six exposés of Masonic ceremony were published, varying in detail and accuracy. The latest of them, Samuel Prichard's *Masonry Dissected*, was very reliable. Within a year it passed through four editions, making the ritual easily accessible to anyone who was interested. Enterprising charlatans began to initiate Masons for a much smaller fee than the duly constituted lodges required. Grand Lodge felt that the situation was getting out of control. At some time between 1730 and 1739 it arbitrarily interchanged the words of the first two degrees. [*Actually the change was somewhat more complicated than this.*] The thinking behind this was that news of the change would be passed on to the brethren by their lodges, whereas irregular Masons would at once betray themselves by their ignorance of the alteration.

The measure generated a good deal of bad feeling from brethren who felt that this was an unwarranted violation of ancient tradition. To add to the problem, soon afterwards the premier Grand Lodge was subjected to a sequence of indifferent or incompetent leaders, and a good many lodges were erased. Some independent lodges were still meeting by immemorial right, and others had been established by brethren who had come over from Ireland.

In 1751 six such groups formed themselves into the Grand Lodge of England according to the Old Institutions. They claimed to preserve the ancient practices pure and unsullied, whereas the premier Grand Lodge had introduced innovations. And so, by a masterful stroke of oneupmanship, they fastened upon the appellation of the "Antients" for themselves, and succeeded in affixing to the older body the name of "Moderns." From 1771, when the Duke of Atholl was elected Grand Master, the Antients were also known as "Atholl Masons." (Actually a Duke of Atholl headed the Antients from 1771 to 1774, from 1775 to 1781, and from 1791 to 1813.)

Among the accusations leveled at the Moderns by the Antients were the following: (1) interchanging the modes of recognition; (2) de-Christianizing the ritual; (3) preparing candidates improperly; (4) abbreviating or omitting lectures and ancient charges; (5) abbreviating or omitting the ceremony of installation; (6) placing officers incorrectly, and introducing variations in opening and closing the lodge. (Masonry of today is influenced by both sides. For example, from the Moderns is derived the acceptance into lodge of men who profess religions other than Christianity. The existence of the office of Deacon, on the other hand, was a hallmark of the Antients.) The Grand Lodges of Ireland and Scotland were much more sympathetic to the Antients than to the Moderns.

The real founder of the Antients was Laurence Dermott (1720–1791), who became Grand Secretary, and later Deputy Grand Master. It was he who in 1756 produced their book of constitutions, which bore the curious name of *Ahiman Rezon; or a Help to a Brother*. The first part of the title is apparently intended to be Hebrew, and is supposed to mean "Brother Secretary."

The Grand Lodge of the Moderns had fallen on evil days, as we have seen, partly because of a lack of vitality. It was largely revitalized through the agency of one remarkable man, Thomas Dunckerley (1724–1795), said to have been a bastard son of King George II. He was at different times Provincial Grand Master of eight counties, and he re-established Masonry in several counties of southern England where it had died out altogether. He worked hard to recruit converts from the Antients, and to make them feel at home.

Rivalry between the two English grand lodges was fierce. Both were active in the New World. The Antients issued a warrant to the Provincial Grand Lodge of Nova Scotia in 1758; the Moderns, apparently through the mediation of Dunckerley, to that of Quebec in 1760. The situation became very difficult. Attempts were made to effect a reconciliation, but the mechanical obstacles seemed to be insuperable. In 1809 a first step was made, when the Moderns rescinded the change they had made three-quarters of a century earlier in the modes of recognition. The same year they established a Lodge of Reconciliation, to study the differences between the practices followed by the two grand lodges, and to make recommendations.

Finally, in 1813 the Duke of Sussex, son of King George III, was chosen Grand Master of the Moderns. Later in the same year his older brother, the Duke of Kent, was chosen Grand Master of the Antients. The time was ripe, and the Royal brethren moved quickly to accomplish the reconciliation. On the Festival of Saint John the Evangelist, December 27, 1813, the two grand lodges amalgamated, to form "The United Grand Lodge of England"; the Duke of Sussex was elected as Grand Master on nomination of the Duke of Kent.

CONCLUSION

We have now traced the main developments in Freemasonry from its origin until the Union of 1813. Incidentally we have shed some light on those enigmatic words from which we set out, "Ancient Free and Accepted Masons." Of necessity our survey has been concerned chiefly with the British Isles. We have noted in passing how the four British grand lodges disseminated the Craft over the face of the whole globe. One particular region to which Freemasonry spread, North America, is of such concern to us that it merits special and more detailed treatment.

THE OLD CHARGES

[William Preston (lived 1742–1818) was a notable English Free-mason who did much to improve the wording of the Masonic cere-monies. Every year, in his memory, the United Grand Lodge of England names a Prestonian Lecturer, who is expected to speak on some topic of his own choosing. In 1986 this honor fell to me. What follows is a shortened "reading" version of the talk.]

"THE CHARGES OF A FREE-MASON"

The "Old Charges" have kindled the imagination of Freemasons for centuries, and hundreds of pages have been written about them. We might therefore imagine that the topic was by now exhausted. Even so, the younger brethren may need to be reminded of these remarkable relics, that are sometimes called the "Title Deeds" of the Craft. And who knows? Perhaps after all we shall be able to say something new about them.

Many jurisdictions have in their law-code or their Book of *Constitutions* a section entitled "The Charges of a Free-Mason." These pages occur in *The Book of Constitution* of the Grand Lodge under which I was initiated, and that is what got me started on this subject.

Thirty-five years ago, when I became a Mason, I read through these pages. Because they came near the beginning, it seemed natural to assume that they were important. Some parts sounded a little like the ritual. "The persons made masons or admitted members of a lodge must be good and true men, free-born, and of mature and discreet age and sound judgment, no bondmen, no women, no immoral or scandalous men, but of good report." "A man . . . is not excluded from the order, provided he believe in the glorious architect of heaven and earth."

Other parts seemed perfectly true, and beautifully expressed in the kind of English that we have forgotten how to write. "Masonry is the center of union between good men and true, and the happy means of conciliating friendship amongst those who must otherwise have remained at a perpetual distance." This much could be related to the Craft as I understood it, and it lent credence to the remainder.

I remember being upset when I was urged to stay for the festive board, because I felt I should go home and attend to my studies. Didn't my brethren know their Masonic law-code? There it was in black and white. "You may enjoy yourselves with innocent mirth, treating one another according to ability, but avoiding all excess, or forcing any brother to eat or drink beyond his

inclination, or hindering him from going when his occasions call him. . . ."
My occasions were calling me, and they were hindering me from going.

But what was one to make of other portions? "No master should take an apprentice unless he has sufficient employment for him." "The master, knowing himself to be able of cunning, shall undertake the lord's work as reasonably as possible, and truly dispend his goods as if they were his own; nor to give more wages to any brother or apprentice than he really may deserve." "All the tools used in working shall be approved by the grand lodge."

Such rules as these cannot apply in any literal sense to most of us. Why then are they printed in some jurisdictions for every Mason? The reason is historical. In its present form more than 99% of the wording goes back two hundred and fifty years.

This is not the occasion to rehearse the tale of how the Premier Grand Lodge of England was instituted on 24 June 1717; or to tell the full story of the learned but undisciplined Presbyterian clergyman, the Reverend James Anderson, late Grand Warden. We simply note that in 1723, Anderson, with the approval of the Grand Lodge, published the most influential work on Masonry ever printed, the first book of *The Constitutions of the Free-Masons*. Suffice it to say that he included a section entitled: "The Charges of a Free-Mason, extracted from The ancient Records of Lodges beyond Sea, and of those in *England*, *Scotland*, and *Ireland*, for the Use of the *Lodges* in London: to be read At the making of New Brethren, or when the Master shall order it." Apart from a dozen or so tiny changes, the modern wording is identical.

ANDERSON'S SOURCES FOR "THE CHARGES OF A FREE-MASON"

Where did Anderson find this material? The second edition of his *Constitutions*, printed in 1738, has a historical section that reveals a bit more. He reports that at the Annual Festival on 24 June 1718, when the Grand Lodge was one year old, the new Grand Master, George Payne, "desired any Brethren to bring to the Grand Lodge any old *Writings* and *Records* concerning *Masons* and *Masonry* in order the shew the Usages of antient Times; And this Year several old Copies of the *Gothic Constitutions* were produced and collated."

Even in those early days there were reticent Masons who did not choose to risk disclosure. In his narrative of 1720, Anderson says, "This Year, at some *private* Lodges, several very valuable *Manuscripts* . . . concerning the Fraternity, their Lodges, Regulations, Charges, Secrets, and Usages . . . were too hastily burnt by some scrupulous Brothers, that those Papers might not fall into strange Hands." Presumably these manuscripts so wantonly destroyed were copies of the old Gothic Constitutions.

The next year, at the Quarterly Communication in September 1721, the Grand Master, His Grace the Duke of Montagu, and the Grand Lodge, "finding Fault with all the Copies of the *Old Gothic Constitutions*, order'd Brother *James Anderson*, A.M., to digest the same in a new and better Method." The end result of these labors was the first book of *Constitutions*, which was duly approved by the Grand Lodge, and printed in 1723. Even as he asserted, James Anderson did make use of the old manuscripts which he termed "the Old Gothic Constitutions." We can tell from the wording of his text that by the time of his second edition, in 1738, he had obtained access to at least six of them, and that he quoted and paraphrased them quite extensively.

THE OLD CHARGES: NUMBER, DATE, LOCATION, FORM, NAMES, MASONIC AFFINITIES

What then are these Old Gothic Constitutions that were so highly regarded in the early days of the premier grand lodge? Today they are usually known as the "Old Charges" or "Old Manuscript Constitutions," and we know a fair bit about them. Despite the destruction wrought by zealous brethren in 1720, the texts of 113 copies of these Old Charges have come down to us, and there are references to fourteen more that are now lost.

Nearly two-thirds of them are earlier than the first Grand Lodge of 1717— perhaps as many as 75. Fifty-five go back before 1700. Four were written about 1600, one is dated Christmas Day 1583, one is about 1400 or 1410, and one goes all the way back to 1390.

Most are located in England; London alone has fifty-two. Eleven are in Scotland—none of them earlier than 1650; four are in the United States, in such old centers as Boston and Philadelphia; one was last heard of in Germany; and one has wandered to Canada—the Scarborough Manuscript of about 1700, which is kept in the offices of my mother Grand Lodge.

The Old Charges present various aspects. Some fourteen are known only from printed transcripts. A few are written on separate sheets of paper or vellum; about thirty-three are written on sheets that are fastened together in book form; but the typical form, represented by more than fifty versions, is a scroll or roll of paper or parchment, between three and fourteen inches wide, and anything up to fourteen and a half feet in length.

Their connection with operative lodges is guaranteed by the contents; but their association with speculative Freemasonry is also well attested. Nearly a quarter have been owned for over 200 years by private lodges in England or Scotland. Another 20 have some traceable connection with lodge meetings or lodge officers; for example, one, as we can tell by the handwriting, was copied by the man who was Clerk of the lodge at Edinburgh from 1675 to 1678; three are by the Clerk to the London Masons' Company at about the same date; another five are by the Secretary to Grand Lodge some fifty years later.

THE OLD CHARGES: CONTENTS

The strangest thing about these one hundred and thirteen texts is that they all say basically the same thing. If you think about it for a minute, you will see that the only possible explanation is that they are all related, and go back to a single original, now lost. Evidently it was edited and reedited dozens of times, and copied and recopied hundreds of times in the years between 1350 and 1717, all over England and Scotland. The versions that survive represent only a small fraction of the ones actually penned. The text is relatively short, and in its most common form runs to about 3500 words, that is, a bit more than half a page of a standard newspaper.

Let us summarize the contents, with a few typical examples of the wording.

They all begin with an Invocation: "The might of the Father of Heaven, with the wisdom of the glorious Son, through the grace and goodness of the Holy Ghost, that be three persons in one Godhead, be with us at our beginning, and give us grace so to govern us here in our living that we may come to His bliss that never shall have ending. Amen."

Then comes an announcement of the purpose and contents, followed by a brief description of the **Seven Liberal Arts or Sciences;** one of them is Geometry, or Masonry, **originally synonymous terms**. Then we have a proof of the fundamental nature of Geometry.

Then there is an extended Traditional History of Geometry, Masonry, and Architecture, taking up over half of the text. It is based in the first instance on the Bible, the only book that most people ever saw or heard of in the Middle Ages. The art of building was invented, we are told, before Noah's Flood, by Jabal; and metal-founding was discovered by his brother **Tubal-cain**. They knew that God would send destruction for sin, so they wrote their arts on **Two Great Pillars**, that were found after the Flood.

Then we hear about Nimrod, and the Tower of Babel; and how Abraham went to Egypt, and taught the Liberal Arts and Sciences to the Egyptians; and how he had a student Euclid (That's an incredible blunder! It brings together two men who lived 1600 years apart); and then how King David loved Masons well; how **Solomon** built the **Temple**, with the help of **King Hiram** and his Master Builder—whose name is not what we would expect.

One man who worked at Solomon's Temple later went to France, and taught the art to Charles Martel (Another howler! In real history **he** came 1700 years after Solomon); subsequently the Craft was brought to England, in the time of Saint Alban (a leap backwards of 500 years); and finally about the year 930, Prince Edwin called a great assembly of Masons in the city of York, and established the regulations used "from that day until this time."

Then we have the manner of taking the oath; usually, for some reason, given in Latin; a literal translation runs, "Then let one of the elders hold the Book, so that he or they may place their hands upon the Book, and then the rules ought to be read."

Next comes the admonition: "Every man that is a Mason take right good heed to these charges, if that you find yourselves guilty in any of these, that you may amend you against God. And especially ye that are to be charged, take good heed that ye may keep these charges, for it is a great peril for a man to foreswear himself upon a Book."

Next come the regulations or Charges proper. Some are to administer the trade: "No Master shall take upon him no lord's work, nor no other man's work, but that he know himself able and cunning to perform the same. . . ." "Also that no Master take no work but that he take it reasonably. . . ."

These are the ones that are still quoted almost *verbatim* in "The Charges of a Free-Mason." Others do not concern trade matters at all, but are intended to regulate behavior. No doubt they were essential in a community of tradesmen who were thrown together in close proximity for twenty-four hours a day. Still, they are unexpected, and serve to mark the masons' lodge as different from most other craft organizations. "Every Mason keep true counsel of lodge and of chamber. . . ." "And also that no Fellow slander another behind his back, to make him lose his good name or his worldly goods." "And that no Fellow go into the town in the night time there as is a lodge of Fellows, without a Fellow with him, that may bear him witness that he was in honest places." "And also that no Mason shall play at hazard or at dice."

Finally comes the Oath: "These charges that we have rehearsed, and all other that belong to Masonry, ye shall keep, so help you God and Halidom, and by this Book to your power. Amen."

THE OLD CHARGES: PURPOSE AND FUNCTION

This text, as we said, runs to some 3500 words. To write it out by hand represents a substantial investment of time and effort, and yet it was copied repeatedly. In the circumstances, it is fair to ask what the Old Charges were used for. To begin with, the rules and orders served a practical purpose. They clearly were intended to regulate the Craft. Twenty-five of the copies actually bear the heading "Constitutions;" two more are hand-written on extra sheets of paper bound in with the printed text of the *Constitutions;* four were written in lodge minute books, and one in the lodge's mark book.

We also know that occasionally they were treated like a Warrant of Constitution. The old Scottish lodge at Stirling had a copy of the Old Charges, written on a single sheet of parchment; it had been mounted and framed, and the members believed that their meetings would not be legal unless the manuscript was exhibited in the lodge room. Another text has the heading "The Mason Charter." In former days the Lodge of Hope, in Bradford, regarded its scroll as the authority for conferring the Mark Degree.

In a sense, the Old Charges also served as The Work, because they described certain procedures that were to be followed when any man was made a Mason, and they included little bits of ritual, such as the Invocation and the Obligation. It is clear that some of them were actually used at lodge meetings. One (the one in Canada) bears an endorsement, describing a gathering at Scarborough in Yorkshire, in 1705. Yet another, dated 1693, includes a list of the members of the lodge.

We see then that they provided **ordinance, authority**, and **ritual**, three practical matters. But as well they must have had a psychological effect. They inculcated in masons a sense of respect and reverence for their craft. They told how it went back to antediluvian times, how it was connected with famous buildings in the Sacred Writings, and how it could number among its votaries even monarchs themselves. This was no servile trade of recent devising, but an ancient and honorable institution.

TEXTUAL CRITICISM AND ITS ROLE

The next question is, what do you do with 113 texts, all nearly identical? Do you copy out each of them as accurately as you can, and then publish your transcription? Well, you may. In fact, this is what has been done with the Old Charges. Exactly one hundred of them have been published. But there is another way of approaching them, and that requires a digression.

The craft of printing from movable type reached Europe at some time about 1450. Before that date, all literary works, all legal documents, all political propaganda, had to be transcribed by hand. Copies were few in number, and no two were identical. Each one was unique, laboriously written one at a time by an individual scribe. If you have ever had to copy out an extensive text, you will realize that mistakes were inevitable.

So far as books by ancient authors are concerned, someone has said that the transmitted text "in physical terms means a monk whose knowledge of Latin hovers between insufficient and non-existent, copying in a bad light from a manuscript in an unfamiliar hand, feeling miserably cold and looking forward to his dinner." No doubt much the same could be said of those who copied out the words of the Old Charges.

The introduction of the printing press had two wonderful effects. It meant that a large number of identical copies could be made. And it introduced a standard of accuracy previously undreamt of. Before publication the editor now could read proof and correct his type as often as he wanted. When we come to consider literary works written since 1500, we can normally assume that almost every word of the printed page accurately reflects the intent of the author.

For older works the case is far otherwise. We do not in most instances have the author's own handwritten text. What we do have are transcripts, at an unknown number of removes. Sometimes there are a very few copies, or even only one (for example, the Anglo-Saxon poem *Beowulf*). At other times a great many copies exist (thus, *The Bible*). In either event, if we want to recover the author's actual words, we cannot simply transcribe the text of a single manuscript, for, as we have seen, scribes are prone to error. We must make use of a discipline known as "Textual Criticism." "The business of textual criticism" in the words of one authority, "is to produce a text as close as possible to the original."

An example or two may serve to establish the utility of the process. In the Greek text of the Old Testament, in the Book of *Ecclesiastes*, some manuscripts read, "or the pitcher be broken at the fountain" (*epi tēn pēgēn*), but Tischendorf's great *Codex Sinaiticus* has "or the pitcher be broken on the ground" (*epi tēn gēn*). When we print our authoritative text, how do we choose between them? Or to take another example, in Chaucer's *Troilus and Cressida*, Book 1, line 949, some versions have, "The rose waxeth swoote and smothe and softe." Others have, "The lilie wexith white, smothe and soft." Presumably **both** cannot be correct. We must choose. But on what basis?

Or again, consider Shakespeare's *Richard III;* towards the end of Act 4, when William Catesby enters with news of the fugitive traitor, the first Quarto edition of 1597 has him announce:

> My liege, the Duke of Buckingham is taken,
> That's the best newes; that the
> Earle of Richmond
> Is with a mightie power landed at Milford,
> Is colder tidings, yet they must be told.

An edition published in London in 1700 lets Catesby say,

> "My liege, the Duke of Buckingham is taken,"

and then has Richard interrupt him with the words,

> "Off with his head. So much for Buckingham."

A very good line! So good in fact that Sir Laurence Olivier kept it in his film version of the play! But how do we decide whether it really belongs there?

A century and a half ago it was the rule to count the manuscripts and trust the majority. But now we know that manuscripts must be weighed, not counted, and one good one outweighs forty bad ones. Should we then follow the best one, correcting it here and there from other sources when it falls into manifest error?

This procedure attracted the scorn of one of the masters of invective, who commented as follows. "To believe that wherever a best MS gives possible readings it gives true readings, and that only when it gives impossible readings does it give false readings, is to believe that an incompetent editor is the darling of Providence, which has given its angels charge over him lest at any time his sloth and folly should produce their natural results and incur their appropriate penalty. Chance and the common course of nature will not bring it to pass that the readings of a MS are right wherever they are possible and impossible wherever they are wrong: that needs divine intervention; and when one considers the history of man and the spectacle of the universe I hope one may say without impiety that divine intervention might have been better employed elsewhere. How the world is managed, and why it was created, I cannot tell; but it is no feather-bed for the repose of sluggards." Clearly we don't dare move in that direction!

Well, then, we can guess, on the strength of our understanding of the author's practice, or the sense demanded by the context. If we are well-trained and sensible, we shall be right some of the time.

But there is another way, which minimizes the guesswork. It involves determining the family relationships of the various manuscripts, and then inferring what must have stood in the ancestor of all the extant versions. That is the way in which the text of ancient authors is normally recovered. That is "textual criticism." Though many of the manuscripts of the Old Charges postdate the introduction of printing, they behave much like earlier manuscripts, and they may be approached in exactly the same way.

THE FAMILIES OF THE OLD CHARGES

The manuscripts of the Old Charges exhibit a basic similarity, but they fall readily into "families," each of which displays a large measure of textual uniformity. This classification was first worked out by the great Masonic scholar Dr Wilhelm Begemann in 1888. There are eight families.

Actually, apart from one copy which is in a class by itself, the families fall into two great groups. One (which has nine descendants) clearly stems from an original composed before 1400; it was wordy, repetitive, and slow-moving, like so many other works composed in the Middle Ages. At some date in the sixteenth century it was completely revised; a lot of the excess verbiage was pruned away, and the whole thing was made much crisper and easier to read. This new text, which is called the "Standard Original" Version, does not survive, but was the ancestor of 95 copies.

What needs to be done is to recover the original text of the "Medieval" version and of the "Standard Original." This can be accomplished with a fair measure of certainty. The Medieval Version is not hard to reconstruct. The Standard Original is somewhat more laborious, but in an Appendix to the printed version of this paper, we present a tentative text of it. Before we turn to consider it, we may appropriately explain how it was reconstructed.

WORKING OUT THE RELATIONSHIPS

First we must work out some of the relationships of the various copies. We do this by making detailed comparisons of the readings of individual passages. We take a portion of the text in which we are reasonably sure what the original said, and then we note which manuscripts diverge from it. We shall generally find that a certain group of texts will share a whole series of these new readings, and we may safely assume that they are all descended from a common ancestor. Sometimes the new reading will arise from a misunderstanding; sometimes it will be a modernization of an old word; sometimes it will be an expansion of the text, or an abbreviation of it. A few examples will make the process clear.

At the very beginning of the text, the Invocation starts off, "The might of the Father of Heaven." Apparently in one copy the first three words were illegible or torn away, and the transcriber filled in the gap by writing in their place, "*O Lord God* the Father of Heaven." There are eight descendants, all in the Tew Family.

When the author is talking of Egypt in the time of Abraham, he says: "And in his days it befell that the lords and estates of the realm had so many sons that they had gotten, some by their wives and some by other ladies of the realm, for that land is a hot land, and plenteous of generation." Someone had trouble with the writing, and converted the passage into nonsense: "for that land is a holy land and plenished generation." Fifteen manuscripts have this or something like it. They belong to the Sloane Family.

By proceeding in this fashion, it is possible eventually to draw up a full table of the relationships of all the manuscripts in the branch. Then we can use the table to reconstruct the ancestors of each of the branches. From them, we can recover the progenitor of the family, and then the Standard Original.

SCRIBAL PERSONALITIES

As we work through the individual copies, we find that each writer has his own personality, and some of them are quite strongly marked. Most of them try conscientiously to copy exactly what is before them. If the words they imagine they see don't make sense, well, so be it! They still transcribe them. Thus, in one passage, the writer of the Embleton Manuscript read "craft" as "ghost" ("Our purpose is to tell you how . . . this worthy GHOST of Masonry was begun"). The Phillipps Manuscript No 3 has "nurses" instead of "nuncheons" ("Saint Alban . . . gave them two shillings sixpence a week and threepence to their NURSES"). And three members of the Hope Branch transcribed "stones" as "sconder" or "scounder" ("if he have no SCONDER for him, he shall refresh him with money"). Some of these corruptions would be utterly unintelligible if we did not have other texts to provide the correct reading.

Unfamiliar names are particularly vulnerable, and so frequently we meet such monstrosities as "Harmonise" instead of "Hermarines;" "Mirth" for "Nimrod;" "Nimmorah" for "Nineveh;" "Fireland" for "Jerusalem;" "Brenithmen" for "Frenchmen;" and "Hoderine" in place of "Edwin."

Some scribes, if they come to a passage they could not read at all, would leave a space just the right length. Thus, the writer of the Antiquity Manuscript could not decipher the word "pagan," and left a blank ("In his days the King of England . . . was a [BLANK]"). Of course, if in turn a later copy is made, then sometimes the blank is closed up, or filled in by guesswork, and we lose all indication that anything is awry. So two younger relatives of the Antiquity Manuscript filled in the gap for the word "pagan" by guessing "mason."

Occasionally we encounter somebody with a bit of initiative, someone who is not afraid to rewrite a phrase or two in the interest of clarity, or what he takes to be clarity.

From time to time a studious type intervenes. A few of them made a habit of checking assertions against their Bible, and sometimes they would substitute a scriptural quotation for the original version. Thus, the original told how Tubal-cain "found smith's craft, of gold, silver, copper, iron and steel." One group of copies carries instead the statement that Tubal-cain was the "instructor of every artificer in brass and iron"—words which come from *Genesis* 4:22.

THE RECONSTITUTED TEXT

The text that we finally recover does not hold any real surprises. It is close in wording to many of its offspring, though it does not coincide with any of them. It is certainly more authoritative and readable than its earliest surviving descendant, the Grand Lodge Manuscript No 1. In hundreds of places the readings differ. In most, to be sure, the difference is not substantive; but in several dozen there is a real distinction.

The exact date of the Standard Original is uncertain, but we can determine the limits within which it was composed. The extreme limits are 1470 and 1560. Perhaps Poole's pronouncement, "some such date as 1520–40," is as good as any.

The text has a distinct flavor of Middle English. Words that were current 450 years ago, but are now obsolete or changed in meaning, occur regularly: "land of behest" (meaning land of promise); "clerk" (for scholar); "made a cry" (for made a proclamation); "cunning" (for skillful); "hight" (for called); "journey" (for day's work); "mete" (for measure); "nuncheons" (for light refreshments); "travel" (for exertion); "tree" (for timber); and so on.

WHY BOTHER?

Perhaps at this juncture I hear someone say, "Why bother?" Why go to the effort of reconstructing a lost manuscript? There are many reasons that make it worthwhile. Not least is the sheer intellectual satisfaction of bringing order out of chaos. There are practical benefits as well. If you are concerned with the contents of the Old Charges, the material you need to consider is reduced to manageable bulk.

Now, instead of arguing about which one of the 113 variant readings we should follow, we have a single text. Let us take a passage with a wide range of variants. In one portion of the traditional history we are told that St Alban raised the wages of masons from a penny a day, and made it right good. But what did he raise it to? Some versions say two shillings a week, others two and six, yet others three, or three and six, or even four or four and six.

What was the original figure? Textual criticism enables us to say that the Standard Original and the Medieval Original both had two shillings and six-pence. It is at least possible that this figure may have some implications for dating the original composition of the Medieval Version. If it represents the actual wage that was then current, it points to the mid-fourteenth century. The average pay for masons was fivepence a day (or 2 / 6 a week) at Oxford during the years between 1351 and 1360. On other grounds the date of this early version had been set between 1350 and 1390.

Or again, consider the name of the architect of Solomon's Temple. In modern Masonry of course he is called Hiram Abif, a form which goes back ultimately to the Bible. You will see it hinted from time to time that the name of Hiram was a Masonic secret, transmitted by word of mouth through the middle ages, while written texts carried instead the "substitute name"

Aymon; this (we are told) is a corruption of the Hebrew word meaning "master workman."

In two texts the architect is called "Apleo," which (we are assured) is another Hebrew "substitute name," meaning "the secret." Speaking for myself, I do not believe **any** of this. Aymon, or more probably Aynon, was certainly the form in the Standard Original. Where other names appear instead, they arise from one of two causes. One is a simple misunderstanding, of the sort that we have noted elsewhere. Aymō (in which the suprascript stroke represents a final N) as written in a script of about 1600 could easily have been misread as Apleo. The second is conscious correction.

The name Hiram begins to appear about 1675, and it occurs in eighteen copies. And we can **prove** that in each of these texts the new name was introduced by one of those scribes who consulted their Bibles, and found the name Hiram there; we can prove it because **without exception** he gives a Biblical reference or allusion. Probably in at least some of these instances he checked his Bible because the name in front of him was illegible or unfamiliar. In short, there is no evidence for any "secret doctrine" here.

DIVIDENDS

There are occasional dividends that arise out of our study. As you browse among the Old Charges, from time to time you find little extra bits added in a single copy, or a set of manuscripts. Sixteen versions have a further body of regulations, apparently added about 1650, headed "The Apprentice Charge," including: "And that he shall not purloin nor steal the goods of his master or dame, nor absent himself from their service, nor go from them about his own pleasure by day or by night without license of one of them." This is clearly operative.

Another special group of rules, called "The New Articles," is found in four members of the Roberts Family. They are said to have been adopted in 1663. They include: "That no person shall be accepted a free mason unless he be one and twenty years old or more." This probably concerns the non-operative Craft.

There are scriptural tags that allude to the craft of building, and to craftsmen, to the works and wisdom of God, and to the raging of the heathen (this last in Hebrew); there are citations of the traditional verses that commence, "In the beginning" (both *Genesis* 1:1 and *John* 1:1). There are texts on scorning the profane, and on the virtues of the mathematical sciences (in both Latin and Greek). There are notes on the size of the stones in Solomon's Temple; on the date at which the Company of Masons was incorporated.

There are sometimes brief hints of ritual or procedure beyond what we already know. The Dumfries Manuscript No 4, of about 1710, has a whole series of questions and answers, of the sort that we know were used in early lodges ("Where lies the key of your lodge? In a bone box . . ."). The Carmick Manuscript of 1727 has a drawing of the lodge. It is triangular in shape; at the corners are placed the Master, the Warden, and the Fellowcraft; the Entered Apprentice is set to the Master's left; in the body of the lodge are drawn a mosaic pavement, the square and compasses, a plumb-rule, a hammer, a trowel, a mariner's compass, and two great pillars.

Six manuscripts have an oath of secrecy, that must go back at least to 1650. "These charges which we now rehearse to you, and all other the charges, secrets, and mysteries belonging to Free Masonry, you shall faithfully and truly keep, together with the counsel of this lodge or chamber. You shall not, for any gift, bribe or reward, favor or affection, directly or indirectly, for any cause whatsoever divulge or disclose the same to either father or mother, sister or brother, wife, child, friend, relation or stranger, or any other person whatsoever, so help you God, your Halidom, and the contents of this Book."

RETROSPECT AND PROSPECT

That perhaps is almost enough for us to say today. In this paper I have tried to do several things: first, to introduce you to the *Old Charges*; second, to explain how we can work out the relationships of the various copies; third, to recover a text which is older than any surviving copies; fourth, to argue that this is worth doing.

Incidentally, I hope that you have learned a bit more about the men who wrote our manuscripts. We have seen the constant tension between fidelity and utility. Some scribes regarded the texts they were copying almost as sacred relics; they transcribed what was before them with as much accuracy as they could muster, even when it had gaps in the text, or did not make sense. Others treated the *Old Charges* as working documents, which had to be intelligible; they modernized the language, filled the gaps, corrected the errors. But most of their alterations were casual surface changes, and had little fundamental effect on the contents.

What now remains to be done? Well, we can attempt to improve the text of the Standard Original Version. We can continue to study the text in detail, and see what it tells us about the Craft in the first half of the sixteenth century—a period from which this sort of evidence has hitherto been lacking. We can set out the evidence for the affinities of the various families of the Old Charges; then it will be easy to describe the peculiarities of each new descendant, and to set forth its relationships. And we can proceed to trace the paths by which this text spread across England and even into Scotland.

CONCLUSION

There is one other class of dividend that I neglected to mention in its proper place, and it might be an appropriate note on which to close. From time to time the manuscripts include poems or songs about the Craft. As the great Carl Claudy observed, there are not many Masonic poems that "satisfy the critical ear as well as the loving heart." To be at once "metrical, poetic and Masonic" is a rare gift. In some specimens of doggerel we can derive a perverse sort of delight from the combination of banal sentiment and bold assonance. (Bold assonance! That's what they say now when they mean "bad rhyme.") I think of Rob Morris's lines, written in 1854.

We could compile an anthology of such things from the *Old Charges*. Let me give you an example or two. From the *Newcastle College Manuscript*, of before 1750:

> Come all you Masons, hear what I do say.
> Here is a strict account for you this day. . . .
> If that a mason or brother some relief do crave,
> Do not requite him like unto a slave.
> You know that charge that we have heard all over,
> That we must be kind the one unto the other.

From the *Woodcock Manuscript*, of before 1740:

> To our Lodge we invite
> Lords, Gentlemen, and Knights.
> None of any low degree are admitted.
> We think it no disgrace
> To go to such a place,
> Where kings and volunteers may be lifted.

From the *Dumfries Manuscript No 2*, of before 1700:

> Masters kind,
> Prove true in mind;
> I pray you, love your fellow well.
> And Brothers, then
> Prove true again.
> This day your Craft all crafts excelled.

But besides all the bad verses, there are a couple of nice pieces that say something worthwhile. There is one entitled "The Prophecy of Brother Roger Bacon," which comments pungently on the political situation of Europe in 1713, and reveals something of the ritual of the time. But of them all, my favorite is a bit of verse copied at the beginning of three texts of the Old Charges. It's hardly great poetry, but it is technically competent, and it carries a certain intellectual and emotional freight. It alludes to the traditional history of the Craft, and reminds us that monarchs themselves have been promoters of the art. It's very early, not too far from 1600, but despite the date it expresses an affection for the fraternity that sounds strangely modern. It is an acrostic; that is, if you take the first letter of each line in order, they spell a word: M A S O N R I E.

> **M**uch might be said of the noble art,
> **A** craft that's worth esteeming in each part.
> **S** undry nations' nobles, and their kings also—
> **O** h, how they sought its worth to know!
> **N** imrod, and Solomon the wisest of all men,
> **R** eason saw to love this science then.
> **I** 'll say no more, lest by my shallow verses I,
> **E** ndeavoring to praise, should blemish Masonrie.

WHY I STILL BELIEVE IN THE TRANSITION THEORY: OPERATIVE TO SPECULATIVE

[In recent years a new theory about the origins of modern specu-
lative Freemasonry has come into fashion. Several of its strongest
supporters are my friends and colleagues from Quatuor Coronati
Lodge. In this matter I think that they are wrong, and that the
older view still provides a better explanation of the evidence. The
following pages attempt to explain why.]

THE PROBLEM

The traditional view, ever since the time of Anderson's *Constitutions* of 1723, has been that in some way the modern speculative Freemasons are the successors of the English operative stonemasons of the Middle Ages, and that they hardly existed before the year 1717. You will find this idea set forth more than once in the pages of this book.

A few years ago some of the evidence began to be interpreted in a different way. "In England . . . in the 17th century . . . lodges began to appear which from their inception were independent of the mason trade" (Eric Ward, *AQC* 91 [1978] 81).

This new speculative Masonry "may first have been devised as a cover for conspiratorial meetings of Royalist groups" (F. W. Seal-Coon, *AQC* 92 [1979] 200). "Records which . . . relate to speculative Masonry . . . date from before 1600" (Colin Dyer, *AQC* 95 [1982] 120). "By the 1600s the guild system . . . was virtually moribund. . . . Accepted masonry . . . simply seems to have appeared in England as a new organization without any prior connections with the operative craft" (John Hamill, *The Craft*, Wellingborough, Northamptonshire, 1986, page 19).

THE SO-CALLED GAP FROM ABOUT 1400 to 1583

I still subscribe to the outmoded view that speculative Freemasonry "descends" from operative stonemasonry. I am pushed in this direction by certain questions that arise out of the evidence. One of the points that is regularly noted in support of the new theory is that no copies of the Old Charges survive from the period between the two oldest versions, the *Regius* and *Cooke Manuscripts* (conventionally abbreviated **A** and **B.1**; both written in the years around 1400) and the *Grand Lodge Manuscript No 1* (**D.a.1**, of

1583). This seems at first blush to argue against the notion that the older and the more recent versions belong to the same tradition. And it is further suggested that while the older copies may well be operative, the ones after 1583 on are speculative from the very beginning.

In fact this "gap" is more apparent than real. In the first place paper and even parchment are hardly the most durable of human artifacts. With constant use they become soiled, dog-eared, and illegible. They are liable to damage or destruction by fire, moisture, mildew, by insects or animals. They may come into the hands of new owners who discard them, or use them to kindle the fire or wrap the garbage. And these threats to their existence are cumulative; early specimens are scarcer than later ones. Evidently thousands of scraps of paper from the fifteenth and sixteenth centuries have vanished without trace.

The lost copies of the *Old Charges* have **not** vanished without trace. We can readily establish the existence of some eight texts which were written in the period under review. Some are known only from allusions or quotations made before their disappearance. (Further details may be found in Douglas Knoop and G. P. Jones, *A Handlist of Masonic Documents*, Manchester, 1942, and in Herbert Poole's revision of *Gould's History of Freemasonry*, London, 1951, volume 1, pages 48–76.)

(1) *Dermott's Manuscript* (**X.4**). According to the Minutes of the Grand Lodge of the Antients for 6 December 1752, "The Grand Secretary [Dermott] produced a very Old Manuscript written or copied by one Bramhall of Canterbury in the Reign of King Henry the Seventh" (who ruled 1485–1509). We know that the Premier Grand Lodge had been interested in the Old Charges, and that its officers had sought them out, and copied them, and displayed them at meetings. It is generally conceded that the Antients were trying to do the same thing, and that therefore this must have been a copy of the *Old Charges*.

(2) *Wilson's Manuscript* (**X.5**). A marginal note to Preston's *Manifesto of the . . . Lodge of Antiquity* (1778) mentions a manuscript "in the hands of Mr Wilson, of Broomhead, near Sheffield, Yorkshire, written in the reign of K. Henry 8th" (1509–1547). It is hard to imagine that this old Masonic manuscript was anything but a copy of the *Old Charges*.

(3) *Levander-York Original*. At the end of the one of the versions of the Old Charges, the *Levander-York Manuscript* (**D.b.41**, which is dated about 1740) is a note explaining that it was "Copy'd from the Original engross'd on Abortive" [that is, on parchment] "in the Year 1560."

(4) *Melrose Manuscript No 1.* (**X.1**). A Scottish copy of the Old Charges, known as the *Melrose Manuscript No 2* (**D.sundry.12**, 1674) closes with a somewhat cryptic note suggesting that the text was transcribed from an older manuscript that had been written in 1581 by Robert Winsester.

The existence of other lost manuscripts must be postulated in order to account for the distribution of readings in the extant texts.

(5) Plot Family Archetype (**C**). One group of the Old Charges is known as the "Plot Family." Its six surviving members are all later than the period in question. Four of them, however (Poole Abstract, **C.5**, 1665; *Heade Manuscript, C.4*, 1675; Plot Abstract, **C.1**, 1686; *Watson Manuscript, C.2*, 1687), include a statement that in its original form ran something like this: "These charges have been seen and perused by our late sovereign lord King Henry the Sixth and the Lords of his Honorable Council; and they have allowed them well, and said that they were right good and reasonable to be holden." Henry VI died in 1471. It follows that the statement, and the text in which it is embedded, must have been composed within the next two generations, 1470–1530, while the king's memory was still fresh.

(6) Standard Original (**TDE**). The ancestor of most (95) of the Old Charges is generally known as the "Standard Original" version. It is lost, but in the Appendix to the printed version of my Prestonian Lecture I try to reconstruct its text. It was clearly a rewriting of a member of the Plot Family. It is therefore later than number (5) above; it was composed at some date within the period 1520–80, probably during the first half.

(7) Grand Lodge Family Original (**D**). The fifty-three texts of the Grand Lodge Family are all descended from a single version, which (like so many others) has not survived the centuries. It was a copy of number (6) above, but one that incorporated a few distinctive changes that were passed on to its descendants. Clearly this "Grand Lodge Family Original" must have been written later than the Standard Original.

(8) Grand Lodge Branch Original (**D.a**). The eight texts that are classified as the Grand Lodge Branch are descended from a single manuscript, which no longer exists. It was a copy of number (7) above, again one which introduced a few easily recognizable changes. It in turn gave rise to the oldest member of the branch, the *Grand Lodge Manuscript No 1* (**D.a.1**), of 1583. It therefore falls between the dates of those two texts.

There is no reason to assume that these eight are the only versions of the *Old Charges* written between c. 1400 and 1583. No doubt there were others. In short, the alleged "gap" is more apparent than real. That is, an interest in the old charges does not suddenly spring up in 1583. Can we make the evidence go away by ignoring it?

OTHER ARGUMENTS FOR CONTINUITY

(1) The "Charges Singular," found in most versions of the *Old Charges*, contain regulations that are clearly intended for operative masons. For example, "No Master shall take upon him no lord's work, but that he know

himself able and cunning to perform the same. . . . No Master nor Fellow set no layer . . . to hew mould stones with no mould of his own making." This text was copied hundreds of times in the years after 1583. If it was all a fantasy or a sham, intended for non-operatives, why bother?

(2) It is usually assumed that Elias Ashmole, whose diary reports that he was made a Free-Mason in 1646, was a gentleman mason, unconnected with operative masonry. Dr David Stevenson, Director of the Centre for Scottish Studies at the University of Aberdeen, has noted that he was in fact a master gunner, and that there was an affinity between the two mathematical crafts (masonry and artillery). In Scotland the King's Master Gunner was often the same man as the King's Master of Works (*Proceedings of the Society of Antiquaries of Scotland*, volume 114, 1984, page 410). When an operative connection is pointed out, do we ignore it in order to accommodate our presuppositions?

(3) The so-called "Apprentice Charge" occurs in sixteen versions of the old charges (Herbert Poole, *The Old Charges*, London, 1924, page 38). It was composed no later than 1650, the approximate date of the two oldest texts that include it (Grand Lodge MS No 2, **F.2**; Hope MS, **E.c.5**). It uses language appropriate to operative masons. It is clear that the apprentice for the term of his service is expected to dwell in the household of his master. Some of the terms include: "You shall truly honor . . . your Master and Dame; you shall not absent yourself but with the licence of both or one of them by day or night. . . . You shall not disclose your Master or Dame's Counsel or Secrets which they have imparted to you, or what is to be concealed, spoken or done within the precincts of your house by them or either of them."

Seven more copies appear before 1700. Are we to imagine, if operative Masonry was extinct in England by that date, and the manuscripts were being copied exclusively for non-operative use, that some creative genius, not content with the revised text of the Old Charges that was in current use, composed a new completely fictional set of regulations, out of whole cloth, as it were, for the edification of non-operative lodges?

(4) The newly discovered Dundee Manuscript No 2 (found a year or so ago in the documents belonging to the Mason Trade in the Royal Burgh of Dundee) is dated to about the year 1650. This version, a perfectly normal text of the old charges belonging to the Grand Lodge Family, was held by an operative lodge that never evolved into a speculative one. It poses, in a more pointed form, the same problem as do the other Scottish texts that come from lodges that **did** pass through a transitional stage (none of the Scottish texts antedates 1650.) Are we to imagine that when the Scottish operative lodges decided to take over the English text of the Old Charges, they were prepared to adopt a text that was used only by non-operative gentlemen Masons in the Southron realm?

(5) At some date between 1672 and 1675 the antiquary and herald Randle Holme III recorded the members of a lodge at Chester. Most of the twenty-six names have been identified in municipal documents. Eighteen, and perhaps as many as twenty, were directly engaged in occupations associated with domestic architecture (masons, bricklayers, carpenters, slaters, plasterers, glaziers; Poole, *Gould's History of Freemasonry*, volume 2, pages 114–120). Does this suggest that the lodge was divorced from the trade?

(6) In 1686, Robert Plot, Professor of Chemistry at the University of Oxford, published a book called *The Natural History of Stafford-shire*. In it he included a description of the Society of Free-Masons. He says that "persons of the most eminent quality . . . did not disdain to be of the *Fellowship*." It is clear from his description that gentleman masons, that is to say, non-operatives, were being accepted at this date. But other parts of his description make it clear that there was still a strong operative component in the lodges. If a stranger appears and gives a Masonic sign, another Mason is obliged to come to him at once, "tho' from the top of a *Steeple*."

Plot goes on to state that the members of the lodges "advise the *Masters* they work for, . . . acquainting them with the badness or goodness of their *materials*; and if they be any way out in the *contrivance* of their *buildings* modestly to rectify them in it" (Douglas Knoop, G. P. Jones, Douglas Hamer, *Early Masonic Pamphlets*, Manchester, 1945, pages 31–32). This language is not compatible with purely speculative lodges.

(7) Three of the texts of the old charges have additional "orders" for operative masons, with fines assessed for infractions. Two are from the "late" operative lodges at Gateshead (**H.2**) and Alnwick (**E.a.10**). The third is the Taylor MS (**E.a.19**), which antedates 1700. For example: "No Mason shall take any work by task or by day, other than the King's work, but that at the least he shall make three or four of his Fellows acquainted therewith, for to take his part; paying for every such offense the sum of £3 6s. 8d." "That no rough layers or any other that has not served their time, or Admitted Masons shall work within the lodge any work of Masonry whatsoever, except under a Master; for every such offense shall pay £3 13s. 4d." Did some speculative mason invent these "orders" for non-operative lodges, with penalties that were never meant to be exacted? Or did some operative mason append them to a speculative document?

These, and questions like these, are never *asked*, let alone *answered*, by those who want to see only speculative masonry in the seventeenth century. They persuade me that we still have operative lodges, or largely operative lodges, flourishing in mid-seventeenth century England, at the time when a broadening interest in the old charges is evident.

EARLY MASONRY IN AMERICA

[Another book that was published by the Grand Lodge of Canada in the Province of Ontario was concerned with the history of Free-masonry in Province of Ontario. One section told how the Craft came to America.]

THE ORIGIN OF MODERN MASONRY

Whence comes Freemasonry? Are modern Masons the spiritual heirs of the initiates in the Mystery Hall at Eleusis? Or of the craftsmen of King Solomon's Temple? Or even of the builders of the Great Pyramid of Gizeh? To be sure, there are similarities; but great gulfs of time and space lie between, gulfs that cannot be bridged except by the eye of faith.

Let us turn aside from what "may have been," and look at what actually "was." Beyond any question, modern speculative Freemasonry springs from the British stone masons of the Middle Ages. Not long after 1350, they began to form trade guilds, and then lodges. The story is too long to rehearse in full here. Enough to note that, from about 1600, lodges began to accept non-operatives, thereby ushering in the "transitional period."

Over the next century and a quarter several lodges are known in which the non-operatives outnumbered the operatives: Warrington in 1646, Aberdeen in 1670, Chester about 1673, Dublin in 1688, Chichester in 1695, and several places in London and Yorkshire from 1693 on.

One lodge may properly claim our attention; it is known only from a document in the possession of the Grand Lodge of Canada in the Province of Ontario. This parchment scroll, eight feet six inches long and six and a quarter inches wide, bears on its front a hand-written version of the "Old Manuscript Constitutions" which governed the operative craft. It is endorsed as follows.

Memorandum: that at a private Lodge held at Scarborough in the County of York, the tenth day of July 1705, before William Thompson, Esq., President of the said Lodge, and several others, brethren, Free Masons, the several persons whose names are hereunto subscribed were then admitted into the said Fraternity: Ed. Thompson, Jo. Tempest, Robt. Johnson, Tho. Lister, Samuel Buck, Richard Hudson.

The era of modern Masonry begins on 24 June 1717, when four London lodges constituted themselves into a grand lodge, which eventually grew into the Grand Lodge of England (the "Moderns"). A few years later the Grand

Lodge of Ireland was organized (about 1725), and then that of Scotland (1736). In 1751 a number of brethren accused the Original Grand Lodge of making innovation in the body of Masonry, and formed the rival Grand Lodge of England, the "Ancients." These four bodies—England ("Moderns"), Ireland, Scotland, and England ("Ancients")—have been the sources from which Freemasonry has spread across the whole globe. . . .

THE EARLIEST MASONS IN AMERICA

Long before any lodges were organized in America, individual members of "operative" or "transitional" lodges reached the New World. The earliest trace is a flat slab of stone from the shore of Goat Island, in the Annapolis Basin, Nova Scotia. Cut into one face are the square and compasses and the date "1606." No doubt it was the grave marker for a French stonemason who had settled at Port Royal with DeMonts and Champlain in 1605.

From 1628 to 1630 Sir William Alexander of Menstrie (lived about 1605–1638) was in Port Royal, Nova Scotia, where his father had sent out a band of Scottish settlers. After returning to Scotland, Lord Alexander was admitted a Fellowcraft in the Lodge of Edinburgh in 1634; but there is no evidence that he engaged in Masonic activity, or even that he was a Mason, during his time in America.

Older books mention the Jewish lodge that met in Newport, Rhode Island, at the house of Mordecai Campunnall, in 1656 or 1658; and John Moore, Collector of the Port of Philadelphia, who in 1715 wrote a letter telling how he had "spent a few evenings in festivity with my Masonic Brethren." Sad to say, both stories seem to be untrue, and the papers which gave rise to them, pious forgeries.

The first undoubted accepted Mason on this side of the Atlantic was John Skene (who died in 1690). In 1670 he is listed, as "Merchant and Mason," on the membership roll of the Lodge at Aberdeen. He came to America in 1682, settling at Burlington, New Jersey, and served as Deputy Governor of East Jersey from 1685 to 1690.

Jonathan Belcher (1681–1757), a native of Boston, graduated from Harvard in 1699, and promptly went to England. He was initiated into Masonry there in 1704, and the next year he returned home. He was Governor of Massachusetts from 1730 to 1741. On 25 September 1741 he wrote to the First Lodge in Boston:

> It is now Thirty Seven years since I was admitted into the Ancient and Honorable Society of Free and Accepted Masons, to whom I have been a faithful Brother, and well-wisher to the Art of Masonry. I shall ever maintain a strict friendship for the whole Fraternity; and always be glad when it may fall in my power to do them any Services.

EARLY LODGES "ACCORDING TO THE OLD CUSTOMS"

Dozens of other Masons must have lived in pioneer America, but their very names are lost to us. Sometimes they banded together into lodges, not by any warrant of constitution from grand lodge, but simply "by immemorial right." The grand lodges had not yet established their authority, and Masons still had this ancient prerogative.

One such group was in Boston by May 25 1727, when the *Boston Weekly News Letter* carried a report of the meeting of the Grand Lodge in London. After all, who but Masons would care to read a news item like that? According to one story, this lodge had met in King's Chapel, Boston, as early as 1720.

Another "immemorial right" lodge met in Philadelphia, at the Tun Tavern, from February 1731 (when Benjamin Franklin was initiated), and perhaps even from July 9 1730, when a bit of Masonic news is repeated in the *Philadelphia Gazette*. A good deal is known about this lodge; its account book for the years 1731–1738—the famous "St John's Lodge Libr B"—can still be seen.

Yet another lodge met "according to the Old Customs" at the Black Horse Tavern in New York in 1731. There were others at Annapolis, Maryland (from February 1733), Savannah, Georgia (from February 1734), possibly at the Cape Fear settlement (later Wilmington), North Carolina (from some time in 1735), and possibly at Charleston, South Carolina (likewise from 1735). Within a few years all were either extinct or had requested warrants from the Grand Lodge of England.

THE ADVENT OF "DULY CONSTITUTED" MASONRY

On 5 June 1730 the Grand Master of England appointed Colonel Daniel Coxe (1673–1739) as Provincial Grand Master of New York, New Jersey, and Pennsylvania, for a term of two years. He was a lawyer, and eventually became "one of the Justices of the Supreme Court of the Province of New Jersey." On 29 January 1731 he visited the Grand Lodge in London, and "his health was drunk as Provincial Grand Master of North America." It used to be thought that he spent these two years in England, but now we know that he passed nearly the whole time in New Jersey, where he owned property. There is still no evidence that he exercised his Masonic authority.

On 13 April (or possibly 30 April) 1733 the Grand Master of England named Major Henry Price (1697–1780) as Provincial Grand Master of New England and the Dominions and Territories thereunto belonging. He was a native of London, and a tailor by trade; "by his Diligence & industry in Business," says his gravestone, "he Acquired the means of a Comfortable Living." In August 1734 his sphere was extended, and he was named P.G.M.

of North America. On 30 July 1733 he formed his Grand Lodge; and immediately, in response to a petition from a number of Masons who had been meeting "according to the Old Customs," he warranted a lodge to meet at the Sign of the Bunch of Grapes, on King Street, in Boston. This lodge, which is still working today under the name "St John's Lodge," Boston, is the oldest duly constituted lodge in America.

During the next few years warrants were issued to several lodges, either by the Grand Lodge of England or by the P.G.L. of North America: Montserrat, in the Leeward Islands (warrant from London, 1 October 1734); Philadelphia, with Benjamin Franklin as Master (from Boston, 21 February 1735, in response to a petition dated 28 November 1734); Savannah, Georgia (from London at some date between 30 October 1735 and 1 March 1736; still working, as Solomon's Lodge, No 1, Georgia); Portsmouth, New Hampshire (from Boston, in response to a petition dated 5 February 1736; now St John's Lodge, No 1); and Charleston, South Carolina (constituted 28 October 1736, by virtue of a deputation from London dated after 15 April 1736; now Solomon's Lodge, No 1). By the end of 1736, regular Masonry was well established in America. . . .

MASONIC BENEVOLENCE

[The Grand Lodge of Canada in the Province of Ontario, like many other jurisdictions, has a charitable foundation which works outside the limits of Masonry. In 1989 the Masonic Foundation of Ontario celebrated its 25th Anniversary, and a short history was authorized, to tell something of its activities. The following pages provide the background.]

THE FUNCTION OF FREEMASONRY

What is the purpose of Freemasonry? What do the Freemasons think they are doing? These questions are often asked by non-Masons, and even by Masons themselves, and various answers might be given.

In the first place, Freemasonry explicitly defines itself as a "system of morality," and says that its meetings are intended "to induce the habit of virtue." But it has other functions as well.

It is also "the happy means of conciliating friendship amongst those who must otherwise have remained at a perpetual distance," and it is shown in its true light when its meetings are "blended with social mirth, and a mutual interchange of fraternal feelings;" that is, it is an affinity group, a group of men who enjoy each other's company.

In addition, it encourages its members to "contemplate the intellectual faculties," and exhorts them to "make a daily advancement in Masonic knowledge;" its objectives, we are told, include "the cultivation and improvement of the human mind." As well, it patiently ministers "to the relief of want and sorrow," and calls upon its members to "exercise that virtue" which Masons "profess to admire," that is to say charity; it instructs them to extend "relief and consolation to [their] fellow creatures in the hour of their affliction."

Here are four functions, to some extent related, but still distinct: teaching virtue, encouraging friendship, fostering education, and prompting benevolence. All four are very old within the Craft, and go back to the days of the operative stonemasons. The regulations of those craftsmen, even as early as the year 1540, included exhortations to do unto others as you would they should do unto you; they directed Masons to be true each one to another; they spoke in praise of the seven liberal sciences; and they said that a stranger was to be given work or else refreshed with money.

Virtue, friendship, education, and benevolence again. They have obviously been a part of Masonry for more than four hundred years, and a book could be written about each of them. In these pages we propose to limit ourselves to the question of benevolence, particularly one form of it that is practiced in the Province of Ontario.

MASONIC BENEVOLENCE BEFORE THE FOUNDATION OF THE GRAND LODGE OF CANADA

All over the world, Freemasons have been providing assistance to those less fortunate than themselves for over three hundred years. In Scotland, in 1670, the lodge at Aberdeen pledged itself to make contributions to the Mason Box, for the support of distressed brethren and the education of their children.

In England, in 1686, a local historian of Wiltshire stated that whenever a Freemason falls into financial difficulty, "the brotherhood is to relieve him."

In Ireland, in 1688, we have a report from Dublin that the members of the Fraternity of Freemasons had recently presented a "well stuffed" purse of charity to a destitute brother. In 1724 the Premier Grand Lodge in London decided that every lodge should take up a monthly collection for a general charity fund, to assist poor brethren.

In 1733, in Massachusetts, the by-laws of the first lodge in Boston specified that each member was to pay at least two shillings per quarter, for the relief of brethren who had fallen upon evil times.

In 1781, in Nova Scotia, the Masters of the three lodges in Halifax were directed to act as a Charity Committee, to assist Masons who had escaped from the American Revolution. And in Ontario, the *Upper Canada Gazette* for June 28 1797 told of a lodge that had set up a fund to help Freemasons' widows, and to educate orphans and the children of poor brethren. The picture is universal, and consistent.

MASONIC BENEVOLENCE IN THE GRAND LODGE OF CANADA

The Grand Lodge of Canada was founded in 1855. From almost the beginning there is evidence of traditional Masonic charity. In 1863 a Benevolent Fund was established, and its procedures were worked out by the efforts of the first Chairman of the Committee on Benevolence, Otto Klotz (who lived 1817–1892). It was intended to provide assistance primarily to Masons who were in need, and to their families.

As years passed, the need continued to grow. In 1917, to meet the increasing demands, it was decided that every Mason would pay one dollar each year to Grand Lodge, of which eighty cents was to be used for benevolent purposes alone and for no other purpose. This, together with transfers from the special funds and the General Fund, was enough to meet the claims made upon the Grand Lodge.

In 1934 at the height of the Great Depression, the committee had its heaviest year, considering 867 applications for assistance from needy and distressed Masons and their dependents, and paying out $122,146.75. At least as much again was paid out in grants by the individual constituent lodges. Since then, Grand Lodge's good works have continued, but never at such a high level. In more recent times, the committee has dealt with more than 60 applications annually, and has authorized the expenditure of more than $80,000 each year.

SELFISHNESS?

All the Masonic benevolence that we have mentioned so far has been directed to Masons, their wives, and families. This gave rise to a saying, "The Masons look after their own." Over a century ago the evangelist Charles G. Finney attacked Masonry on the grounds that it was nothing but a selfish "mutual insurance company." The American scholar Henry Wilson Coil on the other hand tried to justify this exclusiveness, saying that it was actually harmful to act as if Masonry had a responsibility to care for all mankind, because this would open the Fraternity to charges of hypocrisy; there are simply not enough Masons in the world to provide for all those who need help.

DONATIONS TO NON-MASONIC RECIPIENTS

The truth, as so often, lies somewhere between the two extremes, absolute selfishness and total altruism. From time to time, as opportunity has arisen, Freemasons have directed their assistance to non-Masons as well as to their own. It seems likely that this began with help for victims of wars and natural disasters.

In 1867 the Grand Master of the Grand Lodge of Canada, William Mercer Wilson, reported that he had received an appeal on behalf of the widows and orphans of the state of Georgia, who were in dire straits after the American Civil War, but that Grand Lodge had no funds to help. That was the last time that an appeal was made in vain.

From then on, aid was provided where necessary, in such situations as the Franco-Prussian War ($250 in 1871), the Chicago Fire ($2000 in 1872), the Louisiana Floods ($200, in 1874), and many subsequent emergencies of the same sort. At first these were all for strictly Masonic purposes, but during the First World War donations began to be made with no strings attached.

In 1915 $45,000 was transferred to the King of the Belgians, for him to use "among his distressed subjects, irrespective of class or creed, as in his judgment he deemed advisable." Again, in the Second World War, during the years 1941–1946 the Masons of Ontario sent more than $251,000 to England and Scotland, primarily to relieve the suffering caused by bombing; and in 1948–1951, nearly $254,000 was collected for food parcels for Britain.

About this same period another innovation took place. The Grand Master, on behalf of the Grand Lodge, began to make donations to established charitable foundations. In 1943 he authorized $2500 to the Canadian Red Cross, as well as $1000 each to the Chinese Relief Fund, the Greek Relief Fund, and the Canadian Aid to Russia Fund. Thereafter, donations were approved every year.

In 1860 William Mercer Wilson spoke of the mission of Freemasonry: "It comforts the mourner, it speaks peace and consolation to the troubled spirit; it carries relief and gladness to the habitations of want and destitution; it dries the tears of the widow and orphan; it opens the sources of knowledge; it widens the sphere of human happiness; it even seeks to light up the darkness and gloom of the grave, by pointing to the hopes and promises of a better life to come." Here is ample scope for generosity of the spirit, even more than generosity of the pocket book. Today we have publicly funded social security programs that did not exist a century ago. As a result, Masonic benevolent funds may have fewer demands made upon them, proportionally, than was formerly the case. Nevertheless, there is still lots to do. In concluding this section, I can hardly do better than to quote the words of Bro. T. Richard Davies, the Chairman of the Committee on Benevolence of my mother Grand Lodge, in his report for 1988: "Assistance . . . may consist of visitation when ill, advice on personal problems, sympathy during bereavement, help in procuring employment. . . . The opportunities are endless. . . . Supplementary support, whether it be financial or just supportive in general, can add a little light and encouragement to any situation of difficulty, whether it be related to health, family, and so on. . . . Benevolence and caring involvement is one of the fundamental precepts of our fraternity." And our activities, after all, do not have to be restricted to our Masonic brethren. One thinks for example of the splendid Christmas dinners that the Masons of Des Moines provide every year for those who would otherwise have no chance, or cause, to celebrate the festive season. Truly, an example to emulate!

THE EFFECT OF VICTORIAN OBSCENITY LAWS ON MASONIC HISTORIANS: AN ALLEGEDLY OBSCENE POEM OF 1723

[The largest American organization that is devoted to educating Freemasons is The Philalethes Society. Every year at its Annual Assembly and Feast, some Masonic student is invited to address the brethren on a subject of his own choosing. For the year 1986 I was honored with this responsibility, and used the occasion to talk a bit about cultural history.]

Good Queen Victoria ruled Britain for sixty-four years, and by the end of her life she was revered and loved as the earnest, moral and benevolent mother and grandmother of half the world. Her long reign was an age of wars: the Crimean War, the Indian Mutiny, the Boer Wars. By 1901, when she died, the British ruled an Empire "on which," they were proud to say, "the sun never sets." Prince Albert, her husband, had died in 1861, and she lived on as a widow for another forty years. Bro. Rudyard Kipling referred to her as "The Widow at Windsor," and he called her military forces "the sons of the Widow." Queen Victoria gave her name to an age marked by a constellation of major writers, and by astonishing progress in science and technology.

It is of course utterly improper to apply the name of an English queen to an age in the United States of America, and it goes without saying that the same period in America is not so clearly marked. Nevertheless it does exhibit many of the same characteristics.

During these years the United States grew from a small country, with few inhabitants, to an imperial power with twice Britain's population. We have the same age of wars: the Mexican War, the Civil War, the Spanish American War. We have the same array of writers: Emily Dickinson, Henry James, Henry Wadsworth Longfellow, Herman Melville, Edgar Allan Poe, Mark Twain, Walt Whitman. The same technological advance took place: for example, Elias Howe's sewing machine (1846); Bro. Edwin L. Drake's oil well in Titusville, Pa. (1859); Edison's phonograph (1877); and George Eastman's dry photographic plate (1880).

The Victorian Age, both in Britain and in America, was marked by another characteristic, perhaps less commendable, that began before her reign, and lasted long after it; I mean a certain reticence, or even prudishness, in matters of sex, and a hostility to any sort of plain-spokenness. It was not simply a provident sort of puritanism, designed to protect the young and innocent from the baneful effect of obscene French romances. It also looked at literature of the past, weighed it, and found it wanting.

This Victorian Age of prudery lasted from 1820 to 1960, and it was general throughout the English-speaking world. The eighteen twenties were a highpoint of squeamishness so far as the writing of literature was concerned, and we find novels becoming more prudish then (see Walter E. Houghton, *The Victorian Frame of Mind 1830–1870*, New Haven, 1959, page 357, note 48).

The reading public began to demonstrate a concern for "purity." About the same date Keats's poem *Endymion*, Byron's *Don Juan*, and Shelley's play *The Cenci*, were all savagely pilloried by critics on moral grounds when they first appeared. Of the last, *The Literary Gazette* said, "We now most gladly take leave of the work and sincerely hope that should we continue our literary pursuits for fifty years we shall never need to look into one so stamped with pollution, impiousness and infamy."

When Shelley's *Queen Mab* was printed in 1823, it was attacked by the Society for the Suppression of Vice, and the publisher was imprisoned for four months (see Norman St John-Stevas, *Obscenity and the Law*, London, 1956; reprinted 1974, pages 46–48).

Only in England, you say? H. L. Mencken notes that in America from the 1820s on, perfectly ordinary words were suppressed because they sounded taboo. He refers to some letters written in 1822, telling how in the New World the bird that greets the dawn is called not by its old English name of **cock**, but by the newly invented term **rooster**. And, in the same way the insect which the Spanish call **la cucaracha**, and the English call **the cockroach**, in America was abbreviated as early as 1837 to **roach**, to get rid of the offensive first syllable.

The Bible often mentions an animal which it calls the **ass**, but in America this word sounded objectionable, and was displaced by the slang term **donkey** (see H. L. Mencken, *The American Language*, 4th edition, abridged, 1963, pages 356–357).

And there were court cases here too. 1821, Commonwealth of Massachusetts v. Peter Holmes: "The defendant was indicted at a Circuit Court of Common Pleas . . . for . . . a certain book entitled 'Memoirs of a Woman of Pleasure.' . . . The indictment . . . alleges that the defendant, 'being a scandalous and evil disposed person, and contriving, devising and intending, the morals as well of youth as of other good citizens . . . to debauch and corrupt, and to raise and create in their minds inordinate and lustful desires, . . . knowingly . . . did . . . publish . . . a certain lewd, wicked, scandalous, in-

famous and obscene printed book. . . .' The defendant stands convicted . . ."
(Edward De Grazia, *Censorship Landmarks*, New York, 1969, pages 40–41).
    This new age of prudery was also heralded by the appearance, in 1818, of
the Family Shakespeare, from which "those words and expressions are omitted which cannot with propriety be read aloud in a family." It was edited by
Thomas Bowdler, whose name was made into the verb "bowdlerize," meaning "to expurgate by omitting or altering words or passages considered indel-
icate." Bowdler's Shakespeare was reprinted in Philadelphia.
    All these signposts point to 1820 as marking the beginning of a new age of
modesty. In its earlier years this age gave rise to pious statements such as that
made by Tennyson's Sir Galahad,

> My strength is as the strength of ten,
> Because my heart is pure.

And let there be no doubt what "purity" means here. According to Tennyson's vision of the world, King Arthur's monarchy fell because of sexual
licentiousness.
    The first major piece of anti-obscenity legislation in England was Lord
Campbell's Act in 1857, which "gave magistrates the power to order the
destruction of books and prints if in their opinion their publication would
amount to 'a misdemeanor proper to be prosecuted as such' " (St John-
Stevas, *Obscenity and the Law,* page 66).
    The first real definition of obscenity, the so-called Hicklin Rule, was enun-
ciated by Sir Alexander Cockburn in 1868: "I think the test of obscenity is
this, whether the tendency of the matter charged as obscenity is to deprave
and corrupt those whose minds are open to such immoral influences, and into
whose hands a publication of this sort may fall." This definition came to be
followed in courts both in Britain and America. In 1873, in the U.S.A.,
Anthony Comstock persuaded congress to pass a law banning the transportation through the mails of obscene material.
    In 1878 Gilbert and Sullivan could ridicule the whole attitude to profanity
by having Captain Corcoran boast,

> I never use a big big D----.

Let me give you an example or two of the effects of this prudery on my
own life. I am by trade a student of literature, and I make my living by
teaching the Greek and Latin Classics. There is not a tremendous market for
this sort of thing, and since new textbooks in a foreign language are expensive to print, we tend to keep reprinting the same old texts as long as possible. And so, when I began teaching at my present position 24 years ago,
many of the books that the students used had originally been issued in the

Victorian Age. We had to use W. W. Merry's bowdlerized schoolboy edition of the *Clouds* of Aristophanes (revised 1889); and since these were university students who were expected to know the whole play, I had to hand out a sheet of paper with all the lines that the Victorian editor had left out.

Or again, one time we were reading from Homer's *Iliad*, and we came to a mildly risqué part at the end of Book Three. So as not to embarrass the students, I translated it myself. I could do it without blushing; but when I was finished I got the most baffled stares from my class! They had copies of the edition of Leaf and Bayfield (1895), which omitted seven lines. I guess they thought I was making it up.

One of the most useful sets of standard texts in Classical studies is the Loeb Classical Library, which has many volumes, with the Greek or Latin text on the left-hand page, and an English translation facing it. This is extremely convenient; except where the editor sees something obscene. For example, there is a collection known as *The Greek Anthology*, made up of a whole lot of epigrams or brief poems. Some are dull, some are beautiful, some are funny, a few are wildly obscene. The questionable ones W. R. Paton translated—not into English, but into Latin.

With regard to Petronius' *Satyricon*, the great portrait of a decadent society, Michael Heseltine says, "His book is befouled with obscenity. . . . The translator . . . must leave whole pages in the decent obscurity of Latin." Picture the paradox of that: a book which masquerades as a simultaneous translation, with the Latin text on the left-hand page, and facing it, where one would expect the translation, the same Latin text repeated.

There were occasional hints of impending liberalization, but they were few and far between.

In 1933 James Joyce's *Ulysses* won the right to come to the U.S.A.; Federal Judge John Munro Woolsey, of the Southern District of New York, said, in part, "Joyce . . . has honestly attempted to tell in full what his characters think about. . . . His attempt . . . has required him incidentally to use certain words which are generally considered dirty words and has led at times to what many think is a too poignant preoccupation with sex in the thoughts of his characters. The words which are criticized as dirty are old Saxon words known to almost all men and, I venture, to many women, and are such words as would be naturally and habitually used, I believe, by the types of folk whose life, physical and mental, Joyce is trying to describe. In respect of the recurrent emergence of the theme of sex in the minds of his characters, it must always be remembered that his locale was Celtic and his season Spring. Whether or not one enjoys such a technique as Joyce uses is a matter of taste . . ., but to subject that technique to the standards of some other technique seems to me to be little short of absurd. . . . I am quite aware that owing to some of its scenes *Ulysses* is a rather strong draught to ask some sensitive, though normal, persons to take. But my considered opinion, after long reflection, is that whilst in many places the effect of *Ulysses* on the reader undoubtedly is somewhat emetic, nowhere does it tend to be an aphrodisiac . . . *Ulysses* may therefore be admitted into the United States" (St John-Stevas, *Obscenity and the Law*, pages 162–163).

But despite this progressive judgment, by and large the old Victorianism lingered on. As late as 1961, C. J. Fordyce produced a new text of the exquisite Latin poet *Catullus;* he said, "A few poems which do not lend themselves to comment in English have been omitted." Out of a total of some 116 poems, he omitted 35, or 30%.

I don't know if you realize it, but we have lived through a cultural revolution of our own in the last thirty years. The revolution was brewing in the late 1940's, both in England and America. Perhaps it arose out of the Second World War, with its violent actions and violent words.

In 1948 Kathleen Winsor's raunchy historical novel *Forever Amber* was ruled not to be obscene by the Supreme Judicial Court of Massachusetts. And the same year Alfred C. Kinsey published his report on the *Sexual Behavior in the Human Male*.

But the revolution really began in earnest in the middle fifties, probably in England, with the group known as the Angry Young Men, and in America with the Beat Movement, who habitually employed language that their elders regarded as unacceptable, partly to signify their rejection of the standards of the older generation.

The watershed came in 1959. In that year D. H. Lawrence's novel, *Lady Chatterley's Lover*, which had been printed in Italy in 1928, but was banned from the mails by the Comstock Act, was published by the Grove Press in New York and by Penguin Books in England. It was challenged at once in the law courts of both Britain and America. And in both the decision was that it could be distributed.

Federal Judge Frederick van Pelt Bryan, in delivering his decision, said, "The material must be judged in terms of its effect on those it is likely to reach who are conceived of as the average man of normal sexual impulses. . . . Moreover, a book is not to be judged by excerpts or individual passages but must be judged as a whole. . . . The book *Lady Chatterley's Lover* . . . contains a number of passages describing sexual intercourse in great detail with complete candor and realism. Four-letter Anglo-Saxon words are used with some frequency. These passages and this language understandably will shock the sensitive minded. Be that as it may, these passages are relevant to the plot and to the development of the characters and their lives as Lawrence unfolds them. . . . Even if it be assumed that these passages and this language taken in isolation tend to arouse shameful, morbid and lustful sexual desires in the average reader, they are an integral, and to the author a necessary part of the development of theme, plot and character. . . . The book is not 'dirt for dirt's sake.' Nor do these passages and this language submerge the dominant theme so as to make the book obscene even if they could be considered and found to be obscene in isolation. . . . The decision of the Postmaster General that it is obscene and therefore non-mailable is contrary to law and clearly erroneous" (St John-Stevas, *Obscenity and the Law*, pages 157–158).

This was 1959 in the United States. The next year a similar decision was reached by a Jury in England. Within a few years Henry Miller's *Tropic of Capricorn* (1934) came before the American courts (in 1964), and John Cleland's 1750 novel *Fanny Hill* (1966). The same lawyer, Charles Rembar, defended all three books; and later he said in retrospect, "In the seven years between 1959 and 1966, the language up to then unfit to print became entirely fit" (Harry M. Clor, *Censorship and Freedom of Expression*, Chicago, 1971, page 27).

And in England too, since 1960 certain words that formerly brought automatic prosecution have been allowed to appear in full in print (Mary Marshall, *Bozzimacoo: Origins and Meanings of Oaths and Swear Words*, London, 1975, pages 46–50, 71).

In my own field this new liberalization was quickly felt. In 1966, the British scholar K. J. Dover, in his preface to a new edition of Aristophanes' *Clouds*—the work for which I used to hand out a page of lines that had been censored—said "Many jokes in Aristophanes depend on a fairly detailed knowledge of the physiology and psychology of sex. I have explained these jokes much more plainly than has been the custom hitherto. . . . Whatever may have been the case in the last century, it is obvious nowadays that most of those who are old enough to read Aristophanes already have a sound factual knowledge of the main line and branch lines of sexual behavior."

And in the years since, a number of studies have appeared that once would have been impossible: for example, in 1968 Yale University Press was able to publish the complete poems of the seventeenth century poet John Wilmot, Earl of Rochester (edited by David M. Vieth)—which are awash with four-letter words.

Now don't get me wrong. I'm not in favor of pornography. There are certain four-letter words that I cannot bring myself to say in mixed company, or in my classes. I'm not an advocate of free love, or of open marriage, or of stag movies, or of bondage magazines. I recognize how susceptible the young are, particularly young men, to anything that could be regarded as sexually stimulating. I disapprove highly of some of the words that rock musicians sing; they are not suggestive; they are simply filthy. But as a student of the past, I think it is unhealthy to condemn and ban or censor works that were regarded as great literature in ancient times; or even printed works that were a part of the way of life of our predecessors, and can tell us something about their attitudes.

You've been very patient through this summary of cultural history; but I can see some of you asking, What has this got to do with giving or obtaining more light in Masonry?

In *The Daily Post* of London, for Friday, 15 February 1723, there appeared the following advertisement.

This Day is publish'd

The Free-Masons. An Hudibrastick Poem. Illustrating the whole History of the Ancient Free-Masons, from the Building of the Tower of Babel to this Time, with their Laws, Ordinances, Signs, Marks, Messages, &c. so long kept Secret. Faithfully discover'd and made known, and the Manner of their Installation particularly describ'd. By a Free-Mason.

> *All Secrets, 'till they once are known*
> *Are wonderful, all Men must own,*
> *when found out, we cease to wonder,*
> *'Tis equal then to Fart and Thunder.*

Printed for A. Moore near St. Paul's. Price 6 d.

The work was reasonably popular, and before the end of the year it went through a second edition, and a third.

After that date it appears to have dropped out of sight.

In 1944, three university teachers from the University of Sheffield, in England, Douglas Knoop, Gwillym Jones, and Douglas Hamer, published a book entitled *Early Masonic Pamphlets*, in which they reprinted an incredibly useful collection of old documents that had to do with the early history of the Craft. One of them was our pamphlet of the year 1723. It originally ran to some 366 lines. In the preface to their reprint, Knoop, Jones and Hamer say, "we have omitted portions displeasing to modern taste."; in fact, they leave out over half the poem, and print only 158 out of 366 lines.

The date when this collection came out, 1944, is of course before the end of the Victorian Age of prudery, and that accounts for their restraint. As a student of a later generation, I thought that I was entitled to know the work as a whole, and so I was able to obtain a copy of the Second Edition from the British Library, in London; and of the Third Edition from the Library of Freemasons' Hall, in London. I express my gratitude to the authorities of the British Library, and to the United Grand Lodge of England.

It seemed to me that it might be appropriate for a relaxing after dinner talk to share with you some portions of this poem of 1723, that was too obscene to reprint in 1944. It is called "The Free-Masons: An Hudibrastick Poem," and the subtitle sets it in a particular tradition.

In the year 1662, a man named Samuel Butler published the first part of a poem called *Hudibras*, that eventually ran to over 11,000 lines. It told of the adventures of a knight-at-arms named Sir Hudibras, who was (as his name suggests) foolish and brash, hybristic and brazen; the name comes from Spenser, *Faerie Queene* 2.2.17 (see John Wilders, editor, *Samuel Butler: Hudibras*, Oxford, 1967, page 322). The poem became quite popular, and gave rise to a whole series of imitations over the next century, all of them paying tribute to their source by being called hudibrastick (see Edward Ames Richards, *Hudibras in the Burlesque Tradition*, New York 1937, pp. 171–178; Richard P. Bond, *English Burlesque Poetry 1700–1750*, 1932, repr. N.Y. 1961, pp. 232–453).

There are five particular characteristics of hudibrastick verse:

First, the metre, which is rhymed iambic tetrameter, u / u / u / u / .

Secondly, the rhymes, which are often grotesque; as for example,

> There was an ancient sage Philosopher,
> That had read Alexander Ross over,
> And swore the world, as he could prove,
> Was made of Fighting and of Love:
> Just so Romances are, for what else
> Is in them all, but Love and Battels?

Thirdly, the satirical and unsympathetic treatment of certain real classes of people; thus, the original *Hudibras* was aimed particularly at the religious debates of its time. Butler says, in speaking of his hero:

> For his Religion it was fit
> To match his Learning and his Wit:
> 'Twas Presbyterian true blew,
> For he was of that stubborn Crew
> Of Errant Saints, whom all men grant
> To be the true Church militant. . . .
> A Sect, who chief Devotion lies
> In odde perverse Antipathies.

And again:

> What makes all Doctrines Plain and Clear?
> About two Hundred Pounds a Year.

Fourthly, the humor, of word, of rhyme, and of situation.

Fifthly, the obscenity, which is not particularly gross, but which employs plain speaking for satirical purposes.

66

> Then mounted both upon their Horses,
> But with their faces to the Arses.

Our poem of 1723 tries to fit the pattern; the metre is right, u / u / u / u /, and a few of the rhymes are appropriately violent; for example, when a Mason has passed his test, we're told,

> He's mark'd upon the Buttock right,
> With red-hot Iron, out of sight,
> To shew that he dares then defy all,
> And well can stand the fiery Trial:
> By this the Mason's always known,
> Whene'er his Breeches are pull'd down.
> Some likewise say our Masons now
> Do Circumcision undergo,
> For Masonry's a Jewish Custom,
> And by this means they all will thrust home.

Of course, satire is present, for the poem treats the Freemasons in a mocking and unsympathetic way. But, alas, it is neither very funny, nor very obscene.

The author has divided his poem into sections.

First comes a brief Introduction, in which the author announces that he is at last going to reveal the secrets of the Masons, so long concealed.

> ALL Kingdoms have their Masons-Free,
> Which help to form Society;
> By Signs and Marks they'll know each other,
> In num'rous Crowds spy out a Brother;
> They have their Laws, and Orders good,
> To Govern o'er the Brotherhood,
> That ne'er have been, in Ages past
> Divulg'd, 'till now found out at last:
> But here at length the Secret's shown,
> And faithfully to all made known.

There follows a brief History, telling how the Masonic signs and regulations were devised. Actually, he says, they originated at the Tower of Babel.

> IF Hist'ry be no ancient Fable,
> Free Masons came from *Tower of Babel*;
> When first that Fabrick was begun,
> The Greatest underneath the Sun,
> All Nations thither did repair,
> To build this great Castle in th' Air.

Hundreds of men, the author tells us, were employed in this great project, but it was never completed; as fast as it was built, it collapsed. Finally the workers all decided to return to their own homes, but in order that they might be able to recognize each other for ever after, even if they spoke different languages, they framed certain distinguishing signs and marks. And so that they might restrict these secrets to their own people, they agreed until the end of time to keep the various Rules and Orders relating to the Mason Trade, and they devised a solemn Oath for this purpose.

This business about the Tower of Babel is interesting, because it reflects a genuine Masonic tradition, found in the old manuscript constitutions, and going back before the year 1400. One text, the Roberts pamphlet, was published in London in 1722, and it actually says that "at the Tower of Babylon, Masonry was much made [of]."

But even before this date the connection was known to non-Masons as well; thus, "a Scottish letter of 1697 states that masons believe the Mason Word to be as old as Babel, where they could not understand one another, and communicated by signs" (Douglas Knoop and G. P. Jones, *The Genesis of Freemasonry*, Manchester, 1947; reprinted London, 1978, page 277, which also cites the Briscoe pamphlet of 1724, and an exposure of 1754).

Next we have a section explaining how Modern Masons differ from those of earlier times. Their Working Tools are no longer put to use in building buildings.

> BUT since, 'tis found, the Masons-Free,
> Which in our modern Times we see,
> Workmen are of *another kind*,
> To Sport they're more than Toil inclin'd,
> They have no Trowels, nor yet Lines,
> But still retain their Marks and Signs;
> And Tools they've got which always fit,
> A Lady, Dutchess, or a Cit. . . .

"A cit," that is, a female citizen—a tradeswoman or a shopkeeper. We observe that this equation, in which certain portions of the anatomy are compared to the Masonic Working Tools, was used a generation later in a poem sometimes ascribed to Robbie Burns, and quoted by Robin Carr in the August 1985 issue of the *Philalethes*.

Anyway, to continue with our poem, the task of modern Masons is no longer to build buildings, but to build human bodies. And in this task, their skill and workmanship surpasses that used in the building of the Tower of Babel and the steeple of Salisbury Cathedral. It goes without saying that this section was not reprinted in the Victorian text.

Next we learn how Masons are approved as worthy of being admitted to the fraternity.

> OUR *modern Workmen* naked stand,
> Their Clothes untruss'd by Female Hand,
> And after they've a Flogging bore,
> (But not by Jilt or common Whore)
> When once they're to their Building mov'd
> The Members then are strait approv'd
> By lusty Females, who're best Judges
> Of working Tools for Nature's Drudges.

Then, after the candidate has passed the test, as we have seen, he is branded on his posterior—with the Letter M, no doubt standing for Mason. Then we are told how the new Mason is clothed and "installed";

> WHEN thus the Masons have been stript,
> And well Approv'd, and Mark'd, and Whipt,
> They strait are Rigg'd from Top to Toe,
> And dress'd as fine as any Beau,
> With Gloves and Apron made of Leather,
> A Sword, Long-Wig, and Hat, and Feather
> Like mighty *Quixote* then they swagger,
> And manfully they draw the Dagger,
> To prove that they're all Men of Mettle,
> Can Windmills fight, and Treaties settle.

Then the new brother is required to swear upon the Bible that he'll never reveal the Secrets of Free-Masonry. This is a dim reflection of reality. The Masonic oath of secrecy is reported in manuscript texts as early as 1670 (Douglas Knoop, G. P. Jones, and Douglas Hamer, *Early Masonic Catechisms*, Manchester, 1943; 2nd edition, revised by Harry Carr, London, 1963; page 8). A version of it was published in 1722 in the Roberts pamphlet. Next the candidate is required to kiss the posterior of the Brother that was last made before him. And then:

> A learned Speech is then held forth
> Upon the Breech, and Mason's Worth;
> And he's Install'd at last compleat,
> And led down to his Mason's Seat.

It is interesting to note that the poem uses the word "installed" where we would say "initiated." This probably proves, if proof were needed, that the author is not himself a Mason. From time immemorial the word "installed" has been a Masonic technical term for putting the Master of the Lodge in the Chair of King Solomon (see, e.g., Anderson's *Constitutions* of 1723, page 72; but the usage is older). No Mason could ever use it accidentally when he meant "initiated," or "made a freemason;" and both these terms were current about this date.

The author dwells at length on further details concerning the mason's kiss. In the first place, he says, the posterior, by being kissed, can be said to promote Society. In the second place—a somewhat sordid passage—it may well be that the person whose rump is being kissed may suffer from flatulence.

> And if it haps, by Accident,
> The lower End must needs have Vent,
> He that can best a *Brewer* bear,
> If it does not his Face besmear,
> Is still the most indulgent Mason.

And the reason for all this, it's said, is to aid in keeping the secrets; for nobody in his right mind will boast of having given the Mason kiss.

Then the poem discusses the various subjects of Masonic research. It turns out that every lodge has its own library. These include a bit of philosophy, but most of the collection consists of various well known works which concern sexual impropriety. Some are mild literary pornography from the Restoration period. Others deal with various sexual aberrations.

> This is the Library of those,
> Who're now amongst Free Masons chose;
> And these can ne'er of Knowledge fail,
> Who pry in Secrets of the Tail.

The next topic of concern is the subject of Masonic Toasts. Masons of course are well known to be very serious drinkers:

> They drink, carouse, like any *Bacchus*
> And swallow strongest Wines that rack us;
> And then it is they lay Foundation
> Of Masonry, to build a Nation.

They drink various toasts, but their favorite is to Sally Salisbury, the noted Prostitute, who at this time was in Prison for stabbing a young Gentleman. Then they drink various other healths, down, finally, to the Royal Sovereign.

And then at last we come to the meaning of Masonic Signs:

> And now the goodly Task remains,
> To shew how 'tis they've rack'd their Brains,

> To find out *Marks* and speaking *Signs*,
> Which each within his Breast confines.

In all there are six signs. First is the outstretched arm.

> WHEN once a Man his *Arm* forth *stretches*,
> It Masons round some Distance fetches;
> Altho' one be on *Paul*'s Great Steeple,
> He strait comes down amongst the People.

It doesn't matter if the man who makes the sign proposes to ride a hundred Miles, or hasten to the ancient city of York, or even if he gets the mad idea of going on board ship, the brother to whom he has signaled must still go with him.

> And this is Fellowship indeed,
> Where they thus mutually proceed;
> All Hazards run, without a Slip,
> Risque Life and Limb in Partnership.

The interesting thing here is the mention of a mason sign that will summon a brother from the top of a steeple. This is a recurrent piece of folklore (*Early Masonic Pamphlets* 10). In 1686 Robert Plot, a non-Mason, wrote a description of Masonry, in which he says, "If any man appear . . . that can shew any of these signes to a Fellow of the Society, . . . he is obliged presently to come to him, from what company or place soever he be in, nay tho' from the top of a Steeple, . . . to know his pleasure, and assist him" (*Early Masonic Pamphlets* 32).

Likewise, an old manuscript in the British Library, dating to about 1700, professes to reveal the various masonic secrets, and says, "By the aforementioned sign of the hat or hand you are to come if it were from the top of a Steeple to know their pleasure and to assist them" (*Early Masonic Catechisms* 46).

Again, a printed pamphlet of 1724 includes "A short dictionary explaining the private signs, or signals, us'd among the free-masons," and the first of them runs as follows: "[For] a Member to touch the Right Leg as he goes along the Streets, brings a Member (if he sees him) from his Work on the Top of a Steeple" (*Early Masonic Pamphlets* 126).

We note that at least three different signs are mentioned. Perhaps one may be genuine, but I leave to you to determine which.

The second sign is the raised finger.

> A MASON, *holding* up his *Finger*,
> Shews he has got below a Swinger. . . .

71

> And that the Mason is preparing,
> To drink and whore, and not be sparing.

This of course was not in the Victorian reprint.

The third sign is the wink; it signifies that the Mason will soon be ready to engage in typical Masonic activity:

> To exercise and play the Man.
> For Lady or [for] Courtezan.

The fourth sign, the nod, indicates that the Mason is absolutely ready to begin building at once, after his own fashion.

The fifth sign, a shrug, indicates that the Mason is not in a suitable condition to carry out his trade.

> A SHRUG is Mark of foul Disgrace,
> For when 'tis given, this is the Case
> Of Mason, that his Building fair
> Is worn, and out of due Repair;
> But when 'tis fall'n, all is not vain,
> For it at length will rise again.

And the sixth and last sign: if a Mason swings his arm, this indicates that he is in a masochistic mood, and wants his female partner to beat him with a birch rod until she draws blood.

Having covered some of the Marks and Signs used by Masons, our author then says that he will go on to talk about the messages and letters which Masons send to each other. Even though they are not

> . . . writ upon, [they] yet make known
> The greatest Secrets of the Town.

First come letters. They are of two kinds. One sent to a brother Mason is to arrange a drinking party.

> A MASON, when he needs must drink,
> Sends *Letter*, without Pen and Ink,
> Unto some Brother, who's at hand,
> And does the Message understand;
> The Paper's of the Shape that's square,
> Thrice-folded with the nicest Care;
> For if 'tis round (which ne'er it ought)
> It will not then be worth a Groat. . . .
> And in it there must never be

> Least Writing which the Eye may see,
> For it must prove as empty ever,
> As are their Pates under the Beaver. . . .

The message consists of a piece of paper that is square, not round. This seems to be a misunderstanding of a genuine secret, for a manuscript of about 1700 (that we've already mentioned) writes as follows: "Another signe is by lending you a crooked pin or a bit of paper cut in the form of a Square on receipt of which you must come from what place or company soever you are in by virtue of your oath" (*Early Masonic Catechisms* 46). The square again; but this time it must be the mason's square! Another published exposure, that appeared in 1756, but claimed to give procedures of about 1727, says: "To send for another mason, he does it by sending a piece of paper, with a square point folded in at the corner . . ." (*Early Masonic Catechisms* 104). Once again, the square!

We continue with our poem. If on the other hand the Paper is to be sent to a Woman, then the Mason stamps it with his Finger. And the purpose of the letter is to arrange an assignation, a secret meeting.

Because Masons have all these secrets, and these ways of communicating, some people have thought that they were engaged in foul conspiracies.

> From hence they've been for Traitors taken,
> But still have Masons sav'd their Bacon;
> And tho' in Queen *Eliza*'s Days,
> A Reign that merited much Praise,
> And since they've been, at times, suspected,
> They never once have been detected:
> As *Plotters* and Confederates,
> Whose Heads are plac'd on Poles and Gates,
> They were adjudg'd, in Ages past,
> Which has an Odium on them cast;
> Yet they are very harmless Creatures,
> Have nothing plotting in their Natures,
> But what's against Hoop-Petticoats;
> For they've more Wit than risk their Throats,
> Their valuable Lives expose,
> Or hazard e'er their Ears and Nose. . . .

Finally, the poet concludes by summarizing what he has taught us, and confesses that what he has said applies only to the ordinary Mason, and not to peers of the realm.

> THUS now my Muse has faithful shown
> The History of Masons down,

> Their Secrets set in truest Light,
> And Penance, to the Reader's Sight.
> But here I must, at last, confess,
> This is not with all Men the Case;

L[or]ds and D[uke]s and persons of that class, when they join the Fraternity, do not have to do all the things he has mentioned. They don't have to be beaten, or branded, or give the Mason kiss, or drink the health of any prostitute, or read any of the masonic pornography. No,

> 'Tis only vulgar, common Masons,
> (That build no Churches, Walls, nor Bastions)
> Who feel the Whipping and the Marking,
> Are treated with such Strokes and Jirking;
> And he's not e'er a Mason good,
> Who's sparing of his Breech's Blood;
> Or who can't well a Whipping bear
> By hands of lusty Female Fair;
> Or that will shrug, unmanly start
> At Rods, or Friendly Brewer's Fart.

And that's how the poem ends. Well, what are we to make of this?

First we must set it in its historical context. It came at a time when Freemasonry was developing very quickly, and we must try to keep some of the key events in perspective. Let us recall a few dates:

1717, 24 June: The Premier Grand Lodge was Instituted.

1719: "Some Noblemen were . . . made Brothers" (Anderson's *Constitutions* of 1738, page 110).

1720: The General Regulations were first compiled.

1721, 25 March: The First noble G.M. was installed.

1722: The First Masonic book was published, a version of the *Old Charges* known as the *Roberts Pamphlet*; and in the same year Masonry begins to be mentioned in the newspapers.

1723, 26 February: Anderson's first Book of *Constitutions* was published. And later that same year,

1723, 24 June: The First minute book of Grand Lodge begins.

1724: The Grand Lodge first extended its jurisdiction over lodges outside London.

1725: The earliest notice of a Third Degree being conferred; and also the first lodge was founded outside Britain.

That's a lot going on within the space of eight years!

Now we also recall that our Hudibrastick Poem was published on 15 February 1723—eleven days before Anderson's *Constitutions*. This is a striking coincidence, and it is tempting to conclude that more than coincidence was involved. Anderson's text had previously been approved by the Masters and Wardens of all the lodges, and then by the Grand Lodge. Even outside Masonic circles people may have known that an important new book on the Craft was about to be published, and the author of our poem may have been trying to cash in on the advance publicity. So much is pure surmise; but there are some interesting facts as well that we should note.

In the first place, the hudibrastick poem is generally hostile to Masonry; and so it must count as an attack. Now mounting attacks on the Gentle Craft is a game that has gone on for years. Our beloved friend and Fellow Alphonse Cerza has traced the details in his book on *Anti-Masonry*. And the practice continues right up to the present, for example in that ghastly and dishonest book entitled *The Brotherhood* by the late Stephen Knight.

An Anti-Masonic leaflet attacking the Craft, "this devilish Sect of Men," on religious grounds, had been published in 1698 (*Early Masonic Pamphlets* 35). And an Anti-Masonic letter appeared in a London newspaper on 7 July 1722 (*Early Masonic Pamphlets* 68–71), accusing the Masons of being a pretentious and illegal association, and calling them "a Set of Low Gentry among our Artificers, who lately make a great Bluster among us." But the hudibrastick poem is the first long attack on the Craft, and it introduces two slurs that later became commonplace (*Early Masonic Pamphlets* 22–23; *Genesis of Freemasonry* 308–309); that the Masons were notorious for their heavy drinking (*Early Masonic Pamphlets* 108); and that they were sexual libertines, with a sordid reputation so far as women are concerned (*Early Masonic Pamphlets* 156).

Second point: the hudibrastick poem certainly has a few details about the Craft that seem to be true: that they have their own laws and regulations; that candidates must be investigated before they can be made Masons; that they are required to take an oath of secrecy on the Bible; that they have certain signs and tokens, including one that will serve to summon a brother even from the top of a steeple; that they are clothed in leather aprons; that they continue to make use of the Working Tools, though no longer in their original operative sense; that they have a Traditional History which associates them with the Tower of Babel; that they can arrange a meeting by sending a letter with no writing in it, a letter in the form of a square; that their membership includes certain noblemen and peers of the realm; and that they drink various toasts, including one to the Sovereign. It appears that these details must have been common knowledge, and indeed several of them had been mentioned in earlier publications.

Thirdly: the hudibrastick poem purports to reveal the secrets of Masonry; but its secrets are false. The signs allegedly disclosed are erroneous, and the whole bias is badly skewed against Masonry. There are other exposures that contain misleading secrets. The Briscoe Pamphlet of 1724 has a whole array of false signs: "To touch the Forehead with the right Hand, signifies the Member must be at the Devil Tavern in Fleetstreet, at Eleven of the Clock in the Morning the next Day. . . ." A broadsheet printed in Dublin in 1725 reveals the secrets of the brotherhood, giving one of the authorized responses as "Esimberel" (*Early Masonic Pamphlets* 88). Another broadsheet printed in London in 1726 likewise has a whole collection of spurious double-talk, including the delicious secret exchange: "What is the Square call'd? Whosly Powu Tigwawtubby" (*Early Masonic Catechisms* 97–98). But these all come later, and they all may be written by genuine Masons, with the intention of throwing those who were idly curious off the scent. The hudibrastick poem is the earliest bogus exposure, and it seems to be written by a non-Mason. At any rate the author uses the term "Installed" in a way that no Mason could ever use it.

But there is more to come! It is generally said that the oldest surviving published exposure of Masonry is a catechism known as "A Mason's Examination," that appeared in a London newspaper on 11 April 1723 (*Early Masonic Catechisms* 71–75). Other disclosures followed in rapid order (*Early Masonic Catechisms* 76–80; 87–88; 97–98). But our hudibrastick poem appeared on 15 February 1723, nearly two months before the newspaper one. It must therefore count as the earliest Masonic exposure.

Now at last we can see the baneful effects of Victorian obscenity laws on Masonic historians. The prudery of the great scholars of a generation ago prevented them from paying due attention to the hudibrastick poem. It is a wretched performance, almost without redeeming features. Yet is deserves more interest than it has received.

The date of its publication suggests some connection with Anderson's first Book of *Constitutions*, if only an attempt to profit from the general knowledge that a new book on the history and regulations of Masonry was about to appear. But more significantly, it marks an important stage in the public attitude to the Craft. It comes extremely early in the history of modern Freemasonry. It is the oldest extensive attack on the Fraternity, and it gives voice to a number of slanders that later became commonplace. And most important of all, it is the earliest publication that purports to reveal all the Secrets of Freemasonry. Both as an attack and as an exposure, it stands at the head of a long tradition.

Do not mistake my meaning. Just because the hudibrastick poem comes first, that is not to say that it set the pattern, or that it provided inspiration for the others. Inevitably they would have come in due course on their own. But it does have its place as a sign of the times, marking the fact that there was an increased public awareness of Free Masonry, and interest in it, and that there was very little accurate knowledge about it as early as February 1723. This much we can learn from the poem, so long known, so long neglected.

Appendix

THE *FREE MASONS*; AN Hudibrastick POEM: Illustrating the Whole HISTORY of the Ancient *Free Masons*, from the Building the Tower of *Babel* to this Time. With their Laws, Ordinances, Signs, Marks, Messages, &c. so long kept secret, Faithfully discover'd and made known. And the MANNER of their INSTALLATION Particularly Describ'd. By a FREE MASON.

> *All* Secrets *'till they once are known*
> *Are Wonderful, all Men must own;*
> *But when found out we cease to wonder,*
> *'Tis equal then to Fart and Thunder.*

The SECOND EDITION. *LONDON*, Printed for A. MOORE, near *St. Paul's*. 1723. (Price Sixpence)

To the Worshipful Mr. *********** One of the WARDENS of the Society of *Free-Masons*.

SIR,
Having had the Honour, not long since, when I was admitted into the Society of Masons, of Kissing your Posteriors, (an Honour superior to Kissing the Pope's Toe) I am fully determin'd to make you only the Deserving Patron of these my Labours.

The following Poem is Dedicated to You, as to one who, by Experience, can Vouch it to be True to a tittle, excepting only that small part of it which chiefly relates to the Toasting of Healths, at the Clubs of the Free-Masons; which I must own is a little Fabulous; And that of the Brewer's Fart, at the time of Installation, when the utmost Respect is paid to Mr. Breech, would likewise be thought, by all grave Persons, a little Romantick, if I did not appeal to you my Patron, in the most solemn manner, for its Truth and Confirmation.

It must be confess'd you bore it, from your loose Brother, with Christian Patience. And from thence I may presage, if Examples are to be regarded, that in time you will be advanc'd to the Dignity of a Courtier; because an Eminent * / [Note] * Sir S. F. Knight. / One, in several Reigns, had his first Rise, as Tradition tells us, from a Blast of the like Nature, from a Royal Fundament.

And I take it Court Politicians and Free Masons are oftentimes ally'd; for it is possible the one may build Castles in the Air as well as the other: And whenever they enter upon Chimerical Projects, beyond their Accomplishing, they may be undoubtedly said to build such Castles; so that it will not be a Wonderful Wonder of Wonders if you in time become a State-Politician, and arrive at Immortal Fame.

This, Sir, is all I have to say by way of Dedication, unless it be to assure you I expect no Present for the Honour I do you; for I am no mercenary Scribbler; and telling you as to the Oath I have taken, for keeping the Masonry Secrets, I have a Priest at hand (that was very serviceable during the late Rebellion) who will give me the benefit of Absolution.

This will effectually ease my tender Conscience from the Load it lies under, and I hope entitle me to Pardon and Forgiveness from all Free Masons. I am, SIR, Your most Devoted Humble Servant, The Dedicator.

THE FREE MASONS: AN Hudibrastick Poem:

ALL Kingdoms have their Masons-Free,
Which help to form Society;
By Signs and Marks they'll know each other,
In num'rous Crowds spy out a Brother;
They have their Laws, and Orders good,   5
To Govern o'er the Brotherhood,
That ne'er have been, in Ages past
Divulg'd, 'till now found out at last:
But here at length the Secret's shown,
And faithfully to all made known.   10

IF Hist'ry be no ancient Fable,
Free Masons came from *Tower of Babel*;
When first that Fabrick was begun,
The Greatest underneath the Sun,
All Nations thither did repair,   15
To build this Great Castle in th' Air;
Some Thousand Hands were well employ'd,
To finish what was ne'er enjoy'd;
For as They built, it still gave way,
And made Work for succeeding Day;   20
But after They some Years had spent
In Labour, with a good Intent,
And found that all their Lab'ring Pain,
Was still, alas! bestow'd in vain,
They then resolv'd no more to rome,   25
But to return to their own Home:
Tho' first they Signs and Marks did frame,
To signify from whence they came;
That wheresoe'er these Men shou'd go,
They always might their Breth'ren know;   30
And this was well contriv'd, for want
Of Learning, for the Ignorant,

That without speaking ev'ry Tongue,
(As by an ancient Bard is sung)
All Masons might of ev'ry Land,   35
Their Meaning ever understand;
And that it shou'd a Secret be
Amongst themselves, they did agree,
Their sev'ral *Rules* and *Orders* made,
Relating to the Mason Trade,   40
Shou'd be observ'd as long as Time,
As Records writ in Prose or Rhyme:
And by a solemn Oath enjoin'd,
The only Tye upon the Mind.

BUT since, 'tis found, the Masons-Free,   45
Which in our modern Times we see,
Workmen are of *another kind*,
To Sport they're more than Toil inclin'd,
They have no Trowels, nor yet Lines,
But still retain their Marks and Signs;   50
And Tools they've got which always fit,
A Lady, Dutchess, or a Cit,
To Build upon Foundation good,
Not made of Earth, but Flesh and Blood;
And they ne'er want the strongest Stuff,   55
As it appears when stript to Buff,
When they're in Bed, all Females find
To Build the Fabrick of Mankind:
This still must be allow'd by all,
Who've Skill in Buildings that must fall,   60
That this same Workmanship exceeds
The Labour, Pains, and manly Deeds
So long since us'd by all good People,
On *Babel*'s Tower and *Salisbury* Steeple.

OUR *modern Workmen* naked stand,   65
Their Clothes untruss'd by Female Hand,
And after they've a Flogging bore,
(But not by Jilt or common Whore)
When once they're to their Building mov'd
The Members then are strait approv'd   70
By lusty Females, who're best Judges
Of working Tools for Nature's Drudges:
These 'tis can try the Strength of Bone,
And all Materials made of Stone;
And till they've view'd 'em (O Vexation!)   75
The Mason's in State of Probation;
And after he has stood the Test,

This goes for Truth, and is no Jest,
He's * *mark'd* upon the Buttock right,
  / [Note] * *Letter* M, an *antient Custom*. /
With red-hot Iron, out of sight,   80
To shew that he dares then defy all,
And well can stand the fiery Trial:
By this the Mason's always known,
Whene'er his Breeches are pull'd down.
Some likewise say our Masons now   85
Do Circumcision undergo,
For Masonry's a *Jewish* Custom,
And by this means they all will thrust home:
But still their Privities are hidden,
Till they're Examin'd (but not ridden)   90
And none but Females have the Power,
Their Breeches and their Purse to lower.

    WHEN thus the Masons have been stript,
And well Approv'd, and Mark'd, and Whipt,
They strait are Rigg'd from Top to Toe,   95
And dress'd as fine as any Beau,
With Gloves and Apron made of Leather,
A Sword, Long-Wig, and Hat, and Feather
Like mighty *Quixote* then they swagger,
And manfully they draw the Dagger,   100
To prove that they're all Men of Mettle,
Can Windmills fight, and Treaties settle;
The Leather Apron is the Dress,
If one may be allow'd to guess,
Which represents the martial Buff,   105
And every thing that's Great and Rough:
Now 'tis the Mason is *install'd*,
And to the Book is friendly call'd;
Where after he has sworn upon
The Bible, that he'll ne'er make known   110
The Secrets of the Masonry,
Or aught that shou'd still Secret be,
Then 'tis the Brother last was made,
(This is no part of Mason's Trade)
His Breeches low pulls down, and shows   115
His A—se, this all must here expose,
Which the new Mason close salutes,
For none here durst to hold Disputes;
And when he thus the Bum has slabber'd,
And put his Sword up in his Scabbard,   120
A learned Speech is then held forth

Upon the Breech, and Mason's Worth;
And he's Install'd at last compleat,
And led down to his Mason's Seat.

    HERE only 'tis that we can see   125
The A—se promotes Society;
And it is this alone does prove,
They live in Fellowship and Love;
Whene'er 'tis kiss'd, 'tis understood,
It still promotes the Brotherhood;   130
And if it haps, by Accident,
The lower End must needs have Vent,
He that can best a *Brewer* bear,
If it does not his Face besmear,
Is still the most indulgent Mason,   135
Altho' the A—se be not made Case on:
Then if a Hole's made fit in Leather
To t'other Hole, when put together,
When once the Mason does untruss,
Behind you'll find the sweeter Buss;   140
For this will guide the Lips aright,
When Master Breech is not in sight.
This last has been contriv'd, 'tis said,
To keep the Secrets of their Trade;
And certainly that Man's a Fool,   145
Who'll boast of kissing such an Hole.

    THIS Fellowship has *Lodges* many,
Where when you're strip'd it is they tann ye;
They study well, but 'tis no matter,
The Secrets of their Mother Nature;   150
For if Philosophy they know,
It is of Nature's Charms below,
And in this ev'ry one agrees,
They know all Nature's Privities;
Each Lodge with Library is grac'd   155
In which in Order neat are plac'd
Fam'd *Aristotle's Master-Piece*,
Who was the Midwife of *Old Greece*,
And all the modern Grannies down
To *Ch—bl—n, D—gl—s*, and *B—n*:   160
Here Books are on the Shelves around,
And *Rochester*'s in Folio found;
The Play of *Sodom* likewise here
Does open on each Shelf appear;
For ev'ry unlearn'd modern Student,   165
That whores and rakes, yet still is prudent;

There, on another Side, is seen
The Works of wanton luscious *Behn*;
And that they may be here compleat,
On t'other Shelf's display'd a Set   170
Of *Impotency* and Divorce,
Caus'd by debasing Nature's Force;
Onania likewise has a Place,
And is by all caress'd, alas!
For rather than they'll want Employ,   175
They'll deal in every idle Toy,
They'll practise o'er this Sin unclean,
Read Books of * *Curll*'s the most obscene:
/ [Note] * *Bookseller to the Society.* /
This is the Library of those,
Who're now amongst Free Masons chose;   180
And these can ne'er of Knowledge fail,
Who pry in Secrets of the Tail.

    WHENE'ER they *club* it, 'tis to fuddle,
And try the Strength of each Man's Noddle;
No Charities can these Men boast,   185
For who'll be bounteous at's own Cost;
They drink, carouse, like any *Bacchus*
And swallow strongest Wines that rack us;
And then it is they lay Foundation
Of Masonry, to build a Nation.   190
They various Healths strait put around,
To ev'ry airy Female Sound;
But * *Sally* Dear's the Fav'rite Toast,
/ [Note] * Sally Salisbury, *the noted*
Prostitute, in Prison for stabbing a young
Gentleman. /
Whose Health it is they drink the most;
And tho' she's drunk, in *Newgate*, swearing,   195
Which is no Building of their rearing,
And ev'ry Turn-key has a Taste
Of what lies hid below her Waste,
And revels in the self-same Place,
Where lately did my L—d, His G—e;   200
She common is to all the Town,
From airy Beau to meanest Clown:
Yet is this Toast here drank by some,
As to the *Best in Christendom*.
Next *Berry, Darby*, all the Train,   205
Down to the *Royal Sovereign*,
Are put about by Masons all,

E'er they do for the Reck'ning call;
And none can love a Female more
Than these, if She's no dirty Whore.   210

THIS is the *Converse* when they shine,
And well are rais'd with potent Wine;
And now the goodly Task remains,
To shew how 'tis they've rack'd their Brains,
To find out *Marks* and speaking *Signs*,   215
Which each within his Breast confines.

WHEN once a Man his *Arm* forth *stretches*,
It Masons round some Distance fetches;
Altho' one be on *Paul's* Great Steeple,
He strait comes down amongst the People,   220
His Brother follows, far and wide,
If he a hundred Miles shou'd ride;
If he to antient *York* does haste,
The other must go on as fast;
Or if he should a Maggot take,   225
To ship himself on Sea or Lake,
He still attends, nor hard it thinks,
Altho' he with his Brother sinks:
And this is Fellowship indeed,
Where they thus mutually proceed;   230
All Hazards run, without a Slip,
Risque Life and Limb in Partnership.

A MASON, *holding* up his *Finger*,
Shews he has got below a Swinger;
That he's a Member of *Old Drury*,   235
And dares attack with manful Fury;
This is a Mark of *Mother Wyburn*,
That Hanging means, but not at *Tyburn*;
And that the Mason is preparing,
To drink and whore, and not be sparing.   240

A WINK then signifies 'tis Rising,
(Which is not to all Girls surprizing)
And that they quickly shall be ready,
If they've not drank what's over heady,
For Lady or a Courtezan,   245
To exercise and play the Man.

THE *Nod* doth make us understand
The great Enjoyment's near at hand;
That they're then full prepar'd to show,
And do all that a Man can do: 250

With Female Fair they dare engage,
Encounter with a Godlike Rage.

    A SHRUG is Mark of foul Disgrace,
For when 'tis given, this is the Case
Of Mason, that his Building fair   255
Is worn, and out of due Repair;
But when 'tis fall'n, all is not vain,
For it at length will rise again.

    IT is an ignominious thing,
When e'er the Mason gives a *Swing*;   260
With Arm, downright, wide stretch'd, and jogging,
This shews a Mason dull wants *Flogging*;
(And she that can each Stroke draw Blood,
Is still esteem'd a Flogger good;)
Our Masons ne'er will well be pleas'd,   265
'Till with Dame Birch their Bums are reaz'd,
And jirk'd, and whipp'd, with Rods and Scourges,
Which still the brawny Buttocks purges;
And then they feel the greatest Pleasure,
When they're thus scourg'd beyond all measure: 270
For ev'ry Stroke of pleasing Pain,
That helps to empty Cupid's Vein,
Is usher'd in with tickling Joy,
And Bliss that ne'er will Masons cloy.

    THESE some are of the Marks and Signs,   275
To which each Mason strong inclines;
And to these Signs I'm here to add,
What may be deem'd almost as bad,
Their *Messages*, and Scraps of Paper,
Which are not seal'd with Wax or Wafer,   280
Nor writ upon, and yet make known
The greatest Secrets of the Town.

    A MASON, when he needs must drink,
Sends *Letter*, without Pen and Ink,
Unto some Brother, who's at hand,   285
And does the Message understand;
The Paper's of the Shape that's square,
Thrice-folded with the nicest Care;
For if 'tis round (which ne'er it ought)
It will not then be worth a Groat,   290
Have any Force or Meaning good,
By which it may be understood;
And in it there must never be
Least Writing which the Eye may see,

For it must prove as empty ever,   295
As are their Pates under the Beaver,
Or it is not for Purpose fit,
Or consonant with Mason's Wit.
Whene'er this Paper's sent to Woman,
'Tis then with Finger stamp'd uncommon,   300
To shew it means, what is in Fashion
At Plays and Balls, an Assignation;
And he that can interpret these
Unwritten Scrolls and Messages,
It is alone is welcome Guest,   305
And fit to be at Mason's Feast.

    BUT there's another *Billet-deux*,
Which in times past was much in Use,
It Paper was, all over writ on,
By Spaniard, Swede, by Dane, or Briton;   310
In antient Language, and each Rover,
All Masons cou'd the Sense discover:
But as where Paper has no Writing,
So when 'tis of these Mens inditing,
None but their mighty selves cou'd read,   315
Or Myst'ries know of Mason's Trade;
And Dashes, and no Scribbling, mean
The self same Thing as Paper clean,
To him who knows not one or t'other,
Is not install'd a Mason's Brother.   320
From hence they've been for Traitors taken,
But still have Masons sav'd their Bacon;
And tho' in Queen *Eliza*'s Days,
A Reign that merited much Praise,
And since they've been, at times, suspected,   325
They never once have been detected:
As *Plotters* and Confederates,
Whose Heads are plac'd on Poles and Gates,
They were adjudg'd, in Ages past,
Which has an Odium on them cast;   330
Yet they are very harmless Creatures,
Have nothing plotting in their Natures,
But what's against Hoop-Petticoats;
For they've more Wit than risk their Throats,
Their valuable Lives expose,   335
Or hazard e'er their Ears and Nose;
Tho' he's not worth a single Farthing,
Who'll not endure a strong Bumbarding.

THUS now my Muse has faithful shown
The History of Masons down,   340
Their Secrets set in truest Light,
And Penance, to the Reader's Sight.
But here I must, at last, confess,
This is not with all Men the Case;
For we have L--ds, and D--s, and such,   345
Who do not undergo as much;
Who're free, we'll say (without a Sneering)
From Scourging, and from Buttocks Searing;
Nor must they make a Rout or Pother,
Kiss lower End of any Brother,   350
Or Health's Toast to the famous *Sally*,
Or Drabs that dwell in Street or Alley;
Nor do they study *Onan*'s Crime,
Yet some of these begin betime;
Or Impotency, or Divorce,   355
Altho' some can all Females curse:
'Tis only vulgar, common Masons,
(That build no Churches, Walls, nor Bastions)
Who feel the Whipping and the Marking,
Are treated with such Strokes and Jirking;   360
And he's not e'er a Mason good,
Who's sparing of his Breech's Blood;
Or who can't well a Whipping bear
By Hands of lusty Female Fair;
Or that will shrug, unmanly start   365
At Rods, or Friendly Brewer's Fart.

F I N I S

86

THE CAUSES OF RITUAL DIVERGENCE

[If you visit lodges in other states, you will note that the ritual is different. This essay attempts to explain why. It was delivered before the Maryland Masonic Research Society, Elkridge, Maryland, 13 February 1986.]

INTRODUCTION

We're often taught that Freemasonry is immutable, and that no one is allowed to introduce innovations; but of course that is not true. Enough records exist to show that Masonry is constantly changing—not in its essentials, but in the externals, the trappings, of the Order.

That is what I want to discuss for a few minutes today—changes in Freemasonry. These changes are most frequently reflected, and most readily traced, through the ritual. (I must add here that, even though people think of Masonry as a secret society, actually a great many documents survive, that permit us to see in fair detail how the ritual evolved. Just to cover myself, let me say that we shall not be dealing with the Masonic ritual as it is today; we shall be referring to early documents, most of them more than 200 years old; and of course many changes have been incorporated since those days.)

Much of what I am going to say is not new, but is derived from the work of others. Someone has said that we can see so much farther than our predecessors because we stand on the shoulders of giants. And that is true. I am conscious of the giants on whose shoulders I stand. In particular I rely heavily on the work of several brethren whose names I must mention.

There is my own teacher, Bro. Harry Carr, of England, the world's authority on the evolution of the ritual; and two American students who were concerned with the sources of Masonry in the United States: George B. Clark, who for the Masonic Service Association of the United States prepared a Masonic Digest entitled *From Whence Came We?*; and the great Roscoe Pound, Dean of Harvard Law School, who did a marvelous study of "The Causes of Divergence in Ritual."

I begin by summarizing Pound's introductory remarks. "Every Masonic traveler," he said, "soon becomes aware" that there are differences in the ritual. If he's traveling by himself to a different part of the world, and if he wants to hold Masonic communication with brethren whom he has never met, he will probably have to undergo a Board of Trial. He will recognize the look of frustration on the faces of the examining committee, and he will see them awkwardly trying to "fit two divergent systems of work" together without going into long explanations. He will realize that, while both he and they are confident of themselves, something is very wrong.

This can be seen "in a matter as fundamental as the modes of recognition." In some places they letter or syllable both the word and the password. Elsewhere "the pass is given at once, but the word is divided or syllabled." And if our Masonic pilgrim were to visit the continent of Europe, he would meet an *unfamiliar* substitute word.

But, even if he stays in America, when he gets into the lodge he will probably find more or fewer officers than he is used to at home, he will quite likely find "a radically different method of opening and closing," and he will be "sure to find differences of detail here and there in the work."

Take, for example, the matter of opening and closing. "In some jurisdictions the practice is to open a lodge of Entered Apprentices or of Fellowcrafts or of Master Masons," whatever is required, without reference to any preceding degree, "and then to declare the particular lodge open as such." In other jurisdictions "this is deemed wrong, and the lodge is ceremoniously opened successively from the lowest degree to the one in which work is to be done, and then closed in reverse order."

One could go on and on. Is the word "willingly" or "wittingly"? Should one say "wayfaring man" or "seafaring man"? Precisely what are the details of the search by the Craftsmen? All this within the confines of the United States. And then, of course, if you should happen to visit a lodge in *my* mother jurisdiction, you find even greater differences. There we do not make use of the Due Guard; we have *two* adopted substitute words; our Master Mason's Degree is for the most part narrated rather than dramatized. We do not retain the symbolism of the beehive, or the celestial and terrestrial globes, or the trowel, or the winged hour-glass, or the five senses, or the anchor and the ark, or the pot of incense, or the sword pointing to the naked heart, or the Book of *Constitutions* guarded by the Tiler's Sword.

The Master in our lodges does not wear a hat, and the brethren are at perfect liberty to pass between the Master and the Altar. We do not open our Sacred Volume at the 133rd Psalm, or recite the words, "Behold, how good and how pleasant it is for brethren to dwell together in unity. . . ." For us, the seventh chapter of *Amos*, where the Lord stands upon a wall made by a plumbline, is not a part of the Degree of a Fellowcraft, but is used in another ceremony.

Our Working Tools for the Entered Apprentice Degree include the *Chisel* as well as the Twenty-four Inch Gauge and the Common Gavel. Our Working Tools for the Master Mason are the Skirret, the Compasses, and the Pencil. For us, the Square, Level, and Plumbrule are *Movable* Jewels, and the Rough Ashlar, the Perfect Ashlar, and what we call the *Tracing* Board (rather than *Trestle* Board) are *Immovable* Jewels, rather than the other way around. We have the Point within a Circle, but it is not embordered by two Perfect Parallel Lines, or surmounted by the *Book of Constitution*.

In most American Grand Lodges the sessions of the lodge are held in the Master Mason's Degree; in Ontario the business meeting takes place in the E.A. Degree. Our *Constitution* no longer makes reference to the legendary assembly at York in the year 926.

In fact, after hearing this list, you may be tempted to wonder whether we are even entitled to be called Masons. Yet we are recognized as such, and if you look around our lodge rooms, and listen to our degrees, you will find much that is familiar. Where we differ, it is tempting to ask "Which one of us is right, and which is wrong?" But that is the wrong question, because any Grand Lodge has absolute power to legislate the procedures and ritual for its own lodges; and whatever it has decided upon is *right* for that jurisdiction.

In fact, *not* to "conform to every edict of the Grand Lodge" is a Masonic offense. The proper question to ask is rather "Why are we so different?"

Well, there are several reasons. First, we know that in the 1700s, when the Craft was being transplanted to North America, the Masonic ritual was evolving rapidly. Brethren who came to the New World brought their own local variations of the work. As the ritual evolved in the old land, successive versions would find their way across the Atlantic. Faulty memories caused further divergences, since verbal accuracy was not the fetish it is today. In fact the insistence on uniformity seems to be a North American aberration.

Certainly in England today there is no single authorized form of ritual. There are dozens of printed versions, and theoretically any Mason is at liberty to devise his own ritual, so long as he observes the basic outline. Even beyond these factors, we can say that Masonry did not come to America from any single source.

There were different governing bodies in the Craft, and each of them no doubt had its own distinctive idiosyncrasies. Moreover, new grand lodges were formed by the union of lodges chartered from different sources, and these unions gave rise to all sorts of different combinations.

Each new grand lodge was of course independent, and either preserved the ritual as it had received it, or made it over by way of compromise, or revised it in accordance with its own ideas.

EVOLUTION OF THE RITUAL

Now I want in particular to talk about two of these matters. First, let us look at the way in which our ritual has developed. I take it as proven that our modern Freemasonry is descended in some sense from the operative stone-masons, the cathedral builders of England in the Middle Ages. They gave us our symbolism, and much of our language. These workmen wore aprons to protect their garments from spot and stain, and they used hammers and chisels, square and compasses, level and plumbrule. They drew the design for the building on a tracing board. They cut the rough ashlars from the quarry, and transformed them into smooth ashlars.

These operative stone-masons were mostly skilled journeymen, Fellows of Craft; there were a few Apprentices, signed on to learn the trade; and on each job there was the head man, the Master of the Works. These Masons took their meals, and kept their working tools, in a small shed set up on the south side of their project, that was known as a lodge. They were highly trained, and when they moved on to a new job, it appears that they had secret modes of recognition, to show that they belonged to the trade.

In every large center there was an incorporation or a guild, a sort of union, that controlled all the stone building there, and carried out periodic inspections of the work. This union was a closed shop, and you could not work at the trade in the town unless you were recognized as a member of the guild.

The Unions had a set of rules, and a traditional history, that were supposed to be read to every new Mason when he was made; they are known as The Old Charges. They were usually in the form of a scroll, and we have a number of copies. They reveal a bit about the ritual of those days. The earliest version of the Old Charges, the *Regius Manuscript* of about 1390, actually closes with the words:

> Amen, Amen! So mote it be!
> So say we all for Charity!

The later versions all begin with an invocation, which in its most common form runs like this: "The might of the Father of Heaven, with the wisdom of His glorious Son, through the grace and goodness of the Holy Ghost, that be three persons in one God, be with us at our beginning, and give us grace so to govern us in our living, that we may come to His bliss that never shall have ending. Amen."

Then they go on to talk about the Seven Liberal Arts and Sciences, particularly Geometry. They include a traditional history which tells, among other things, about the first metallurgist, Tubalcain, and the two great pillars, and the building of King Solomon's Temple. Then, before we come to the actual regulations, we are told that the candidate had to place his hands on "The Book" and hold them there while the rules were read to him. And after all this he is given an obligation, that runs something like this:

> These charges that we have now rehearsed unto you, and all other that belong to masons, ye shall keep, so help you God and your halidom, and by this Book in your hand, unto your power. Amen.

90

This particular obligation was familiar to the operative masons in England not too long after 1550; no penalty, no secrets; the candidate simply swears to abide by the regulations. And here's another obligation, 100 years younger, from about 1650:

> There are several words and signs of a freemason to be revealed to you, which as you will answer before God at the great and terrible day of judgment, you keep secret, and not to reveal the same in the ears of any person but to the masters and fellows of the said society of freemasons. So help me God.

These operative lodges lasted about 300 years, from about 1350 to 1650. Then for some reason or other in the years after 1600 the organized building trade collapsed. Perhaps the Reformation had something to do with it. Perhaps the great fire of London was another cause.

So much new building was needed after the fire that the authorities allowed anyone who could hold a hammer to help with the rebuilding. The union closed shop was broken. In order simply to survive, the old guilds, incorporations, and lodges began to admit non-operatives as members, people who belonged to the gentry, who had never held a hammer and chisel, who were for some reason interested in the building trade, and cared enough to pay a fee to join. The earliest examples are in the 1630s and 1640s in England and Scotland.

This ushered in the Transitional period. Lodges would apparently consist of mixtures of primarily operative masons with a few gentlemen attached. As time passed, it appears that they came to include fewer and fewer operative masons in their members. They had to do something else to justify their existence, and first they turned into drinking clubs. Then they began to engage in good works, and moral improvement.

We have some documents that tell us about the ritual that was used in those days, particularly in Scotland. These are the series of papers that are usually called the Old Masonic Catechisms, because they consist of questions and answers. The oldest of them all is the *Edinburgh Register House Manuscript*, which is dated 1696. It includes the Obligation that was used by these transitional Masons. It runs like this:

> By God himself—and you shall answer to God when you shall stand naked before him at the Great Day—you shall not reveal any part of what you shall hear or see at this time, neither by word nor write, nor put it in write at any time, nor draw it with the point of a sword, or any other instrument, upon the snow or sand, nor shall you speak of it but with an entered mason. So help you God.

By now there are secrets, that is, signs and tokens; and something that sounds like the original of our "write, indite, mark, print, carve, engrave;" but still no penalty.

Now, in the year 1717 four of these lodges in the city of London banded together, and formed the first Grand Lodge in the world. Within a generation independent Grand Lodges were formed in Scotland and Ireland; and from them, all Masonry in the world is descended. This mother Grand Lodge was clearly non-operative. But I hardly think that it should yet be called speculative. This non-operative non-speculative period lasts until 1770.

We begin to have more information about the ritual now, both published in newspapers, and preserved on handwritten sheets of paper. One might imagine that they would all be suspect, because, after all, they do disclose things that were not supposed to be disclosed. But in general they show such consistent evolution that we can be almost certain that they reflect reality. The most popular version was provided by Samuel Prichard in his *Masonry Dissected* of 1730. It was very wide-spread, and in fact we know it was used even in America, for the obligation that it gives was quoted in a newspaper, the New York *Gazette*, for 28 November 1737:

> I hereby solemnly vow and swear in the presence of Almighty God and this Right Worshipful Assembly, that I will hele and conceal and never reveal the secrets or secrecy of masons or masonry that shall be revealed unto me; unless to a true and lawful Brother, after due examination, or in a just and worshipful lodge of Brothers and Fellows well met.
>
> I furthermore promise and vow that I will not write them, print them, mark them, carve them, or engrave them, or cause them to be written, printed, marked, carved, or engraved, on wood or stone, so as the visible character or impression of a letter may appear, whereby it may be unlawfully obtained.
>
> All this under no less penalty than to have my throat cut, my tongue taken from the roof of my mouth, my heart plucked from under my left breast, them to be buried in the sands of the sea, the length of a cable-rope from shore, where the tide ebbs and flows twice in 24 hours, my body to be burnt to ashes, my ashes to be scattered upon the face of the earth, so that there shall be no more remembrance of me among masons. So help me God.

Now *that* Obligation is getting to sound a bit more familiar; except of course that the penalties are piled up together in a terrifying way.

With so many exposures being published, anybody who wished could learn the secrets of Masonry, and could gain admission to lodge, or claim charity. Grand Lodge got so upset about this that at some date close to 1739 it actually changed the modes of recognition!

Prichard's *Masonry Dissected* had said that the Entered Apprentice used two pillar words, while the Fellow Craft used one of them. But Grand Lodge arbitrarily decreed that henceforth the word for the First Degree should be the one formerly used for the Second Degree, and that the other one should now designate the Second Degree. This created a tremendous uproar, because of course it was tampering with the Landmarks.

A group of Irish Masons in London said that the Grand Lodge was making innovation in the body of Masonry, and so they formed their own independent Grand Lodge. And for the next sixty years England had these two rival Grand Lodges, known as the Ancients and the Moderns. They used the words in different order in the two first degrees, and they had different words in the Third Degree.

Meanwhile, the ritual continued to evolve. The wording was still pretty threadbare, and there wasn't too much for the mind. Three exposures were published around 1760, and they show us the working of that time. It remained in use in England right up until the Union of 1813. Here is the obligation they give, the one that was current at the time of the American Revolution:

I, A. B., of my own free will and accord, and in the presence of Almighty God and this Right Worshipful Lodge dedicated to Saint John, do hereby and hereon most solemnly and sincerely swear that I will always hele, conceal, and never reveal any of the secrets or mysteries of Free Masonry that shall be delivered to me now or at any time hereafter, except it be to a true and lawful Brother, or in a just and lawful Lodge of Brothers and Fellows, him or them whom I shall find to be such after just trial and due examination.

I furthermore do swear that I will not write it, print it, cut it, paint it, stint it, mark it, stain or engrave it, or cause so to be done, upon anything movable or immovable under the canopy of Heaven whereby it may become legible or intelligible, or the least appearance of the character of a letter, whereby the Secret Art may be unlawfully obtained.

All this I swear, with a strong and steady resolution to perform the same, without any hesitation, mental reservation, or self-evasion of mind in me whatsoever; under no less penalty than to have my throat cut across, my tongue torn out by the root, and that to be buried in the sands of the sea at low water mark a cable's length from the shore where the tide ebbs and flows twice in twenty-four hours.

So help me God, and keep me steadfast in this my Entered Apprentice's Obligation.

SOURCES OF AMERICAN MASONRY

We see then that during the period of the first immigration the ritual was evolving rapidly. The second factor that accounts for differences in the wording is the fact that Masonry did not come to America from any single source. As a matter of fact, there were seven distinct wellsprings.

(1) *"Immemorial Right"*. All through the era before the grand lodges, masons had the right of gathering together in lodges, clearly without any warrant of constitution from a higher authority, because there was no higher authority. They simply came together "by immemorial right." The practice is well documented in England and Scotland. One such gathering was the lodge at Aberdeen, which is still working today.

The earliest undoubted Mason in America belonged to this "immemorial right" lodge. John Skene, of the lodge at Aberdeen, came to America in 1682, and served as Deputy Governor of East Jersey until his death in 1690. Dozens of other Masons must have lived in pioneer America, and sometimes they too banded together into lodges "by immemorial right." The Grand Lodges had not yet established their authority, and Masons still had this ancient prerogative.

One such group was in Philadelphia as early as 1730; this was the lodge that initiated Benjamin Franklin. There were others elsewhere, including one (a bit later) at Fredericksburg, Virginia, where George Washington was initiated in 1752. Once regularly warranted lodges reached the country, all of these old bodies sought warrants of constitution from the British Grand Lodges.

(2) *England (Moderns)*. The Premier Grand Lodge was established in London, England, in 1717, by four lodges meeting there by immemorial right. It grew quickly. In April of 1733 the Grand Master named Henry Price as Provincial Grand Master for New England and the Dominions and Territories thereunto belonging. Later that year he formed his Grand Lodge, and immediately, in response to a petition from a number of Masons who had been meeting "according to the Old Customs," he warranted a lodge to meet in Boston. During the next few years warrants were issued to several lodges in America, either from London or from Boston. By the end of 1736, regular Freemasonry was well established in America.

One gathers that there is a great debate among Masons in the United States about which state is entitled to priority in matters Masonic, Pennsylvania or Massachusetts. Please bear with a foreigner if he attempts to adjudicate this debate, but the matter seems perfectly clear to me. If you are talking about Masonic lodges who constituted themselves according to the old customs, the palm must go to Pennsylvania (1730 or before). At that early date such a procedure was perfectly regular. If on the other hand you are talking about a lodge warranted from a superior body, then the priority goes to Massachusetts (1733). Simple as that. Define your terms, and the problem disappears.

The premier Grand Lodge was the only body of duly constituted Masonry to take any interest in America before 1755. It issued patents to various Provincial Grand Masters to take charge of particular regions.

(3) *France.* Freemasonry was introduced to France from England in 1725. The independent Grand Lodge of France was formed in 1728 or 1729. In 1760, La Parfait Union, a French-speaking lodge, was warranted by the English (M) P.G.L. of New York. From 1798 to 1823 various French bodies warranted lodges in Louisiana, working in French. There is said to be Scottish Rite influence in the ritual of Louisiana, and it probably goes back to French sources. Two French lodges were founded by the Grand Orient in California in 1850 or so, and still work the First Degree in French.

(4) *The Grand Lodge of Scotland* was established in 1736. It founded lodges at Blandford, Virginia, and at Boston, in 1756, and subsequently other Scottish lodges in the Southern colonies.

(5) *The Lodge at Kilwinning* ("Mother Kilwinning") in Scotland withdrew from the Grand Lodge of Scotland in 1743 and acted as an independent warranting body for more than sixty years. It chartered lodges in Virginia between 1755 and 1758.

(6) *The Grand Lodge of Ireland* was instituted about 1725. It warranted no civilian lodges in the colonies before the Revolution, but it issued "traveling" warrants to regimental lodges in the British Army, and many of them came to America during the French and Indian War (1755-1763). They played a significant role in planting Freemasonry in the country.

(7) *The Grand Lodge of England according to the Old Institutions ("Ancients")* was formed in 1751 by six lodges in England made up largely of Irishmen. They claimed that the Premier Grand Lodge had introduced innovations, and therefore they called it the "Moderns," and took for themselves the name of the "Ancients." The "Ancients" warranted Lodge No 69, Philadelphia, in 1758, and subsequently other lodges were formed in Delaware, Maryland, New Jersey, and Virginia.

So we see that Freemasonry came to America from seven different sources: "time immemorial" lodges, England (the "Moderns" and the "Ancients"), Ireland, Scotland (both the Grand Lodge and Mother Kilwinning), and France. But these sources appear in various admixtures in the different states.

Masonry spread across the United States from seven of the thirteen colonies, and each of them drew its traditions in varying proportions from the different sources. North Carolina is said to derive its work entirely from the Moderns, and so perhaps did Georgia. Pennsylvania and New York preserve the traditions of the Ancients almost unimpaired, but New York derived its share not just from the Grand Lodge of the Ancients, but also from Ireland and Scotland, which worked in amity with it.

The other founding colonies were hybrids. Massachusetts and South Carolina are a mingling of both Ancients and Moderns, and Virginia incorporates a component from Scotland and from Mother Kilwinning. There is said to be a trace of "time immemorial" Masonry in Massachusetts, Pennsylvania, and Virginia.

These seven states in turn acted as Masonic colonizers for the rest of the country. Today a few grand lodges are more or less unmixed. Thus, Maryland and Delaware derived their founding lodges from Pennsylvania, and New Jersey largely from New York, and so they are purely Ancients. The first lodges in New Hampshire and Rhode Island were warranted from Boston in the early period before the Ancients arrived, and so they are Moderns. The Craft in Tennessee sprang from North Carolina, and in turn passed the same Moderns traditions unimpaired to Missouri, and from thence to Iowa, Kansas, the Dakotas, and New Mexico.

But most Grand Lodges mingle their components in varying proportions. Just to cite one or two examples, lodges in the District of Columbia were founded from Maryland (pure Ancients) and Virginia ("time immemorial," Moderns, Ancients from Scotland, and Ancients from Lodge Kilwinning). California derives its Craft traditions from the District of Columbia (whose components we have just listed), from Connecticut—which in turn came from a mixture of New York (Ancients) and Massachusetts ("time immemorial," Moderns, Ancients from England, Ireland, and Scotland)—and from Missouri (pure Moderns, deriving from North Carolina).

California in its turn acted as a center of dissemination, and transmitted this very mixed tradition to Arizona, Nevada, Oregon, Washington, and Idaho. It is little wonder that each jurisdiction has its distinctive traditions. It would be too confusing to go though all the states in this fashion. I hope that you get the idea.

Some jurisdictions in America bear the name F. & A.M., and others are A.F. & A.M. The latter is sometimes assumed to point to an Ancients background, but even this signpost can be deceptive. Pennsylvania, pure Ancients, calls itself F. & A.M., and North Carolina, pure Moderns, is A.F. & A.M.

One other reason for change is worth noting.

In 1843 a National Masonic Convention was held in Baltimore. It proposed certain standard innovations, which came to be adopted by many of the grand lodges. (1) It changed the Due Guard in the First and Third Degrees. (2) It interchanged the movable and immovable jewels. (3) It decided that all business would be transacted in the Master Mason Degree.

That perhaps will give you the idea. Roughly the same sort of thing happened in Canada. To begin with, Masonry was implanted in our Atlantic Provinces in the formative period, in 1738; the first implantation came from Boston—and at this period that would mean the Moderns.

Next there was a strong infusion of the Ancients in Nova Scotia in 1757. Right after the city of Quebec was captured from the French in 1759, six military lodges held a meeting—five Irish ones and one carrying a "Moderns" warrant from Boston. Then the Ancients founded Provincial Grand Lodges in Ontario and Quebec in 1792. In fact, our ritual was evolving in much the same way as yours.

In some parts of Canada (particularly the Atlantic Provinces) our working of today is basically indistinguishable from that current in United States of America.

But there is one place that is different, and that is Ontario. The ritual used in my home jurisdiction is fundamentally English, and it is quite different from the American York Rite. This is because in England in 1813 the two rival grand lodges, the Ancients and the Moderns, amalgamated after sixty years of savage hostility, and formed the United Grand Lodge of England.

After the Union the ritual was totally revised, to make it acceptable to both parties. Since they to some extent had different modes of recognition, some compromises were necessary. *That* is when many of the distinctive portions of the pre-Union ritual were jettisoned. That is when the *two* adopted substitute words came into use; one belonged to the Ancients and one to the Moderns, and they couldn't agree which was right, and so they kept both. And while the authorities were at it, they took the opportunity to rewrite the whole ritual, cutting it down and removing the Christian allusions.

And that is why our Working differs so much from American ritual. Yours is basically pre-Union, and ours is post-Union. That is when we dropped so much of the symbolism that is still current in the States.

The reason we have retained this post-Union ritual in my part of Canada is because of one very gifted and strong-willed Mason, who was an early Provincial Grand Master sent out from London. He introduced the new ritual to Canada. While it has changed a bit, it is still clearly recognizable as post-Union, and the only places it is used are those parts of Canada that derived their working from Ontario.

The man responsible is one of my Masonic heroes, Simon McGillivray. He was a Scottish merchant and fur-trader who worked out of Montreal, and was a close personal friend of the Most Worshipful the Grand Master, His Royal Highness the Duke of Sussex. Simon McGillivray was Provincial Grand Master in Ontario from 1822 to 1840; *he* brought the new ritual to Canada in 1825. I have another long talk devoted entirely to his life, but you'll have to ask me back again if you want to hear it. Anyway, as a result of his work, about three-quarters of the lodges in Canada use what is called the Canadian working, which is really a post-Union English ritual. And just under a quarter of the lodges use the Ancient York Ritual, which is really American; there are at least two lodges using it in every province.

So we see that Masonic ritual has been evolving for 600 years, and that to some extent it has evolved differently in different parts of the world. Can we draw any useful lessons from all this? I think we can.

To begin with, as you travel around you will see that the ritual differs from place to place. This serves to remind us that Freemasonry is not absolutely immutable; it *does* change, though only slowly, and because of this evolution, each grand lodge is a little bit different from all others.

Secondly, and more importantly, *despite* these differences, you will observe in your travels that the ritual is basically similar, and that it clearly goes back to a single prototype. Although the Craft has been spread over different parts of the globe for some 250 years, no matter where it is, it still clings tenaciously to those features that it values—and not just the outline of the ritual, but also certain intangibles. It is still an affinity group of brethren who have gone through some of the same experiences, and who share some of the same ideals.

Others may if they choose proclaim that God is dead, but Freemasonry still believes in the existence of a Supreme Being. Others may subscribe to what are called situational ethics, but Freemasonry still holds to *absolute* moral standards. Freemasonry still proclaims that all men are created equal, and are worthy to meet together upon the level.

It still adheres to the tenets or fundamental principles of Brotherly Love, Relief, and Truth.

It still asserts that Faith, Hope, and Charity are more than mere words.

It still exhorts us to unite in the grand design of being happy and communicating happiness.

In short, Freemasonry continues, as it has been in the past, to be an unchanging moral force for good in this changing world.

ANTI-MASONRY IN THE EIGHTIES

*[Many people, incredibly enough, express a hostility to Free-
masonry. This paper attempts to discover some of the reasons and
to suggest how we might react to such people.]*

POLITICAL PERSECUTION

You may hardly be aware, but in 1985 Canada saw two noteworthy trials at
law, both of them concerned essentially with the nature of historical truth.

One was the trial of Ernst Zundel, in Toronto; he used to run a publishing
house called SAMISDAT, from which he sold Nazi propaganda; you could
get tapes of Hitler's speeches, and recordings of German military bands, and
pamphlets arguing that the Holocaust never took place.

The other trial was that of James Keegstra in Red Deer, Alberta; he was a
high-school teacher, and regularly taught that the media were in the hands of
the Jews, and that the Holocaust was a Jewish invention.

In their reports, the newspapers turned most of their attention to a single
question: Did Hitler really cause the death of six million Jews? (A court of
law seems a peculiar place in which to determine the accuracy of the historical record—but let that go.) I have no desire to belittle the significance of the
question, but it is less relevant to my purposes than one of the subsidiary
issues raised at the same trials.

In the course of the proceedings it became clear that both Zundel and
Keegstra believed in the existence of an International Jewish-Masonic Conspiracy to take over the world. This idea of course had achieved great cur-
rency in Germany after the First World War, and was adopted enthusiastically
under Hitler. It served to justify, on the one hand, the death-camps, and, on
the other, the abolition of German Freemasonry in May of 1935. Awareness
of this conspiracy so far as Jews are concerned goes back to 1848. The
Masons were implicated as early as 1797.

It seems that the unsavory reputation of the Freemasons has had repercus-
sions more than once. In 1795 the Emperor Francis II suppressed the Craft
throughout the Austrian Empire, and the lodges remained closed until 1918.

In 1822 Czar Alexander I issued a ukase closing all the lodges in Russia
permanently. The Craft was revived in 1908, but was put out of existence by
the Bolsheviks in 1919. It still attracts Russian thunderbolts. Let me quote
from a column written by Grigory Alexeyev in the English language *Moscow
News* in 1983:

From the outset Freemasonry was a secret organization of the elite. They always came out against social change, against social revolutions. . . . After the October Socialist Revolution the Masons took part in the counter-revolutionaries' armed actions. . . . Their lodges and organizations were eventually outlawed. . . . After World War II New Masonic lodges appeared in [several countries] with the purpose of carrying out subversive activities against the USSR and other socialist countries. . . . Zionist agents are active in those 'new' lodges as well (quoted by Allen E. Roberts, *Philalethes*, September 1983).

In 1925 Mussolini passed an anti-Masonic law in Italy. Masonry was suppressed in Portugal by Salazar in 1931; in Spain in 1941 by Franco; in Rumania in 1948, and in Hungary in 1950, both by the Communists; in Egypt by Nasser in the fifties or sixties, and in Indonesia by Soekarno in the 1960s; in Pakistan by the Interior Minister, Khan Abdul Quayyum Khan, in December of 1972; in Iran by the Ayatollah Khomeini in 1979. Even before word leaked out from Iran that members of the Baha'i faith were being tortured, newspapers reported that Senator Mohsen Khajenouri had been shot by a firing squad for the crime of Freemasonry, and others followed. In his defence the Senator was reported to have said, "There were some good people in it."

I don't know whether you can detect any pattern here. It seems to me that in general a certain kind of regime, either of the left or of the right, tends to prohibit Masonry. The only countries where it exists openly today are those that are more or less democratic: western and northern Europe, Greece, Turkey, Israel, North and South America, India, Australia, Japan.

RELIGIOUS PERSECUTION

But there are others who condemn the Craft on grounds that are not political. In 1738 Pope Clement XII issued a Papal Bull which ran in part like this: "By virtue of the Holy Obedience, we strictly enjoin the Faithful in Christ, all and singular, . . . that no one, under any pretext or excuse whatsoever, venture or presume to enter into the . . . Societies known by the name of **Liberi Muratori** or **Francs Maçons**, . . . under penalty of Excommunication, to be incurred automatically without proclamation."

This was 1738. On 26 November 1983, Cardinal Ratzinger, Prefect of the Sacred Congregation for the Teaching of the Faith, issued a declaration: "The Church's negative opinion about Masonic lodges continues unchanged. . . . Enrolment in them remains prohibited by the Church. The Faithful in Christ who give their names to Masonic Lodges are in a state of grave sin and cannot attend Holy Communion."

In Italy, because of this condemnation, the Masons came to be equated with unbelievers. This notion even finds its way into Hemingway's novel, *A Farewell to Arms*, where two young Italian officers are talking. One of them, the major, says "All thinking men are atheists;" (and then, as if they were the same thing, he goes on) "I do not believe in the Free Masons however." "I believe in the Free Masons," the lieutenant said. "It is a noble organization."

But the Catholic Church does not stand alone in looking askance at the Craft. The Church of Jesus Christ of the Latter Day Saints, the Mormons, has condemned Masonry since the time of Brigham Young.

In 1925 General William Booth, the founder of the Salvation Army, denounced it. So did the Free Church of Scotland in 1927; the Assembly of Bishops of the Church of Greece in 1933, and again in 1970; and a special Commission of the Dutch Reformed Church of South Africa (Cape Synod) in November 1940. Masonry was denounced by the Missouri Synod of the Lutheran Church in June 1950, and repeatedly by the Jehovah's Witnesses, the Seventh Day Adventists, and in general all fundamentalist evangelical Christian denominations.

For example, in 1980 a book was published by Salem Kirban, and distributed by Morris Cerullo World Evangelism; its title is *Satan's Angels Exposed*. . . . And there you will find them all: the Fabian Society, the Bilderbergers, the Trilateral Commission, the Unification Church, the Illuminati—and the Freemasons. The author says that "The basic idealogies of Masonry . . . make it incompatible with Christianity." "Albert Pike . . . writes, . . . 'The Masonic religion should be . . . maintained in the purity of the Luciferian doctrine.' " "Lucifer is God. . . . The Christian God . . . is the God of Evil" (pages 140, 160–161, 165).

And in 1984 a book by Charles G. Finney, called *The Antichrist or the Masonic Society* . . . was published. It first came out in 1868, but was reissued in 1984 with a new foreword by Donald Huffman. It says that Freemasonry is a false religion, that its oaths and obligations are unlawful and void, that its boasted benevolence is a great sham. In the new preface the editor, fortified by liberal quotation from the book of *Revelation*, argues "that the Antichrist will rise to power out of the Masonic Society" (page 9).

In July of 1985 the Faith and Order Committee of the Methodist Church of England presented a recommendation to the General Conference that Methodists should not become Masons. The report was adopted.

Or again, one of the great evangelical churches in my home city of Toronto is The People's Church, which has a marvellous reputation for good works, for magnificent fellowship, for splendid faith, and for superb devotion. And last January, a visiting minister preached from their pulpit: Pastor Ron Carlson, of Milwaukee. The subject of his message was "Freemasonry." it was taped, and copies were distributed. I have one. He quotes extensively from the Masonic classics, particularly Albert Pike's great *Morals and Dogma*; and he concludes that Freemasonry is a religion that claims to preserve the ancient mysteries, that it is in fact a form of nature-worship, which centres on the worship of the principle of reproduction, the male generative organ, the phallus, and that no Christian could be a member with a clear conscience.

In April of this year I gather that on national television the evangelist John Ankerberg has been explaining why Christians should not be Freemasons. And in Grand Lodge M. W. James O. Wood reminded us, in his Report of the Committee on Correspondence, that in England the Church of England has recently set up a commission to investigate Freemasonry.

One hesitates to seek any general pattern in all this, unless it be that the more conservative churches are hostile to Freemasonry.

CRIMINAL CONNECTIONS

But there are other reasons to find the Craft suspicious. In the old cemetery at Batavia, N.Y., stands a gigantic monument carrying the following inscription: "Sacred to the Memory of Wm Morgan, a Native of Virginia, a Capt. in the War of 1812, a respectable Citizen of Batavia, and a Martyr to the Freedom of Writing, Printing and Speaking the Truth. He was abducted from near this Spot in the Year 1826, by Free Masons and Murdered for Revealing the Secrets of their Order." So great was the furore that arose from Morgan's disappearance that it actually gave rise to the Anti-Masonic political Party, that contested the Presidential election of 1832.

In the 1970s one Stephen Knight finally showed that the Jack the Ripper murders were really a Masonic conspiracy, designed to protect the reputation of Queen Victoria's grandson, the Duke of Clarence; he had got himself involved with a lower class girl, and the situation demanded that a number of prostitutes who were in on the secret be silenced. In 1980 the tale was made into a movie, *Murder by Decree*, with Christopher Plummer playing the role of Sherlock Holmes, and even demonstrating his version of some of the notorious Masonic secret signs.

In 1979, the newspapers in New Jersey carried reports that the Cosa Nostra was infiltrating Freemasonry, to use its organization for their own purposes.

In 1981 the scandal broke about Licio Gelli, and the Italian Lodge P2, which was said to be involved in all sorts of criminal activity, and which exerted immense pressure on many aspects of Italian politics.

In 1982 a murder mystery was published, written by Reginald Hill, under the title, *Who Guards the Prince?*. . . . The bad guys in it, who plan to stage-manage the election of the President of the United States, have infiltrated a Masonic Lodge and taken it over. As someone says there, "The best place to hide a poisoned needle . . . is not in a haystack but in a sewing-box. You'd have to prick yourself with each in turn to find out the deadly one. . . . So you hid your secret society in a secret society" (page 262).

In 1983, in his book *The Brotherhood* . . . the late Stephen Knight alleged that the only way to get ahead in the police force was to be a Mason; that Masonic judges often let off Masonic defendants, and that the Russian KGB had slipped into English Masonry, and was using it to place operatives in positions of authority.

In 1984 David A. Yallop, in his book entitled *In God's Name* . . . , disclosed that Pope John Paul I, who died in 1978 after a pontificate of only 33 days, was in fact murdered by the Masons, because he planned to investigate their activities and curb their powers.

About all of this I make no comment. This is simply a catalogue of matters that belong to the public record. Clearly many people and institutions have found ample reason to be hostile to Free Masonry.

CONCLUSION

We think of the Craft as a kindly, benign, moral institution, supporting a brother's personal religion without in any way supplanting it, forbidding any controversy on political or religious topics. But it appears that this Dr Jekyll personality has a darker, Mr Hyde, aspect to it. If most of the things that are said about us are true, than no man of integrity can ever remain in our ranks, and no wife who has any principles at all can be happy so long as her husband is a Mason.

That's the problem, isn't it? Those of us who are associated with Masonry know that all these charges are lies, but we don't do very much to refute them. On the whole we as Masons strive for good, but our good works are seldom regarded as newsworthy. In any event, we have never been very forthcoming about just what it is we do do.

There's really no common feature in the attacks. To start with, we must take them individually, and see if we can determine why each one was made, and how it is made. For example, centralized governments oppose Masonry because in general terms it believes in the dignity of the individual, and this may have led it occasionally to dabble in political topics; the door of the lodge room is closed, and guarded by an armed man, and theoretically the Masons could do anything they want behind that barred door.

So far as political plots are concerned, I was interviewed on the radio several months ago, and I was asked whether there was an international Masonic-Jewish conspiracy. I quoted from the Obligation that all Master

Masons in Ontario have to take—this part of The Working is hardly one of the Masonic secrets: "My heart shall be the safe and sacred repository of all his secrets, when entrusted to my care as such; at all times especially excepting murder, treason, felony, and all other offenses contrary to the laws of God or man." If I adhere to that promise, I cannot be a part of a political plot.

The Catholic church hates us by force of habit; and the present pontificate has shown in more than one aspect that it is inclined to return to old traditions rather than continuing to move ahead. I suspect the Mormons have reasons for hostility associated with their symbolism; so at least goes the rumor. But in general, I'm afraid the churches are running scared. They are attacking Masonry because they're having trouble keeping their members.

Now I should like to consider the fundamentalist evangelicals in somewhat more detail. People like Charles Finney, and Salem Kirban, and Pastor Ron Carlson, but also churches like the Missouri synod, and the Southern Methodists, that profess to be Bible-based.

Freemasons are forbidden to debate contentious matters of religion and politics within their lodges. I certainly am not in a position to criticise other people's beliefs. And yet, I think I'm entitled to ask just what it is that they believe, particularly when they condemn me for something I do. If a person professes to base all his actions upon the Volume of the Sacred Law, and he condemns me on those grounds, I guess there's not much I can say in my own defense.

I mean, the *Bible* is quite explicit on the matter of oaths. Jesus says in *Matthew* 5:34–37: "I say unto you, Swear not at all; neither by heaven; for it is God's throne; Neither by the earth; for it is his footstool; neither by Jerusalem; for it is the city of the Great King. Neither shalt thou swear by thy head, because thou canst not make one hair white or black. But let your communication be, Yea, yea; Nay, nay: for whatever is more than these cometh of evil."

And St James echoes him in his *Epistle*, 5:12: "Above all things, my brethren, swear not, neither by heaven, neither by the earth, neither by any other oath: but let your yea be yea; and your nay, nay. . . ." That certainly sounds as if the Masons are wrong to require oaths! The one thing I want to be sure of is that we are not being discriminated against, and that the people who condemn us on scriptural grounds are equally punctilious about obeying all the other injunctions in the Bible. So I would ask such people a number of questions, something like this:

Do you believe that murderers should pay their debt to society with long prison terms?

The Bible says, at *Deuteronomy* 21:23–24: . . . Thou shalt give life for life, Eye for eye, tooth for tooth, hand for hand, foot for foot. . . . (cf *Matt*.5:38).

(Or conversely, *Exodus* 20:13: Thou shalt not kill. Maybe you can argue it either way.)

I have known many good Jews and good Moslems and good Buddhists. What will happen to them when they die? *Mark* 16:15,16: Go ye into all the world, and preach the gospel to every creature. He that believeth and is baptized shall be saved; but he that believeth not shall be damned.

If a marriage ends in divorce, should the people involved remarry? *Mark* 10:11: Whosoever shall put away his wife, and marry another, committeth adultery. . . .

What about women's liberation, and the equality of the sexes? *Ephesians* 5:22-23: Wives, submit yourselves unto your own husbands, . . . For the husband is the head of the wife. . . .

Should women be ordained as ministers? *1 Corinthians* 14:34: Let your women keep silence in the churches: for it is not permitted unto them to speak.

What about women wearing slacks and fedoras? *Deut.* 22:5: The woman shall not wear that which pertaineth unto a man . . .; for all that do so are abomination unto the Lord. . . .

Surely in this day and age women don't have to wear hats in church any more? *1 Corinthians* 11:5-6: Every woman that prayeth or prophesieth with her head uncovered dishonoreth her head: . . . For if the woman be not covered, let her also be shorn. . . .

From the time of Henry Thoreau on, civil disobedience has been an American tradition. Does the *Bible* have any views on civil disobedience? *Romans* 13:1-2: Let every soul be subject unto the higher powers . . .; the powers that be are ordained of God. Whosoever therefore resisteth the power, resisteth the ordinance of God.

Should one abstain totally from alcohol? *1 Timothy* 5:23: Drink no longer water, but take a little wine for thy stomach's sake. . . .

How about physical fitness, aerobics, and the like? *1 Timothy* 4:7-8: Refuse profane and old wives' fables. . . . Bodily exercise profiteth little: but godliness is profitable unto all things.

What about homosexuality? *Leviticus* 20:13: If a man . . . lie with mankind, as he lieth with a woman, both of them have committed an abomination; they shall surely be put to death. . . .

Do you see the nature of my problem? Now I know that Shakespeare says, "The devil can cite Scripture for his purpose" (*Merchant of Venice* 1.3.99). Maybe I'm the devil. But still, the *Bible* is the *Bible*. It is a great and good book, filled with wisdom, strength, and beauty. We, as Masons, believe that in it the Supreme Being has revealed his will to man. What it says about the nature of God, and the nature of man, is valid for all time.

The two great commandments still summarize the whole of all the law-codes ever written: "Thou shalt love the Lord thy God with all thy heart, and with all thy soul, and with all thy strength, and with all thy mind; and thy neighbor as thyself" (*Luke* 10:27). Then are we allowed to obey it when it suits us, but not otherwise? That's hard!

If an evangelical follows the guidelines laid down by the Volume of the Sacred Law with regard to oaths, but not in other respects, then clearly he is being intellectually dishonest. But if he is consistent, and follows the scripture in every detail, then I cannot communicate with him, because he rejects so many beliefs that seem to me essential if "God is Love" (*1 John* 4:8, 16).

There is one other problem with most of the people who write attacking Freemasonry. To those who are acquainted with the facts, they simply are not credible. Let us just look at a few of the individuals whom we mentioned earlier.

Pastor Ron Carlson, Salem Kirban, and Stephen Knight, all fall into the same mistake as many Masons, that of imagining that thirty-three degrees are eleven times as good as only three; and that therefore the Ancient and Accepted Scottish Rite is higher than Craft Masonry, and controls it. This is of course nonsense. But the belief adds further complications, because the father of the Scottish rite, who devised much of the ritual, and wrote the gigantic commentary on it, *Morals and Dogma*, was the great Albert Pike, a brilliant man of immense but undisciplined learning, and a bigoted, mystical nut. So long as anyone imagines that he speaks for Masonry, we're in deep trouble.

Salem Kirban, the Morris Cerullo man, says that Thomas Jefferson and John Adams, who helped to design the Great Seal of the United States, were both Masons (page 155). This is untrue, and the truth has been readily available since 1965 in Ronald Heaton's book *The Masonic Membership of the Founding Fathers*.

The same author, Salem Kirban, professes to translate the two mottoes on the Great Seal of the United States, and to make them say "Announcing the Birth of a new Secular Order" (page 154). This is an utterly impossible rendering of the Latin. It seems to follow that Salem Kirban, whatever else he is trying to do, is not concerned with being correct. Whether he is incompetent, or just a liar, is not for me to say.

Stephen Knight, the author of *The Brotherhood*? Well, I can say that some of his researches into the history and ritual of Freemasonry are erroneous. I don't want to be too technical, or talk about the so-called secrets of Masonry, but in fact he mixes up American and English ritual, which are quite different.

And the man himself? I'm sorry to tell you that he died in July of 1985 at the age of 33; there were reports that the Masons got him, but apparently it was a brain tumor. It's always sad when anyone dies so young, but I can't pretend to any regret. Mr Knight's concern for honesty, morality, and principle, is shown by the fact that three years before his death he became a disciple of that well known moralist, your former neighbor, the Guru Baghwan Shree Rajneesh.

David Yallop, the man who says we killed the Pope—well, he closes his book with a gloomy picture: "Another change must be bringing a warm smile to the face of Licio Gelli [the head of P2]. The new canon law that took effect on November 27, 1983, has dropped the ruling that Freemasons are subject to automatic excommunication. The survivors on the list of Vatican Masons that [Pope John Paul I] considered are now safe. The purge he had planned will not be reactivated by his successor" (pages 371–372).

And one of those allegedly implicated in the murder of the Pope was Michele Sindona, known as "God's Banker", a member of the lodge P2, whose future, according to Yallop, was much rosier with the Pope dead. All very persuasive. Except that the Holy Office has now banned Freemasonry in much the same terms as it always has, and no good Catholic is allowed to belong.

How has God's banker made out? Is he enjoying life since freeing himself from the threats posed by the Pope? Well, he died in prison on March 22 last, after swallowing a cyanide capsule. If Yallop is wrong in these fundamental predictions, I find it hard to swallow the rest of his picture.

What I really want to say is, Masonry is called "the gentle Craft." It is not in the habit of speaking back to its critics. I think of myself as a tolerant "live and let live" person; I don't want to break anyone's rice bowl. I do think that it is short-sighted for Masons to change their ritual, as some have done, in response to external criticism; that's a no-win situation. But for my part I'm sick of lying down and being kicked.

So if you hear somebody attacking Masonry, and if you believe from your own experience that the Craft is a good institution, or if you think that your husband has benefitted more from Masonry than he has been harmed, then don't sit back and let these people win the field by default. Tell them, "Your facts are wrong and your conclusions are wrong," or "Your prejudices are showing."

If you care, it's time to stand up and be counted.

THE GREAT ARCHITECT
OF THE UNIVERSE

[Sometimes members of religious groups attack Freemasonry, basing their remarks on false premises, simply because they have not bothered to find out the facts.]

In the *Presbyterian Record*, a magazine which is "Published on the first of each month except August by The Presbyterian Church in Canada," in volume 110, number 11 (December 1986), there were two attacks on Freemasonry, largely on the grounds that it is a non-Christian religion. A spirited correspondence ensued over the next six months.

Among the points at issue was the appellation "the Great Architect Of The Universe;" one of the original contributors had said that it "makes God seem like an abstract being;" the other stated that this was the name of the false god "that the Masons worship at their altar."

The sources of Masonic terminology are often interesting, and some time ago Lieut.-Col. Harvey N. Brown, of El Paso, Texas, called my attention to the American magazine *The New Age*, of Washington, D.C., volume 72, number 1 (January 1964), page 58, in which a passage from Calvin's commentary on Psalm 19 was quoted without further remark. This prompted me to submit a rejoinder to *The Presbyterian Record*, which was eventually published (volume 111, number 5, May 1987, page 33). It ran in part as follows:

> Actually this phrase entered Freemasonry by way of the first Book of *Constitutions*, printed in 1723. The compiler was Rev. Dr James Anderson, a graduate of Aberdeen University, and minister of the Scotch Presbyterian Church in Swallow Street, Piccadilly, London, from 1710 to 1734. He did not invent the phrase, but took it over from John Calvin, who uses it, for example, in his *Commentary* on Psalm 19; the heavens "were wonderfully founded by the Great Architect" (*ab opifice praestantissimo*); again, according to the same paragraph, "when once we recognize God as the Architect of the Universe" (*mundi opificem*), we are bound to marvel at his Wisdom, Strength, and Goodness. In fact, Calvin repeatedly calls God "the Architect of the Universe," and refers to his works in nature as "Architecture of the Universe;" ten times in the *Institutes of the Christian Religion* alone. I may be missing something, but it seems to me bizarre that writers in the national publication of The Presbyterian Church in Canada should suddenly find fault with words that have been a part of Calvinism for four centuries.

Possibly the source of Anderson's phrase is familiar to Masonic students, though I have not seen it cited recently.

FREEMASONRY, AS A
MATTER OF FACT

*[Often, "profane" historians are careless when it comes to the
details of Freemasonry. For example, the Dictionary of Canadian
Biography includes a number of errors. The following paragraphs
attempt to set the contributors on the proper path.]*

. . . . [Nine errors of fact are pointed out in the authoritative *Dictionary of
Canadian Biography*.] This misinformation all concerns Freemasonry. Two
questions come to mind. In the first place, why should a social club even be
relevant to a brief biography? Second, how is it possible that such an array of
errors can have arisen with regard to this one topic?

First, relevance. It is worth remembering that Freemasonry is inextricably
interwoven with the early history of Canada[1].

Halifax was founded in 1749, and a year later the First Lodge was established there, its Master being Colonel the Honorable Edward Cornwallis,
M.P., Captain General and Governor of Nova Scotia.

A scant eleven weeks after the Battle on the Plains of Abraham, on 28
November 1759, the representatives of six military lodges in Wolfe's army
met in the city of Quebec, "as soon as Convenient after the Surrender of this
place to His Brittanic [*sic*] Majesty's Arms," and formed themselves into a
Provincial Grand Lodge. The inaugural session of the First Legislature of
Upper Canada was held in the Freemasons' Hall, Niagara, on 17 September
1792.

The Cariboo Gold Rush began in 1858, and on 12 July of that year the first
meeting of Freemasons took place in Victoria, which served as the last out-
post of civilization for the prospectors.

Five years before the outbreak of the Red River Rebellion, Northern Light
Lodge in Fort Garry held its initial meeting on 8 November 1864. Lodges
were formed in Prince Albert in 1879, and in Edmonton in 1882, even before
the arrival of the railroad.

In and out of the pages of Masonic history move some of the more notable
public figures of the past. For example, in the year 1805 the men who held
the highest Masonic office in the colonies of British North America were
H.R.H. Prince Edward Augustus, Duke of Kent and Strathearn (1767–1820),
Provincial Grand Master (Ancients) for Lower Canada (by this time, to be
sure, back in England, but still bearing the title); Sir John Johnson (1742–
1830), Member of the Legislative Council and sometime Superintendent-

General of Indian Affairs in British North America, Provincial Grand Master (Moderns) for Quebec; Sir John Wentworth (1737–1820), former Governor of New Hampshire and now Lieutenant-Governor of Nova Scotia, Provincial Grand Master (Ancients) for Nova Scotia; and William Jarvis (1756–1817), Provincial Secretary and Registrar of Deeds for Upper Canada, Provincial Grand Master (Ancients) for Upper Canada.

Again, in 1890, the Grand Master of the United Grand Lodge of England was H.R.H. the Prince of Wales; the Grand Master of the Grand Lodge of Canada was John Ross Robertson, newspaperman and philanthropist; the Governor-General of Canada (Baron Stanley of Preston), the Prime Minister of Canada (Sir John A. Macdonald), the Lieutenant-Governor of Ontario (Sir Alexander Campbell), the Premier of Manitoba (Thomas Greenway), and the Mayor of the City of Toronto (Edward Frederick Clarke), were all Freemasons.

With ample reason the early settlements reconstructed at Heritage Park in Calgary and at Black Creek Pioneer Village near Toronto both include Masonic lodge rooms.

Evidently the members of the Craft (as it is called) have included some famous men; evidently also Freemasonry filled some necessary social function in early English-speaking Canada. One could attempt to explain both phenomena, but the discussion would be long, largely inconclusive, and not directly related to the present enquiry.

The one point worth noting is that Freemasonry is an affinity group, a collection of men who enjoy each other's company, and share each other's interests and activities. Not surprisingly, these interests are sometimes professional; the evidence, though anecdotal and sporadic, will serve to establish the principle. In 1723 the lodge that met at the Horn Tavern in Westminster had seventy-one members; of these, ten were, or would become, Fellows of the Royal Society[2].

Gordon R. Silber has noted that a Parisian lodge of 1736–37 included a small core of professional musicians[3]. A French lodge that met in Lisbon in 1743 had twenty-seven members, of whom fourteen were associated in one way or another with the jewellery trade (as goldsmiths, silversmiths, watchmakers, diamond traders, and precious stone cutters)[4].

If one may come closer to home, the membership lists of St Andrew's Lodge in Toronto have been published; they show that in the mid-nineteenth century the members included a sizeable proportion of practical scientists. Thus, the three founders of the Canadian Institute, "the oldest [surviving] scientific society in Canada," F. W. Cumberland, Sandford Fleming, and Kivas Tully, all joined the lodge; and of fifty new members who joined between July 1853 and July 1854, nine were, or would become, officers of the Institute[5].

Again, in 1892 Victoria College moved from Cobourg to Toronto, and the new building was formally opened on 25 October 1892. Between October 1892 and October 1896, twenty-one new members affiliated with St Andrew's Lodge (the Masonic home of W. G. Storm, the college's architect); and of this number three were professors there[6].

Again, about the same time Ionic Lodge in Toronto was a nest of lawyers; in the years 1887–1890 sixty-seven new members joined, and of these (in addition to lesser luminaries) eight became jurists of sufficient eminence to earn an entry in *The Macmillan Dictionary of Canadian Biography*[7].

In such lodges as these, men who had certain interests in common would meet together in a relaxed non-competitive social atmosphere. We may readily appreciate, without invoking any sinister notion of conspiracy, that those who encountered each other in such an environment might feel at ease together outside the lodge as well. No doubt a certain amount of "networking" took place.

This is one justification for mentioning Freemasonry in a biography. For example, William Badgley was a devoted member of St Paul's Lodge, Montreal, for sixty-four years (1824–1888), and served as Master for seven years. The members of the lodge in that era included a number of well-known citizens of Montreal; not just John Molson and Peter McGill (Badgley's predecessors as Provincial Grand Master), but also John Bethune, Augustin Cuvillier, Moses Samuel David, Stewart Derbishire, Horatio Gates, Louis Gugy, Moses Hayes, David Kinnear, John Samuel McCord, and David Lewis Macpherson. These were the people, the club-members, with whom Badgley was thrown into social contact on a regular basis[8].

At all events, some of the authors decided that the Masonic connection was worth mentioning. Why then did they not trouble to get their facts right? Evidently we have repeated violations of an elementary rule of professional scholarship, which in another discipline is sometimes called Routh's canon ("I think, sir, . . . you will find it a very good practice **always to verify your references**")[9].

But this procedural lapse cannot in itself account for the startling concentration of error within such a narrow compass. In order to explain it, we must invoke one or another of three attitudes or prejudices that concern Freemasonry. They are to some extent related, they are largely erroneous, but they are explicable. The first is that, without knowing too much about it, outsiders are likely to assume that it is a "secret" society, and that one cannot learn anything about it.

Indeed, most people get their impression of fraternal organizations from Laurel and Hardy in *Sons of the Desert* (1934); or from George "Kingfish" Stevens and the Mystic Knights of the Sea in the old radio programme "Amos 'n' Andy;" or from Polecats Lodge in the comic-strip "Drabble;" or from Christopher Plummer and Sir Anthony Quayle playing Sherlock Holmes and Sir Charles Warren in *Murder by Decree* (1978); or from such irresponsible catchpennies as *Holy Blood, Holy Grail*, by Michael Baigent, Richard Leigh, and Henry Lincoln (London 1982), or Stephen Knight's *The Brotherhood* (London 1983).

But if we may turn from fantasy to reality, the "secret" aspect of Freemasonry is often exaggerated. There is very little about it that cannot be learned, and, in the circumstances, there is no excuse for factual inaccuracy.

Some of the errors noted in the *DCB* arise from loose terminology. Freemasonry has its own technical terms and titles, which have led more than one student into error. We may cite an example from another time and place.

Among the papers of the English free-thinker John Toland (1670-1722) in the British Library is a manuscript entitled "Extrait des Registres du Chapitre Général des Chevaliers de La Jubilation. . . ." It records a meeting that took place on 24 November 1710 at "Gaillardin, Maison de l'Ordre," probably in The Hague. The extract was written by the secretary Prosper Marchand (1678-1756), editor of the 1720 edition of Bayle's *Dictionnaire*, and is signed as well by the six other officers of the order, who were all involved in one way or another with the book trade.

The actual transactions of the meeting are not earth-shaking, or even particularly edifying; it was in effect a bachelor party, to mark the forthcoming marriage of one of the number. The secretary's handwriting seems to deteriorate as he becomes increasingly disguised in liquor.

Margaret C. Jacob, who brought this text to the attention of the scholarly world, deserves gratitude for shedding a flood of light on the members of the order, their activities and their friends. But as well as recognizing this cell as a hive of intellectual activity, she imputes to it one other unexpected characteristic. She calls it "a masonic lodge," "the earliest Masonic group on the Continent," and further asserts that it is derived from English Freemasonry. She is wrong.

Certain characteristic traits and verbal *tics* in English Freemasonry are adequately documented for the period 1621-1717, and their absence from the minutes in question is enough to establish that the gathering was not Masonic. The members are called "Knights" or "Chevaliers," with no mention of "Masons" or "Free Masons;" they are organized into a "chapter-general" (with other "chapters" and "constitutions"), not a "lodge" or "society;" the officers include a "Grand Master" (as in other orders of chivalry), but no "Wardens;" the regulations, which are quoted, bear no relation to the Masonic "constitutions;" there is no hint of various grades or degrees, or of a fixed ritual, or of secrets.

Professor Jacob wonders "what other term could possibly describe this group." Perhaps "drinking club" would be most honest[10].

But to return to the matter at hand, contributors to the *DCB* would be well-advised to recognize the difference in extent between a lodge, a Grand Lodge, and a Provincial Grand Lodge, and the distinction in rank between the Master of a lodge, the Grand Master of a Grand Lodge, and the Provincial Grand Master of a Provincial Grand Lodge, and their respective officers.

The second widespread prejudice is that anything written about Freemasonry is uncritical and unreliable. At one time Masonic history was "by ill luck the happiest of all hunting-grounds for the light-headed, the fanciful, the altogether unscholarly, and the lunatic fringe of the British Museum Reading Room"[11].

Though the Enlightenment came late to this particular sub-discipline, its advent is clearly marked by Georg Kloss's *Geschichte der Freimaurerei in England, Irland und Schottland, aus ächten Urkunden dargestellt (1685 bis 1784)* (Leipzig 1847). Yet the notion persists that the world is still in the Dark Ages. For example, Nina R. Gelbart greeted Margaret C. Jacob's *The Radical Enlightenment* with the words, "This is, to my knowledge, the first scholarly account in our language of the early history of Freemasonry,"[12] an assertion that reflects more enthusiasm than competence.

Kloss found worthy successors in the Germans J. G. Findel (1828–1905) and Wilhelm Begemann (1843–1914), and the Englishmen Robert Freke Gould (1836–1915), Douglas Knoop (1883–1948), Herbert Poole (1885–1951), and Harry Carr (1900–1983).

Besides such serious scholars, at a less sophisticated level there are dozens of "lodge historians," earnest record-searchers who are chroniclers rather than historians. At least they do their best to get the facts right. Their publications are not in every library, but they are in no sense restricted.

The third perception is that Masonic archives are inaccessible. We are told, for example, that "the records of the Grand Lodge are closed to all non-Masonic historians (and therefore, of course, to all women historians);" whatever may have been the practice in the past, that statement is not true today. Or again, "French Masonic records—unlike the British—are available to all historians," a patent overstatement on both counts[13].

Some Masonic bodies have immense collections of old papers. To be sure, access to them by non-members is entirely discretionary, but many officials have shown a disposition to cooperate with serious students, provided that arrangements can be made to suit the convenience of both parties. One might find it useful, for example, to consult the archives of a particular lodge.

Dozens of lodges in Canada have been working for more than a century, and a few are two hundred years old. Some have never been burnt out, and have full documentation from the very start. Again, Freemasons' Hall, in London, has custody of "The Historical Correspondence Files" of the United Grand Lodge of England and its predecessors. They include some five hundred letters, duly calendared, about Canada, mostly from the period 1769–1873. . . .

In matters connected with Freemasonry, then, it appears that the *DCB* includes more errors of fact than any reader would expect. Plato tells us (*Protagoras* 345d-e) that no one makes mistakes on purpose; and surely, at least in the scholarly world, we must believe him. We can only assume that some of the contributors still suppose that exact details are somehow beyond recovery, and in any event do not much matter. Actually, the information is largely available, and, in some instances at least, is probably relevant.

What researcher, knowing that truth is to hand, will prefer falsehood? Perhaps we may venture to hope that forthcoming volumes of the series will not lie open to this particular criticism.

NOTES

Part of this paper was presented at Victoria College, Toronto, on 1 March 1986, as a contribution to a colloquium on "Science and Culture in the Enlightenment," organized jointly by the Institute for the History and Philosophy of Science and Technology of the University of Toronto and the Upper Canada Branch of the Canadian Society for the History and Philosophy of Science. The writer expresses his thanks to J. M. Hamill, Librarian and Curator of Freemasons' Hall, London, and the Board of General Purposes of the United Grand Lodge of England, to R. E. Davies, Grand Secretary, and the Board of General Purposes of the Grand Lodge of Canada in the Province of Ontario, and to B. S. Hayne, the Historian of Ionic Lodge, No 25, Toronto, for permission to refer to unpublished documents. He is also grateful to Alan M. Black, Francis J. Bruce, Margaret C. Jacob, Helen Kilgour of the Royal Ontario Museum, and Gordon R. Silber for their assistance in various matters. . . . [Works cited by short title include] J. Ross Robertson, *The History of Freemasonry in Canada from its Introduction in 1749* (Toronto 1900); . . . A. J. B. Milborne, *Freemasonry in the Province of Quebec 1759–1959* (Montreal 1960); . . . John Charles Hope, *St. Paul's Lodge No. 374 E.R.: The History of the Lodge 1770 to 1970* (3rd edition; Montreal 1972); . . . Wallace McLeod, ed., *Whence Come We? Freemasonry in Ontario 1764–1980* (Hamilton 1980); . . . Henry T. Smith, *History of St Andrew's Lodge, A.F. & A.M., No. 16, G.R.C., 1822–1922,* (Toronto 1922). . . .

[1] This summary reposes on "standard authority;" such works as Robertson, *Freemasonry in Canada*; Osborne Sheppard, *A Concise History of Freemasonry in Canada* (3rd edition; Hamilton 1924); Reginald V. Harris, *The Beginnings of Freemasonry in Canada* (Halifax 1938); James J. Talman, *His-*

torical Sketch to Commemorate the Sesqui-Centenary of Freemasonry in the Niagara District, 1792-1942 (Hamilton 1942); Walter S. Herrington and Roy S. Foley, *A History of the Grand Lodge A.F. & A.M. of Canada in the Province of Ontario 1855-1955* (Toronto 1955); Milborne, *Freemasonry in Quebec*; Ronald S. Longley and Reginald V. Harris, *A Short History of Freemasonry in Nova Scotia 1738-1966* (Halifax, 1966); Robert E. Emmett, *Freemasonry in Manitoba: Part II, 1925-1974* (Winnipeg 1975); McLeod, ed., *Whence Come We?*; C. E. B. LeGresley, ed., *The Papers of the Canadian Masonic Research Association* (1949-1976; reprinted Toronto 1986).

[2] William John Songhurst, editor, *The Minutes of the Grand Lodge of Freemasons of England, 1723-1735* (London, *Quatuor Coronatorum Antigrapha*, X, 1913), 5-6; J. R. Clarke, "The Royal Society and Early Grand Lodge Freemasonry," *AQC* 80 (1967): 110-19; Richard H. Sands, "Physicists, the Royal Society, and Freemasonry," *Michigan Quarterly Review* 20 (1981): 194-209; *Philalethes* 34, 6 (Dec. 1981): 11-16.

[3] Gordon R. Silber, "Poèmes et chansons maçonniques du XVIIIe siècle: un aspect peu connu de la franc-maçonnerie," *Revue des Sciences Humaines* 37, Fasc. 146 (April-June 1972): 171-2.

[4] W. McLeod, "John Coustos: His Lodges and His Book," *AQC* 92 (1979): 119-20.

[5] James Bovell, Alfred Brunel, Cumberland, Fleming, Samuel Bickerton Harman, William Hay, Thomas Ridout, Francis Shanly, and Walter Shanly; the register of members for the first century is given by Smith, *St Andrew's Lodge*, 171-204; the names have been compared with W. Stewart Wallace, ed., *The Royal Canadian Institute Centennial Volume 1849-1949* (Toronto 1949), 171-232; on the seniority of the Institute, see *ibid.*, 167.

[6] Rev. John Burwash, Lewis Emerson Horning, and Rev. Alfred Henry Reynar; see Smith, *St Andrew's Lodge*, 188-9; C. B. Sissons, *A History of Victoria University* (Toronto 1952), 127-9, 193-4, 195, 208.

[7] Sir Allen Bristol Aylesworth, Edmund Bristol, William Henry Pope Clement, William George Eakins, Robert Osborne McCulloch, Cornelius Arthur Masten, Herbert Macdonald Mowat, and Wallace Nesbitt; the membership roll for the first fifty years is published in *Ionic Lodge A.F. & A.M., No. 25, G.R.C., 1847-1897* (Toronto 1897), 78-92; compare W. Stewart Wallace, editor, *The Macmillan Dictionary of Canadian Biography* (4th edition, revised by W. A. McKay; Toronto 1978). . . .

[8] Badgley was initiated 10 February 1824; Milborne, *Freemasonry in Quebec*, 77; for partial lists of lodge members, see Hope, *St. Paul's Lodge*, 9-10, 96-7.

[9] Martin Joseph Routh (1755–1854), quoted in John Edwin Sandys, *A History of Classical Scholarship* (Cambridge 1908), III, 393.

[10] Jacob, "An Unpublished Record of a Masonic Lodge in England: 1710," *Zeitschrift für Religions-und Geistesgeschichte* 22 (1970): 168–71; Jacob, *The Newtonians and the English Revolution 1689–1720* (Ithaca 1976), especially 224–6; Jacob, "Newtonianism and the Origins of the Enlightenment: A Reassessment," *Eighteenth-Century Studies* 11 (1977–8): 1–25, especially 13–16; Jacob, *The Radical Enlightenment: Pantheists, Freemasons and Republicans* (London 1981), especially 155–69, 267–79. The quotations in the body of the text come from *Zeitschrift für Religions-und Geistesgeschichte* 22 (1970): 168; *Eighteenth-Century Studies* 11 (1977–8): 16; and *Newtonians*, 224, n. 75.

[11] John Saltmarsh, *Economic History Review* 8 (1937–8): 103.

[12] *Eighteenth-Century Studies* 17 (1983–4): 186.

[13] Margaret C. Jacob, *Eighteenth-Century Studies* 11 (1977–8): 16; Jacob, review of Albert Ladret, *Le Grand Siècle de la Franc-Maçonnerie*, in Robert R. Allen, ed., *The Eighteenth Century: A Current Bibliography*, n.s., 4 (1978): 144.

WHY SAINT ALBAN?

[Every year there is a reunion of the various lodges named after Saint Alban. The Thirtieth Annual Gathering was held near Toronto. The following address was given on that occasion.]

LIFE OF SAINT ALBAN

Why Saint Alban? Well, the first stage in our quest is to find just who the man is. In 1483 William Caxton published a collection of the lives of the Saints, under the title of *The Golden Legend*. We might summarize one of the stories it includes.

A certain law in force in the Roman Empire stated that no man was permitted to receive the honor of knighthood, save only at Rome, and then at the hands of the Emperor himself. And so it was that about the year 295 a deputation of young noblemen went from Britain to the capital. They included Amphibal, the son of a Welsh prince, and Alban, the son of a lord of the city of Verulamium.

While they were in Rome, Amphibal was converted to Christianity, and left the brotherhood of apprentice knights. A great day was set, and the others were all knighted by the Emperor Diocletian, after which a tournament was held, where Alban won the palm of honor. The blazon on his shield was a cross of gold against a blue background. (This of course is still used as the crest of St Alban's, No 514.) After the tournament all the British knights returned home, except Alban, whom the Emperor kept in his service, on account of his manliness and prowess, for the term of seven years.

In due course a rebellion broke out in Britain, and a Roman army was sent to suppress it, with Alban as chief of the knights. At this same time there was a persecution of Christians in Rome, and the people of the faith were scattered, each one to his own country.

And so it befell that Amphibal, who had gone to Rome with Alban, returned home to Britain, and came to the city of Verulamium, where he found Alban as lord of the city, prince of the knights, and steward of the land, having a great multitude of servants. Amphibal was clothed as a Christian priest, and could find no lodging in the city. He recognized his former friend Alban (who did not however recognize him), and sought hospitality of him. This was granted. They fell into conversation, Amphibal told Alban of his faith, and Alban had a vision, and in short was converted to Christianity, and was baptized.

After they had communed together for six weeks and more, the magistrate heard that a preacher of the new religion lay concealed at Alban's house, and he summoned them to appear before him. Amphibal had to go to South Wales, and to facilitate his escape Alban exchanged clothes with him. Amphibal departed garbed as a knight, whilst Alban, robed as a priest and wearing a cross, went to the judge.

The judge cross-examined him closely, and when he learned his true identity, asked him where his teacher had gone, and directed him to renounce Christianity. This Alban declined to do. Then a great crowd of pagans came forth and tried to force him to offer sacrifice to their false gods, but he steadfastly refused. The judge then sentenced him to be stretched on the rack and scourged. The torturers beat him so long that their hands grew weary.

He was kept in custody for six months and more, and during that whole time there was neither rain nor dew, nothing but the blazing sun, so that neither trees nor fields brought forth any fruit. The judge was afraid to sentence him to death, because he held the Emperor's commission.

Finally the Emperor sent one of his viceroys to Britain, with orders to kill all the Christians except for Alban; he alone had the option of abandoning his faith. If he refused, he was to be beheaded by another knight; and the priest that had converted him was to suffer the foulest death that could be imagined.

Alban was brought forth from prison, but when he refused to relapse into paganism, sentence was passed. First it was decreed that, when Amphibal was found, "he should be scourged, and after bounden to a stake all naked, and then his navel be opened and his bowels to be fastened by that one end to the stake, and he then to be driven to go round and about the stake till all his bowels were wounden out about the stake, and after to have his head smitten off. . . ."

Alban was to be simply beheaded. On the stated day, a great crowd assembled, and he was led forth to Holmhurst Hill for execution.

"The people were so great a multitude that they occupied all the place. . . . And the heat of the sun was so great that it burnt and scalded their feet as they went, and so they led him till they came to a swift running river, where they might not lightly pass for press of people, for many were shifted over the bridge into the water and were drowned, and many, because they might not go over the bridge for press, unclothed them for to swim over the river, and some that could not swim presumed to do the same, and were wretchedly drowned. . . . And when Saint Alban perceived this thing he bewailed and wept for the harm and death of his enemies . . ., and kneeled down holding his hands up to God beseeching that the water might be lessed and the flood withdrawn that the people might be with him at his passion."

In answer to his prayer the waters withdrew. At this miracle the knight who was escorting him threw down his sword and acknowledged his error. The pagan mob seized the new convert, and pulled out all his teeth, and beat him, breaking all his bones, and left him lying on the sand.

When at last they reached the place of execution, there was a great multitude, nigh dead from the heat of the sun and for thirst. Saint Alban prayed for relief for them, and at once a cool breeze sprang up and a fountain gushed from the top of the hill.

Then the pagans fastened his hair to the branch of a tree, and they found a man to cut off his head. And at once the executioner's eyes fell out of his head and lay upon the ground. Then the knight who had been left for dead came crawling up the hill, and reverently loosed Alban's head from the bough. At this act of devotion he was restored to health, and took and buried the body, and raised over it a fair tomb.

Many people were converted to Christianity when they saw this array of miracles. They carried word to Amphibal in Wales, and he returned to suffer the martyrdom to which he too had been condemned. And the pagans, persevering in their malice, threw stones at his dead body; and when a quarrel arose among them, a certain Christian man was able to steal the body away and hide it.

And soon after their deaths the Lord showed forth another miracle, and this was that "the visages of the tormentors were disfigured, their hands, arms and other members dried up, and the judge lost his mind and was mad."

THE INFLUENCE OF SAINT ALBAN

Like many lives of the saints, this is a pretty good story, full of bloodthirsty episodes, and reaching its climax in a suitable punishment for the villains, and an appropriate triumph of the faithful. It shows by example the virtue of steadfastness, and one can readily see why it became popular. Of course the full version of the story contains a certain amount of preaching, which has been curtailed in the version you have just heard.

It would be inappropriate to enquire whether every detail of the life is true, because its function is to inspire people, not to recite history.

According to tradition, Alban died at some time about 303–305, being the first one in the realm to suffer death for the new faith, and he is therefore known as the protomartyr, or "first martyr," of England. The story has it that his death took place at the Roman city of Verulamium, 20 miles northwest of London. He was soon canonized as a Saint, with his festival being set on 22 June. By 429, a century and a quarter after his death, there was a church dedicated to him near his tomb; and Verulamium soon took the name of Saint Albans.

In 793 King Offa is said to have founded a new church here, and a monastery. During the Middle Ages this grew into a great Benedictine Abbey, which was one of the richest in England until King Henry VIII dissolved the

119

monasteries in 1536. Here too was built one of the largest Gothic churches in the world, still in use after nine centuries.

The monastery was of course a centre of literacy, and one of the necessary activities of the monks was to keep the memory of Saint Alban green. And so we know of at least five lives of the Saint that were composed by or for members of the house and disseminated to the world at large in the years between 1166 and 1439. The story was also picked up in other circles, and thereby hangeth a tale.

THE OLD CHARGES

We modern Freemasons are descended, not as we are told in our ritual from the workmen at King Solomon's Temple, but from the operative stone-masons of Britain in the Middle Ages. At some time soon after 1350 these stone-masons began to congregate themselves into formal bodies that were known as Guilds or Lodges; they served some of the functions of the modern trade-union. We know quite a bit about what they did, and we know also something of how they were governed—particularly the Lodges. It seems that each of them had a handwritten scroll containing the laws and regulations of the masons, and also giving a traditional history of the craft of building.

More than a hundred (actually 113) of these old manuscript constitutions have survived; and the strangest thing about them is that they all go back to a single original, that was written not too long after the year 1350. (The coincidence of date is striking.) This was copied and recopied, edited and revised, dozens of times between 1350 and 1750; and it looks as if every lodge of stone-masons had to have its own copy.

These old manuscript constitutions are still reflected in modern Freemasonry today, in various ways. The oldest of them closes with the words "Amen, Amen, So mote it be! So say we all for charity!" So evidently a little of our traditional Masonic language is derived from them.

Again, if you look at the *Book of Constitution* of your Grand Lodge, you will find a section with a title that runs something like this: "The Charges of a Free-Mason, extracted from The ancient records of Lodges beyond Sea, and of those in England, Scotland, and Ireland, for the Use of the Lodges in London: to be read at the making of New Brethren, or when the Master shall order it."

Have you ever looked at them? We don't use them very much any more, but they're still worth reading. They have been reprinted in every book of constitution of modern Freemasonry ever since the first one, in 1717. And the Rev. Dr James Anderson, the editor of that volume (the most influential book of Masonry ever written) "borrowed" them from the old manuscript constitutions of the operative stone-masons.

But we said that the old texts also included a traditional history. And it too is occasionally reflected in our ritual. It tells how the seven liberal arts and sciences (you know, Grammar, Rhetoric, Logic, Arithmetic, Geometry, Music, and Astronomy) were found before Noah's flood by the three brothers Jabel, Jubal, and Tubal-cain, together with their sister.

You will find the story recorded in the Book of Genesis. And then how they wrote their sciences on Two Great Pillars. And then it recounts how masonry was used at some of the great architectural programs of Biblical times: at the Tower of Babel, and at the building of King Solomon's Temple; and how Solomon was helped by Hiram King of Tyre, and by his principal architect. And then we are told how the Art was brought to Western Europe; first it came to France, and from there it was brought to England. And in due course Prince Edwin called a great assemblage of masons in York some time about the year 930, and established the code of regulations that continued in use through the Middle Ages.

SAINT ALBAN IN THE OLD CHARGES

That is not real history. It is really propaganda, that was intended to give the masons a proper sense of their own worth by showing how the Craft went back to Biblical times, and counted even monarchs themselves among its members. But it was heard and believed by our operative brethren. Now of particular interest to us today is the story of how masonry came to England. The most common version runs like this:

> England in all this season stood void of any charge of masonry, until the time of Saint Alban. And in his time the King of England, that was a pagan, did wall the town about that is now called Saint Albans. And Saint Alban was a worthy knight, and chief steward to the King, and had the governance of the realm, and also of the making of the town walls. And he loved well masons, and cherished them much. And he made their pay right good, standing as the realm did then, for he gave them two shillings and sixpence a week, and threepence for their nuncheons. And before that time through all the land a mason took but a penny a day and his meat, until Saint Alban amended it. And gave them a charter of the King and his council for to hold a general council, and gave it the name of an assembly. And thereat he was himself, and helped to make masons, and gave them charges as you shall hear afterwards.

Now, can you see what has happened? The man who made the earliest version of the old manuscript constitutions composed the traditional history, basing himself in the first instance on the Volume of the Sacred Law, the only book ever seen by most people in those days. But he had to find somebody famous to bring Masonry to England. Who better than a notable martyr of the church, a man who had a city named after him. Surely that must have meant that he was himself a builder? Obviously the natural choice! (It may mean that our writer lived somewhere near the monastery of Saint Albans, but of that we cannot be certain.)

LODGES NAMED FOR SAINT ALBAN

And again the fact that lodges are named after Saint Alban is interesting. He is not regarded today as one of the patron saints of Masonry. They are Saint John the Baptist, Saint John the Evangelist, Saint Barbara, and the Four Crowned Martyrs (see Bernard E. Jones, *Freemasons' Guide and Compendium*, pages 338–342). But someone in the very early days of the premier Grand Lodge recalled that Saint Alban was a part of the traditional history, and determined that his name should be perpetuated.

I do not know just when his name was first commemorated in a lodge. There is in London, England, an old lodge, founded in 1728, meeting at Freemasons' Hall, under the name of St Alban's, No 29, but of course that will not be its original name. Lodges were originally named for the tavern in which they met, and the practice of taking permanent names did not become common until the 1760's. Thus, we know that Saint Alban's Lodge, No 29, was originally known as the Lodge that met at the Castle and Leg in Holborn.

It's often interesting to learn where lodges get their titles. There are in Ontario more than forty which are named for saints. The reason for some of them can be guessed. For example, thirteen are named for Saint John, the traditional patron of Masons. There are seven Saint Andrew's Lodges, and I'd bet there is a Scottish connection in most of them. Six are named for Saint George, and it would hardly be surprising if they all claimed a link with England.

There are three Saint Clair Lodges, and the Saint Clairs (or Sinclairs) were in early days the hereditary Grand Masters of Scotland. There are in this jurisdiction two lodges carrying the name of Saint Alban: one, No 200, at Mount Forest (instituted in 1868), and one, our host, No 514, in Toronto (instituted in 1913). I should very much like to learn why their names were chosen. Was it because one of the founders came from Saint Albans in England? Or was there a connection with one of the English lodges of that name? Or did the name perhaps come from a church? (The cornerstone of Saint Alban's Church, Ottawa, was laid with Masonic honors in 1867.) Or is it possible that one of your founders was aware that this saint had a place in the Masonic tradition?

CONCLUSION

Those of you who belong to these lodges, and to others of the same name, hold high your heads with pride. Not only do you commemorate a man who preferred to suffer death rather than betray the sacred trust reposed in him.

You also bear testimony to a Masonic tradition that goes back more than 600 years. Saint Alban has had a demonstrable connection with the Craft since 1350, though latterly it is not much remembered. The name should constantly remind you that you are part of a continuous chain of good men, thousands of them, going back through the impenetrable mists of time.

The vast majority are no longer with us, for they have been summoned to the Grand Lodge Above, but they have left their deeds behind, as monuments for us to emulate. And we may perhaps imagine that though dead they still speak to us through these monuments; and maybe even (who knows?) from on high they look down with interest on the deeds of us, their successors.

It is pleasant to think so anyway. If we bear that picture in mind, perhaps we may, without irreverence, apply to ourselves the words of the apostle: "Wherefore [brethren] seeing we also are compassed about with so great a cloud of witnesses, let us lay aside every weight, and the sin which doth so easily beset us, and let us run with patience the race that is set before us."

Run with patience the race that is set before us. There is lots to be done. Do you make a daily advancement in Masonic knowledge? Do you support the charitable and benevolent activities of your lodge, and of your grand lodge? Do you visit your sick and shut-in members? Do you have an instructional programme in your lodge for your candidates? Is provision made for the training of your officers? Do you investigate the situation of those who come up for suspension for Non-Payment of Dues? Do you tend the widows of your brethren?

In short, do you show by your actions that you believe in the three Tenets or Fundamental Principles of Brotherly Love, Relief, and Truth? "Business?" said Marley's ghost. "Mankind was my business!"

The Brotherhood of Man! Run with patience the race that is set before us. Think about it.

JOHN COUSTOS: A VICTIM
OF THE INQUISITION

*[One of the early martyrs of Freemasonry was John Coustos. Here
we attempt to tell his story.]*

HIS BOOK

"As for himself, he would rather suffer death than betray the sacred trust
reposed in him."

Some of you may have heard those words somewhere. I want to remind you
of a man, now forgotten, who was once regarded as a hero of Freemasonry,
because he followed that ideal. Long, long ago, more than two centuries ago,
a book was published in London, England. Its title was, in the fashion of the
day, amply descriptive.

It ran as follows: *The Sufferings of John Coustos, for Free-Masonry, and
for His refusing to turn Roman Catholic, in the Inquisition at Lisbon; Where
he was sentenc'd, during Four Years, to the Galley; and afterwards releas'd
from thence by the gracious Interposition of his present Majesty King George
II.* The book was incredibly popular. It went through nineteen editions over
the next seventy-five years.

Here is the story it tells. John Coustos was born in Switzerland in 1703. As
a child he was taken to England, and was trained as a diamond cutter. He
went to France in 1736, and worked in Paris for five years. Then he went to
Lisbon, Portugal. His original hope had been to go to America, to the Portuguese colony of Brazil, where diamonds had been discovered in 1729, and
where there are still rich diamond mines; but he was unable to get authoriza-
tion, so he stayed in Lisbon, plying his trade. While there, he established a
Masonic Lodge, with himself as Master; and that was the cause of his troubles. Masonry had been banned by the Catholic Church in 1738, and was
illegal in Portugal.

Apparently the wife of another jeweller in the city was jealous of Coustos's
success, and in order to remove one of her husband's competitors, she denounced Coustos to the authorities as a Free Mason. In March of 1743 he
was arrested and taken to the Prison of the Inquisition. Let us hear his own
words:

> A little after, the . . . Officer . . . bid the Guards search me; and take away
> all the Gold, Silver, Papers, Knives, Scissars, Buckles, &c. I might have about
> me. They then led me to a lonely Dungeon, expressly forbidding me to speak

loud, or knock at the Walls; but that, in case I wanted any Thing, to beat against
the Door, with a Padlock, that hung on the outward Door; and which I could
reach, by thrusting my Arm through the Iron Grates.

After a few days he was shaved, and his hair was cut short, and he was led
before the Inquisitors for the first time. After a little beating about the bush,
they made it clear that he had been arrested for the crime of Masonry, and
that they wanted more information. So he told them that it was a society
devoted to Charity, where religious controversy was forbidden. He was exam-
ined a number of times, and after each interrogation was remanded to his
solitary cell for a longer or shorter period.

During the fifth examination, the following exchange took place:

Inquisitors: [We insist that you reveal to us the Secrets of this Art.]
Coustos: [The Oath I took] at my Admission . . . will not permit me to do it;
Conscience forbids me; and therefore I hope your Lordships are too equitable to
use Compulsion.
Inquisitors: Your Oath is as nothing in our Presence, and we shall absolve
you from it.
Coustos: Your Lordships are very gracious; but as I am firmly persuaded,
that it is not in the Power of any Being upon Earth to free me from my Oath, I
am firmly determin'd never to violate it.

And so, back to the dungeon.
In the ninth examination, he was strongly urged, with threats, to turn Catholic; but Coustos expressed his firm resolution to live and die a Protestant.
Finally, he was brought before the tribunal for the thirteenth time. He tells
us what happened then:

The President . . . order'd a Paper, containing Part of my Sentence, to be
read. I thereby was doom'd to suffer the Tortures employ'd by the Holy Office,
for refusing to tell the Truth . . .; for my not discovering the Secrets of
Masonry. . . .
I hereupon was instantly convey'd to the Torture-Room, built in the Form of a
square Tower, where no Light appear'd, but what two Candles gave: . . . the
Doors are lin'd with a sort of Quilt. . . . At my entring this infernal Place, I
saw myself . . . surrounded by six Wretches, who, after preparing the Tortures,
strip'd me naked (all to Linen Drawers); when, laying me on my Back, . . .
they put round my Neck an Iron Collar, which was fastned to the Scaffold; they
then fix'd a Ring to each Foot; and this being done, they stretched my Limbs
with all their Might. They next wound two Ropes round each Arm, and two
round each Thigh, which Ropes pass'd under the Scaffold, through Holes made
for that Purpose; and were all drawn tight, at the same time, by four Men, upon
a Signal made for this Purpose. . . . These Ropes, which were of the Size of

one's little Finger, pierc'd through my Flesh quite to the Bone; making the Blood gush out at the eight different Places that were thus bound. As I persisted in refusing . . . , the Ropes were thus drawn together four different Times. At my Side stood a Physician and Surgeon, who often felt my Temples, to judge of the Danger I might be in; by which Means my Tortures were suspended, at Intervals. . . . The last Time the Ropes were drawn tight, I grew so exceedingly weak, occasioned by the Blood's Circulation being stopp'd, and the Pains I endur'd, that I fainted quite away; insomuch that I was carried back to my Dungeon. . . .

They were so inhuman, six Weeks after, as to expose me to another kind of Torture. . . . They made me stretch my Arms in such a Manner, that the Palms of my Hands were turn'd outward; when, by the Help of a Rope that fastned them together at the Wrist, and which they turn'd by an Engine; they drew them gently nearer to one another behind, in such a Manner that the Back of each Hand touch'd, and stood exactly parallel one to the other; whereby both my Shoulders were dislocated, and a considerable Quantity of Blood issued from my Mouth. This torture was repeated thrice; after which I was again taken to my Dungeon, and put into the Hands of Physicians and Surgeons,

Two Months after, . . . I was again conveyed to the Torture-Room; and there made to undergo another Kind of Punishment twice. . . . They tortur'd me, on this Occasion, to such a Degree, that my Wrists and Shoulders, were put out of Joint. The Surgeons, however, set them presently after. . . .

He was remanded back to the dungeon. "The Reader may judge . . .," he says, "of the dreadful Anguish I must have labor'd under. . . . Most of my Limbs were put out of Joint, and bruis'd in such a Manner, that I was unable, during some Weeks, to lift my Hand to my Mouth; my Body being vastly swell'd, by the Inflammations caus'd by the frequent Dislocations. I have . . . Reason to fear, that I shall feel the sad Effects . . . so long as I live. . . ."

Finally, on 21 June 1744 Coustos was taken out and sentenced to four years in the galleys. After four months, the British Minister at Lisbon intervened, and got him his freedom. He returned to London, and wrote his book. He died the same year that it was published.

Well, from this summary you can see why Coustos was regarded as a Masonic hero. Here was a Man who remained steadfast to his obligations in the face of the most appalling mistreatment. A real example for us all to follow!

THE HISTORICAL SITUATION

If you know a little bit about British history, you can perhaps see another reason for the popularity of his book. The year was 1745. The British throne was held by George II of the House of Hanover, sixty-two years of age, stupid, graceless, and Protestant; "snuffy old drone from the German hive," as Justice Oliver Wendell Holmes called him. On the continent of Europe, Great Britain was at war with France and Prussia. Bonnie Prince Charlie, clever, charismatic, and Catholic, had landed in Scotland on 25 July, and raised the Jacobite standard of rebellion. He routed Johnnie Cope at Preston-pans on 21 September, and marched south into England, reaching Derby, a scant 120 miles from London on 4 December.

The English countered with the pen as well as the sword. The newspapers declaimed a litany of hatred against the Stuarts, and their Scots Highlander and Roman Catholic supporters.

Printing presses flooded the country with shrill anti-Romanist propaganda, all duly heralded in the London journals: *A Faithful Portrait of Popery: By which it is seen to be the Reverse of Christianity*, by William Warburton; *The Papists bloody Oath of Secrecy*, by Robert Bolton; *The bloody Cruelties of the Papists against the Protestants*, by "D. W.;" *Popish Intrigues and Cruelty, plainly exemplified in the afflicting Case and Narrative of Mrs Frances Shaftoe*; and dozens of others.

Two days before Christmas the newspaper advertised another book that seemed cast from the same mold: *The Sufferings of John Coustos*. What an appropriate time for a good bit of anti-Catholic propaganda! And Coustos's book was certainly that! It is easy to see why the establishment might have encouraged its sale.

LODGE RECORDS

But let us leave that. In the past thirty years, a wealth of new material dealing with John Coustos has been found. We now know a bit about the two lodges that he joined in London around 1730. One of them, No 75, which met at the Rainbow Coffee House, was quite large for those days. It had 63 members, and they included the Honorable James Cavendish, son of the Duke of Devonshire; Vincent LaChapelle, who became Master of the first lodge in the Netherlands, founded in the Hague in 1734, and who also published in 1735 the first collection of Masonic songs in French; Thomas Lance, who translated into French two of the songs in Anderson's *Constitutions*; Lewis Mercy, a minor composer and recorder-player; Colonel James Pitt, the uncle of William Pitt the elder, Minister of State for Britain at the time of the French and Indian War; Valentine Snow, the trumpeter for whom Handel composed the *obbligato* parts in the *Messiah*; and Henry Price, who introduced regular Freemasonry to America, founding a lodge in Boston in 1733.

Coustos's other London lodge, No 98, which met at Prince Eugene's Coffee House, worked in the French language. It had only thirty members. Nine of them came from the other lodge, No 75, including three whom we have already mentioned besides Coustos—Vincent LaChapelle, Thomas Lance, and Lewis Mercy. Another member was Louis François de la Tierce, who helped found the first lodge in Frankfurt (1741), and who also published a French translation of Anderson's *Constitutions* in 1742.

In Paris, we have discovered the actual minute book of the lodge to which Coustos belonged; it was seized in a police raid in 1737. This was a large and important lodge, and Coustos was its Master. The 68 members were a cosmopolitan group, with brethren from all over Europe. They included L'Abbé d'Aunillon, a comic playwright; Charles J. Baur, a German banker who later became Substitute Grand Master of France; Bontems, the *valet de chambre* of King Louis XV; Count Czapski, a Polish nobleman, and cousin of the Queen of France; Philippe Farsetti, a Venetian nobleman and art connoisseur; Claude Jacquier de Geraudly, a dentist at the Royal Court; Jean Pierre Guignon, a leading violinist; Pierre Jeliotte, an outstanding tenor; Johann Daniel Krafft, a leather-merchant of Hamburg, who founded the first lodge in Germany in 1737; Thomas Pierre LeBreton, a goldsmith, concurrently Master of another lodge in Paris; Prince Lubomirski, Grand Marshal at the Polish Royal Court, and a member of the first lodge in Warsaw in 1744; Jaque Christophe Naudot, a flute-player and composer; Bro. Ricault, a minor poet; Count Carl Fredrik Scheffer, later Grand Master of Sweden, 1753.

The list goes on and on: Baron de Bousch, Count de Gatterburg, Count de Swirby, Duke de Villeroy, Baron de Wendhausen. Two features are striking: the number of brethren connected with music, and the number of Masons who were instrumental in spreading the Craft over much of the world. It is clear moreover that Coustos was held in high esteem by this body of distinguished brethren. We read as follows in the lodge minutes of 30 April 1737.

"Since an ill-founded slur had been cast on our W. Bro. Coustos, that he had not taken the usual Masonic obligation, he took it [again] . . .; even though he had been Master of five lodges in England, and though he is the one, so to speak, who brought Masonry here, who has kept regular lodge, and established the Order on its present footing, since it is from him that we hold those admirable Masonic secrets which he possesses to perfection; and we are happy only insofar as we follow his instructions faithfully."

THE ARCHIVES OF THE INQUISITION

But of all the new information on Coustos, most important, the Portuguese archives have yielded up a full record of his trial, with transcripts of the denunciations against him, and a complete file of his examinations by the Inquisitors. And this material confirms virtually every statement made by Coustos: the repeated interrogations, the torture sessions, the pressure on him to reveal what he knew about Masonry, his refusal to turn Catholic.

There is one difference, an important one. According to the Inquisitorial Archives, the very first time he was brought before the Tribunal, a week after his arrest, Coustos made a full confession, a full disclosure of the nature of Masonry as it was in his time—the arrangement of the lodge, the modes of recognition, the penalties of his obligation, the method of initiation, the procedure at the banquet. All there!

Let us take an example (I translate from the original, which is written in Portuguese).

> And then the said Master teaches him the signs he should observe so as to be recognised in any part of the World by the other Brethren, and to be able to warn himself against those who are not: which is the putting of the right hand in front of the throat in the manner of seeking to cut it, and then allowing the right arm to fall straight down remaining fully extended; and also gives him the following signs: to take the right hand of another person and place his thumb upon the last joint of the other finger next thereto, there thus being embraced the greater part of the hand, and saying at the same time "Jaquem;" as also placing the right hand on the left breast, and from thence placing the hand on the last joint of the middle finger, saying at the same time the word "Boas."

We know from other sources that these details are correct for that date. It's the fullest description we have of the way in which Freemasonry was conducted in the 1740s. Coustos sang like a canary, and before they even laid a hand on him! And the irony of it is that they didn't **believe** he'd told it all! **That**'s why he was tortured.

CONCLUSION

Now it is my conviction that any Masonic talk that is presented in public should lead to a fuller recognition of general principles, as well as simply communicating certain specific facts. That is, in the true sense of the word, it should be Educational. Well, then, what do we learn from the sufferings of John Coustos? Two things, as it seems to me.

First, that there are still some interesting Masonic stories lurking about for us to root out. And secondly, that perhaps we shouldn't make snap judgments. It is tempting, and easy, to condemn the Catholic Church for torturing Coustos because of his Masonry.

His book was, as we have seen, an effective piece of anti-Catholic propaganda. But I would not want you to go away thinking that I was anti-Catholic, or that this talk was anti-Catholic. We have to look at the way of life 240 years ago. In those days torture and harsh punishment were still the custom of the time, even for what seem to us trivial offences. In 1772 a boy named Peter M'Cloud was hanged in London for an attempt at housebreaking which failed, so that he was caught. In 1789 a woman by the name of Christian

129

Murphy was burnt at the stake in London for counterfeiting. In France in 1757, Robert François Damiens, who had tried unsuccessfully to kill the king, had his hand burnt, his body pinched with red hot pinchers; boiling oil, melted wax and rosin, and melted lead were poured into all his wounds, and then he was torn asunder by four horses. A turn or two on the rack seems mild enough in comparison!

And what of the charge of Freemasonry? Well, the Craft had been condemned by the Church on suspicion of heresy; that means that, in the Church's eyes, Masons were putting their immortal souls in hazard of everlasting hell-fire. Not something the Church could accept without exerting strong efforts for Salvation!

What does a little temporary physical discomfort count, when measured against the whole of eternity? Better to suffer a bit on earth than to burn for ever in the afterlife. One can even see why Masonry was suspect. It came from a Protestant country—a country of heretics; a country of radicals, which had killed one king (Charles I) and driven out another (James II) within the course of the preceding century. Furthermore, the doors of the lodges were tyled, and the members took an oath to veil in impenetrable secrecy everything that went on. Who could say what pagan rites, what vile orgies, what diabolical plots were being hatched by that bunch of radical heretics! Small wonder the Church imagined the worst!

And what are we to think of Coustos himself? Contempt is the easy first reaction towards a man who so violates the sacred trust reposed in him. Yet the Inquisitors had ways (as the saying goes) to loosen tongues. They had great powers, they knew how to use them, and they saw to it that people realized the extent of these powers.

Arrest by the Holy Office was practically as good as a conviction; rare was the prisoner who did not confess whatever was wanted of him. The officials would take him to the torture chamber, and show him all the instruments, and explain their use to him, so that "he would readily understand how arduous and thorough would be his examination."

Again and again they would give him time by himself, to ponder his situation. He could brood about whether he would rather talk now or later. For talk he certainly would. In this century we have seen how effective psychological pressure can be when exerted by a powerful institution against an isolated individual. Certain regimes have honed the technique to a fine art.

We hear regularly of the "confessions" of political prisoners in Russia, China, North Korea, and Eastern Europe. The name given to the procedure, "brain-washing," is new; its methods, we now perceive, are not new. Seen in this light, Coustos's capitulation is quite intelligible; there is no reason to spurn him for his confession, given the extremity to which he was reduced. Which of us would be brave enough to endure the *strappado*, or the rack, or even the threat of them, without succumbing?

In Coustos we see a man who was a leader of the Craft in three countries. We know from the record that he won the respect and admiration of the lords and barons of Paris. His lodges in London and Paris were the centres from which the Craft spread to America, to Holland, to Germany, to Sweden, and even to Poland. He was a man who, though not an accomplished writer, determined to win his revenge on his tormentors by telling the world of his sufferings. And he did so with simplicity and with a wealth of circumstantial detail.

His early death at the age of forty-three, less than two years after his deliverance, was undoubtedly hastened by his torture and imprisonment. He is worthy to be enshrined among those who gave up their lives for a principle.

In my books he is still a Masonic hero.

BATTY LANGLEY: WRITER OF ARCHITECTURAL HANDBOOKS

[Another early English Mason whose activities are not without interest is Batty Langley. Here is his story.]

LIFE OF BATTY LANGLEY

The main question is, can we learn anything about Freemasonry from a man who did not make his mark in either the Craft or the profane world? I would argue that we can, and I offer an example for your consideration.

On 14 September 1696, at Twickenham Parish Church, just west of London, was baptized Batty Langley, the son of Daniel Langley, a gardener. His first name, which today would make him a laughing-stock, was originally a diminutive for Bartholomew.

Batty followed in his father's footsteps, and started out as a landscape gardener in Twickenham. Somewhere, we don't know where, he got professional training, and soon set up as an architect. By 1729, when he moved to London, he had already produced six or seven books, mostly manuals in gardening and building.

He was a fair draftsman, and submitted designs in two large public competitions: for the Mansion House (the official residence of the Lord Mayor of London) in 1735, and for the New Westminster Bridge across the River Thames in 1736. If his drawings for either had been selected, his future success would have been assured. Failure in both (probably a fair reflection of his talents) marked him as an also-ran. In fact altogether he had few architectural commissions: several out-buildings for the Duke of Kent at Wrest Park, Bedfordshire (1735), and "a curious grotesque temple in a taste entirely new" at Parliament Stairs, Westminster, for Nathaniel Blackerby (likewise 1735).

Simply in order to keep body and soul together he continued to produce popular handbooks for journeyman builders. Such books by their very nature are not original, and Langley borrowed heavily from the writings and drawings of others. About thirty works are ascribed to him, which is not bad when you consider that he was doing other things as well.

In his titles, whether from stupidity or cupidity, he tended to repeat himself (*The Builder's Chest-Book*, June 1727; *The Builder's Compleat Chest-Book*, November 1738; *The Builder's Compleat Assistant*, March-April 1739; *The Builder's Director*, April 1747; *The Builder's Jewel*, about May 1741; *The Measurer's Jewel*, November 1742). His books were filled with concise instructions and clear illustrations. The early ones, which dealt primarily with the classical tradition, culminated in *Ancient Masonry, both in the Theory and Practice* (1736), with its three thousand examples, engraved on four hundred and ninety-four large folio copper-plates.

In 1737 Batty Langley moved to the part of London known as Soho, and with the help of his younger brother Thomas, an engraver, opened a school of architecture. The advertisement runs, "Workmen from 7 to 9 in every Evening, Saturdays and Sundays excepted, and young Gentlemen and others by the Year, are taught Drawing, Geometry, Architecture, Mensuration, Mechanicks, &c."

It was hardly one of the great academies. "His disciples were all carpenters," according to one who knew them. In 1742, after more than twenty years of study, Langley published his most original work, an attempt to recover the rules by which the great English cathedrals had been built. It was entitled *Ancient Architecture, restored and improved by a great Variety of Grand and Useful Designs entirely new in the Gothick Mode*; the plates were re-issued in 1747 under the title, *Gothic Architecture improved by Rules and Proportions*. In it he devised five orders of **Gothic** architecture, corresponding to the five **Noble** orders.

This is interesting, because, at the time at which he was writing, the Gothic style of building was no longer in fashion. The dominant school, known as Renaissance Architecture, was marked by an imitation of classical forms. It had been introduced into England from Italy soon after 1600, and the tradition was too well established for Langley to have any immediate effect. He was clearly ahead of his time, and his efforts won him only ridicule. Critics spoke contemptuously of his "book of bad Designs," and of "Batty Langley's Gothic." Yet in some ways he was a forerunner of the Gothic revival.

He had other irons in the fire as well. He advertised himself as a surveyor of homes and estates and a valuer of timber, growing or felled. He was prepared to construct "Engines for raising Waters to any height required, for the service of Towns, private Families, Canals, Fish-ponds, &c." He continued to provide advice on the "Laying Out, Planting, Government, &c.," of gardens. In 1729 he invented an artificial stone (made of "a Composition of Clays &c.") which could be used for columns, statues, and architectural decorations. He even offered himself as what we would call a consumer's advocate, and was prepared "at honest living Prices" to reduce the "exorbitant Bills of Workmen."

THE MASONIC CONNECTION

Langley was certainly a Freemason. Even though his name does not appear in lodge records, his books from 1736 on provide eloquent testimony, which we shall consider in a moment. As early as 1726 his *Practical Geometry* was dedicated to Lord Paisley, "the Head of a most Ancient and most Honorable Society, whose profound Knowledge, in these Affairs, is their Pride and Distinction." (Lord Paisley was Grand Master of the Premier Grand Lodge in 1726.) Langley signed the dedication as "Your Lordship's most Obedient, Most Humble, And most Devoted Servant," which rather sounds as if he were an admirer, but not yet a member.

The Builder's Compleat Chest-Book (1738; later editions were entitled *The Builder's Compleat Assistant*) provided a list of subscribers that includes the Sun Lodge of Free and Accepted Masons, in St Paul's Church-Yard (No 40), and the Talbot Lodge of Free and Accepted Masons, at Stourbridge (No 119). Stourbridge is outside Birmingham, at some distance from London, and Langley will not have had any Masonic roots there. Quite probably the other lodge, No 40, had initiated him. It was warranted in 1725, took the name Lodge of Cordiality in 1796, and lapsed in 1830. Grand Lodge archives list the members of No 40 in 1725 and 1730.

Batty's name does not appear, and so he must have joined later. Members whom he will have known include the actor John Hippisley (died 1748), the antiquarian Richard Rawlinson (lived 1690–1755), and Daniel Delvalle, who in 1732 became the first Jewish Master of a lodge. Batty must have been initiated within a year or two of 1730. Beginning on 11 July 1734 he published in *The Grub-Street Journal* a series of articles on architecture. His pen-name, "Hiram," indicates that by now he belonged to the Craft. (He actually named one of his fourteen children, born 2 January 1742, Hiram; other young Langleys included Euclid, Vitruvius, and Archimedes.) We cannot be absolutely certain, but the balance of probability is that he became a Mason in Lodge No 40 at some date between 1730 and 1734.

He had professional dealings with more than one notable Mason. In 1732 he sold some sculptured busts, no doubt made of his artificial stone, to Charles, Duke of Richmond (G.M., 1724–1725). And, as we have already seen, he did some building for Nathaniel Blackerby (S.G.W., 1728; Deputy G.M., 1729–1730; Grand Treasurer, 1727–1737).

There is at least one Mason with whom he was at variance. When he submitted his unsuccessful design for Westminster Bridge, the winning entry came from Bro. Charles Labelye (lived 1705–1762), a native of Switzerland, who in 1725 belonged to a French-speaking lodge in London. Langley took his defeat badly, and twelve years later still spoke bitterly of his competitor, referring to him as "an Insolvent, Ignorant, Arrogating Swiss," and even publishing a sketch of him being hanged on a gallows beneath his bridge, labelling it "The Swiss Impostor rewarded, as his Ignorance justly deserves."

MASONRY IN HIS BOOKS

Some of Langley's books reveal a detailed acquaintance with the Craft and its members. About this time the Rev. James Anderson wrote, "Many Noblemen and Gentlemen of the first Rank desir'd to be admitted into the *Fraternity*, besides other Learned Men, Merchants, Clergymen and Tradesmen, who found a *Lodge* to be a safe and pleasant Relaxation from Intense Study or the Hurry of Business, without Politicks or Party." A few years earlier an Oxford clergyman had said that Freemasonry "has been an honor much courted of late by quality." Langley's gigantic collection of plates, *Ancient Masonry* (1736), which we mentioned a moment ago, provides a striking commentary. It was dedicated to Francis, Duke of Lorraine (the first royal prince to become a Mason), and **forty** British noblemen, duly named, and "to all others The Right Honorable and Right Worshipful Masters of Masonry," by "Your Most Obedient, Humble Servant, and Affectionate Brother, B. Langley."

The list includes seven Dukes, sixteen Earls, seven Viscounts, and ten Barons; there are fifteen brethren who either had been or would become Grand Masters of one of the British Grand Lodges. This dedication has been neglected by Masonic historians, and would repay further study. Several of the noblemen listed here are not otherwise known to have belonged to the Craft.

In both *The Builder's Chest-Book* (1727) and *The Builder's Compleat Chest-Book* (1738) he gives instructions by way of dialogue, in what he calls Lectures, between Master and Prentice. The earlier book begins as follows:

M. What is an Architect?

P. A Person Skilful in the Art of Building.

M. How many principal Parts is Architecture divided into?

P. Three. Civil, Naval, and Military. . . .

M. How many Conditions doth well Building consist of?

P. Three. Commodity, Firmness and Delight.

The later book starts off after this fashion:

P. What is Arithmetick?

M. Arithmetick, is a Greek Word, and imports an Art or Science, that teaches the Use and Properties of Figures, or right Art of numbering.

P. What doth right numbering consist of?

M. To denote any given quantity with proper Characters, and to express them by Words, which is called Notation.

Some students have compared these dialogues with the Masonic Catechisms current at the time, but it is hard to see much resemblance, except in the format of question and answer.

Another pocket-sized manual is *The Builder's Jewel: or the Youth's Instructor, and Workman's Remembrancer.* It is illustrated by upwards of two hundred examples, engraved on one hundred copper-plates. The frontispiece was designed by Batty Langley, and engraved by his brother. It is dated in the Masonic fashion, "A.L. 5741." It depicts three Great Pillars (Doric, Tuscan, Corinthian), their pedestals bearing the letters W, S, and B (for Wisdom, Strength, and Beauty), and (from right to left) the Roman numerals 3, 5, 7.

On the architraves stand representations of the Sun, Moon, and M(aster) M(ason). The Pillars stand upon Holy Ground, duly labeled H. G. Overhead is a clouded Canopy. In the background is a high Hill and a low Vale, with a Shrub on the Brow of the Hill, and the number 15, alluding to the Fifteen Loving Brothers. Suspended from the left-hand pillar are the Bible, Compass and Square, and a drawing of a Point, a Line, a Superficies and a Solid.

At the top of the centre pillar is the Wind which blows due East and West, and fastened below it are a Clock with its hands set at High Twelve, and a drawing of the Lodge, with its Mosaic Pavement, Blazing Star, Border, and two columns labeled I and B flanking the northern entrance. Hanging from the right-hand pillar are the Square, Level, and Plumb-Rule, together with a drawing of Squares, Angles and Perpendiculars.

These are all Masonic symbols that were current in Langley's time; most of them occur for example in Samuel Prichard's ritual exposure *Masonry Dissected* (1730). In fact, this frontispiece foreshadows the later Masonic Tracing Board, Trestle Board or Monitorial Chart. Yet it has nothing to do with the text of the book. It is an irrelevant insertion, and must be Langley's gesture of affection towards the Craft.

THE TRADITIONAL HISTORY OF GEOMETRY

One of Langley's other books carried the title, *The Builders Compleat Chest-Book, or Library of Arts and Sciences, Absolutely Necessary to be understood by Builders and Workmen in general.* The title-page is dated 1738, and in fact the publication was announced in *The Gentleman's Magazine* for November of that year.

The book is relentlessly practical, and offers instruction in Arithmetick, Geometry, Architecture, Mensuration, Plain Trigonometry, Surveying, Mechanick Powers, and Hydrostaticks. After Langley has finished giving "all the useful Rules in Vulgar and Decimal Arithmetick both in whole Numbers and in Fractions," he moves on to Geometry. He begins with a short introduction, tracing the Science from Biblical Times on down.

"PART II. OF Geometry.

INTRODUCTION.

THE next Science in order after Arithmetick is Geometry, the most excellent Knowledge in the World, as being the *Basis* or Foundation of all Trade, and on which all Arts depend.

Geometry is speculative and practical; the former demonstrates the Properties of Lines, Angles and Figures; the latter teaches how to apply them to practice in *Architecture, Trigonometry, Mensuration, Surveying, Mechanicks, Perspective, Dialling, Astronomy, Navigation, Fortification,* &c. This Art was first invented by Jabal the Son of Lamech and Adah, by whom the first House with Stones and Trees was built.

Jabal was also the first that wrote on this Subject, and which he performed, with his Brethren, Jubal, Tubal Cain, and Naamah, who together wrote on two Columns the Arts of *Geometry, Musick, working in Brass and Weaving,* which were found (after the Flood of Noah) by Hermarines, a descendant from Noah, who was afterwards called Hermes the Father of Wisdom, and who taught those Sciences to other Men. So that in a short time the Science of *Geometry* became known to many, and even to those of the highest Rank, for the mighty Nimrod King of *Babylon* understood Geometry, and was not only a Mason himself, but caused others to be taught *Masonry,* many of whom he sent to build the City of *Ninive* and other Cities in the *East.* Abraham was also a Geometer, and when he went into *Egypt,* he taught Euclid, the then most worthy Geometrician in the World, the Science of Geometry, to whom the whole World is now largely indebted for his unparalleled Elements of Geometry. Hiram, the chief Conducter of the Temple of *Solomon,* was also an excellent Geometer, as was Grecus, a curious Mason who worked at the Temple, and who afterwards taught the Science of Masonry in *France.*

England was entirely unacquainted with this noble Science, until the time of St Alban, when Masonry was then established, and *Geometry* was taught to most Workmen concerned in Building; but as soon after, this Kingdom was frequently invaded, and nothing but Troubles and Confusion reign'd all the

Land over, this noble Science was disregarded until Athelstan a worthy King of *England* suppress'd those Tumults, and brought the Land into Peace; when *Geometry* and *Masonry* were re-established, and great Numbers of Abbys and other stately Buildings were erected in this Kingdom.

Edwin the Son of Athelstan was also a great lover of Geometry, and used to read Lectures thereof to Masons. He also obtained from his Father a Charter to hold an Assembly, where they would, within the Realm, once in every Year, and himself held the first at York, where he made Masons; so from hence it is, that Masons to this Day have a grand Meeting and Feast, once in every Year. Thus much by way of Introduction, to shew the Use, and how much the Science of Geometry has been esteemed by some of the greatest Men in the World, and which with regard to the Publick Good of my Country, I have here explained, in the most plain and easy manner that I am able to do, and to which I proceed."

And with these words Langley turns to the mechanical details of Geometry, beginning (like Euclid in his First Book) with Definitions, Axioms, and Postulates. In March or April of 1739 the same book was re-issued under the title *The Builders Compleat Assistant,* and a number of subsequent editions followed in quick succession. They all contain the same potted history of Geometry.

THE SOURCE OF LANGLEY'S INFORMATION

The historical preamble is unexpected in such a utilitarian context. It recites a series of incidents, in each of which Geometry and Masonry are treated as synonymous terms:

(1) how Jabal invented Geometry before the Flood;

(2) how Hermarines discovered it after the Flood;

(3) how Nimrod fostered it;

(4) how Abraham's pupil Euclid taught it in Egypt;

(5) how Hiram, King Solomon's Architect, was a Geometer;

(6) how Grecus introduced the science into France;

(7) how it spread to England in Saint Alban's time; and

(8) how King Athelstan and his son Edwin reorganized it.

Batty is clearly drawing on a copy of the documents known as "the Old Charges" or "the Old Manuscript Constitutions," where all eight episodes are found. These Old Charges exist in various forms, but the typical one is a parchment roll or scroll, with the regulations used to govern the operative craft, but including as well a traditional history. In its most common form the text runs to under four thousand words, roughly the equivalent of two-thirds of a page from *The New York Times*.

The *Old Charges* were first put together about the year 1350, and were copied and recopied, edited and re-edited dozens of times over the next four centuries. One hundred and thirteen versions are known, all telling basically the same story, and all derived ultimately from the same original. Each one is identified by a name and a code abbreviation that indicates its affinities. The "Langley Abstract" is conventionally designated **H.4**, No 4 in the category "Sundry Versions," because no one has ever worked out its relationships. The first question is, can we determine precisely which version was consulted by Batty Langley?

The wording provides several clues. To begin with, Hermes is usually described in the Old Charges as "the father of wise men," but twenty-one copies make him "the father of wisdom," as does Langley. Again, the Architect of the Temple is most often named Aynon or Aymon; eighteen texts call him Hiram, the way Langley does.

Finally, the "curious" (that is, careful) Mason from King Solomon's Temple who carried the craft to France is generally called Naymus Grecus, or something like that. Seven other versions call him simply "Grecus." Only one manuscript of the Old Charges exhibits all three of these peculiarities. It was written on thirteen sheets of paper about the year 1725, and now belongs to Quatuor Coronati Lodge, in London. Nothing is known of its history before it turned up in Margate, north of Dover, in 1888. It was secured for the lodge with the assistance of Bro. Dorabjee Pestonjee Cama, Past Grand Treasurer, and is therefore known as the Cama Manuscript; it is designated by the code abbreviation **D.a.29**. Evidently Langley had access to it or to something very similar.

We do not know who wrote the Cama Manuscript, but we can make certain inferences. It is (as its text shows) closely akin to the ancestor of the Spencer Family (G), a thoroughly modernized revision carried out by parties unknown at some date between 1722 and 1725. Three copies of this prototype were transcribed about 1726 by the man who became Secretary to Grand Lodge a year later. The same text was engraved on copper plates and published in 1729 by a member of the old Lodge No 1, who later served as the official printer to Grand Lodge. Clearly the Spencer ancestor had some official status.

Now here we have Batty Langley, a man who was certainly a devoted and vociferous Freemason, who had business dealings with senior Masonic officers. He too publishes a summary of the Old Charges, founded upon a text which is related to the Spencer ancestor. Where does he get it? Evidently he must have obtained it from his acquaintances in high places.

We know that during the first decade of the premier Grand Lodge (1717–1727) the authorities were at great pains to locate and copy as many texts of the Old Charges as they could. It appears that the Cama Manuscript and its relative the Spencer Original were in the hands of the Grand Lodge, and in fact may even have been edited by an executive officer.

This is odd, because the Rev. James Anderson says that in 1721 the Grand Master had ordered him to digest the Old Charges "in a new and better Method." The result of his work was the first Book of *Constitutions*, published in 1723. And yet the Cama and Spencer revisions were being carried out at the very same time, or shortly after. It is almost as if some of the senior brethren were not completely in favor of Anderson, and were preparing a rival or alternative text.

CONCLUSION

Batty Langley died 3 March 1751 in London.

The one portrait of him was engraved in 1741 when he was 46 years of age. It shows a fat miserable looking man, with a double chin and a discontented mouth. He holds in his hands the plan of a semiformal garden.

Architectural historians, even those who try to be fair, cannot find much significance in his career. He was not a great creative architect, but was rather a mass popularizer at a vulgar level. "As a matter of fact Batty Langley was really an excellent practical builder who had mistaken his vocation when he set up as an architect. . . . He was an excellent builder of many of the edifices which he had himself indifferently designed" (E. Beresford Chancellor).

He "won the gratitude of village craftsmen and local builders trained in classical ways" (J. Mordaunt Crook), and his portfolio of Gothic patterns became "the oracle and text book of carpenters and bricklayers when employed by churchwardens and country gentlemen" (James Dallaway). All over England, and even in Scotland and Ireland, you will find doorways, windows, and fireplaces, that are clearly designed after his pattern books. They turn up in such unexpected places as the Police Station at Ludlow, a gate lodge at Castletown in County Kildare, and a mausoleum in the Calton Hill Cemetery in Edinburgh.

Batty Langley was not rich, or successful, or important, or even particularly attractive. He was not an officer of Grand Lodge, and there is no evidence that he ever presided in lodge. He contributed nothing to the evolution of the Craft. He was however a devoted Mason, and a prolific author who was ready on occasion to refer to Masonry in his writings. He offers an impressive list of Masonic noblemen for the year 1736. He publishes a sym-bolic chart that confirms many details of early ritual, but must have baffled the tradesmen who tried to use it. He prints a summary of the Old Charges that hints at certain behind-the-scene rivalries.

In short he helps to illuminate the obscure early days of the first Grand Lodge.

WELLINS CALCOTT: EXPOUNDER OF THE RITUAL

[We owe much of the wording of our Masonic ritual to the work of "the three great expounders." The earliest of them was Wellins Calcott.]

PRELIMINARY REMARKS

There are in the world several groups of people that are noticeably conservative. I don't mean conservative in a political sense. I mean simply that, when these people are called upon to perform certain age-old ceremonial acts, they symbolically recall their long history by wearing traditional articles of clothing.

In this connection one thinks of university professors, with their robes and hoods; and priests of the church, with their cassocks and surplices; and British lawyers, with their gowns and tabs; and Freemasons, with their aprons and gauntlets. Sometimes these groups are conservative in the wording of their ceremonies as well.

Someone has said that the Masonic ritual came to King Solomon inscribed on tablets of stone, and has been passed down without change ever since. This is an exaggeration. But the ritual does go back a long way. Those who have looked into the matter say that much of the modern working was already a part of the Craft by 1745, but that it was still rude and unpolished.

Not until some time around the year 1770, when the three great expounders of the ritual came on the scene, did the wording begin to assume a more attractive form, closer to what is familiar today. These three men, Wellins Calcott, William Hutchinson, and William Preston (all of whom worked in England), wrote longer charges and for the first time included something for the mind. Preston, the latest and greatest of them, eventually took what was best in the other two, and consolidated it. His handbook became so useful that it was adapted for use in America by Thomas Smith Webb, and by this means was carried across the Atlantic.

Within the past fifteen years, the works of two of the expounders, William Preston's *Illustrations of Masonry* and William Hutchinson's *Spirit of Masonry*, have been reprinted more than once, and have become available to a new generation of students. They can provide endless entertainment for the ritualist, for time and again he will find in them addresses that are still well known. Thus, the following prayer appears in Preston:

Vouchsafe thine aid, Almighty Father and supreme Governor of the world, to this our present convention; and grant that this candidate for Masonry may dedicate and devote his life to thy service, and become a true and faithful brother among us. Endue him with a competence of thy divine wisdom, that, by the secrets of this Art, he may be better enabled to unfold the mysteries of godliness, to the honour of thy holy name. Amen.

Even today these words, or something like them, are heard when a candidate is initiated into Freemasonry.

In the same way, the charges that are delivered to the Wardens at their investiture, or that in other jurisdictions form a part of the ceremony of passing, are edited versions of Hutchinson's "Moral Observations on the Instruments of Masonry":

The Plumb-line admonishes us to walk erect and upright . . .; not to lean to a side, but to hold the scale of justice in equal poise; to observe the just medium between temperance and voluptuousness; . . . and to make our several passions and prejudices . . . coincide with our line of duty. . . . The level should advise us that . . . we are all descended from the same common stock, partake of the like nature, have . . . the same hope . . .; and though distinctions necessarily make a subordination among mankind, yet eminence of station should not make us forget that we are men, nor cause us to treat our brethren, because placed on the lowest spoke of the wheel of fortune, with contempt; because a time will come, and the wisest of men know not how soon, when all distinctions, except in goodness, will cease, and when death—that grand leveller of all human greatness—will bring us to a level at the last.

The earliest of the three expounders was Wellins Calcott. His *Candid Disquisition* (1769), which has been not been reprinted for 130 years, has been chosen by The Masonic Book Club as its volume for 1989. Calcott's words, like those of Preston and Hutchinson, can still strike a responsive chord. Here, for example, is one of his charges:

Right Worshipful SIR, BY the unanimous voice of the members of this lodge, you are elected to the mastership thereof for the ensuing half-year. . . . What you have seen *praise-worthy* in others, we doubt not you will *imitate*; and what you have seen *defective*, you will in yourself *amend*. . . . For a pattern of imitation, consider the great luminary of nature, which, rising in the *east*, regularly diffuses light and lustre to all within its circle. In like manner it is your province, with due decorum, to spread and communicate light and instruction to the brethren in the lodge.

Part of this is now used in the address to the Master, and part of it, in some grand lodges, in the address to the Wardens.

LIFE OF CALCOTT

Clearly Wellins Calcott merits a closer look. Not much is known of his life. He was born in the Parish of St Chad, at Shrewsbury, in Shropshire, England, on 27 January 1726, the son of Mathias Calcott and Sarah Heady. His family seems to have been reasonably well off, and his father had been a member of the Shrewsbury Corporation, or town council. For some reason or other young Wellins fell upon evil times. The details are not clear, but he leads us to believe that he was treated unjustly and cheated by dishonest men of superior wealth. He tried to improve his fortune by producing books. He wrote two, both of which found a ready market and came out in more than one edition. In each, he made sure that he would be able to cover expenses, and even to turn a profit, by drumming up subscribers; they paid in advance, and received the honor of being listed at the front of the publication.

In 1756 he came out with his first book, *Thoughts Moral and Divine; Collected and intended for the better Instruction and Conduct of Life*; it was so popular that it went through five editions (London, 1756; Birmingham, 1758; Coventry, 1759; Manchester, 1761; Exeter, 1764). The first edition lists 339 subscribers, including twelve peers of the realm. The book is a collection of clever sayings and popular philosophy, largely borrowed from earlier writers.

You know the sort of thing: a catchy turn of phrase that sounds as if it embodies a great truth, and will stick in your mind. "Gaze not on Beauty too much lest it blast you, nor too long lest it blind you, nor too near lest it burn you." "He is a wise Man that can avoid an evil, a patient Man that can endure it, but a valiant Man that can conquer it." "No Men are so oft in the Wrong, as those who pretend to be always in the Right." "To laugh at wise Men is the Privilege of Fools." "Why should Death be so formidable when life is so miserable?" "Yesterday cannot be recalled; to-morrow cannot be assured; only today is yours."

HIS MASONIC CAREER

Calcott was also a Freemason. We do not know when he joined the Craft, but in December 1758 he was present at a meeting of Lodge No 71 (Ancients), at Birmingham. In December 1761 he is listed in the register as a visitor to Lodge St David, No 36, Edinburgh, being described as "R[ight] W[orshipful] M[aster] of the Lodge at Holywell, Flintshire," and the next year he joined two Scottish lodges by affiliation. In 1767 he delivered two addresses at the ceremony of Installation and Investiture of the Palladian Lodge (Moderns), Hereford (now No 120); his name is subscribed to them with the rank of Past Master, and this has led some students to believe that he had ruled the lodge. At any rate, he was Master of the Lodge of Regularity,

London (now No 91), in 1768. In 1779 he was made an honorary member of Apollo Lodge at York, England. He is last heard of on 4 August 1779, when he delivered a lecture in Phoenix Lodge, now No 94, in Sunderland. Thereafter he disappears from the scene.

His second book concerns Freemasonry. It was published in London in 1769 under the title, *A Candid Disquisition of the Principles and Practices of the Most Ancient and Honourable Society of Free and Accepted Masons; together with Some Strictures on the Origin, Nature, and Design of that Institution.* . . .

THE SUBSCRIBERS

In the days before a regular postal system as we know it was in operation, the surest way to find advance subscribers for a book was by going on speaking tours, and then, after the lectures, giving the audience a chance to place orders. It is a tough way to make a living, but clearly Calcott did a fair bit of talking on Masonic subjects. We know that in the 1760s he was delivering formal addresses in the County of Durham, and from 1761 on he lectured even in Scotland. He must have been an accomplished speaker. The minutes of Phoenix Lodge in Sunderland report "that Bro. Calcott's Lecture was the best and most informative ever heard in this Lodge."

One other index of his success is to be found in the list of people who were prepared to order his book and pay in advance. His London edition carries the names of 1164 subscribers. Most of his sales came from London (more than 300 names), and the southwest (the region embracing Devon, Somerset, and Cornwall; over 500 names).

He recruited some fairly respectable people; he has the Duke of Beaufort, who was Grand Master of England (Moderns) 1767–1771, as well as three Past Grand Masters, the Deputy Grand Master, both of the Grand Wardens, the Grand Treasurer, and the Grand Secretary; he also has twenty-three holders of hereditary titles (Dukes, Marquesses, Earls, Viscounts, Barons, Baronets—including two royal princes), and sixteen Members of Parliament. The list includes several subscribers who one might have thought could receive copies without paying: Calcott's printer, James Dixwell, and five of those whose words he quotes at length, Rev. Mr Chalmers, James Galloway, J. S. Gaudry, Alex. Shedden, and John Whitmash. Four other names are of particular interest: one is William Cole, the engraver (died 1803), the man who produced and printed the lists of "Modern" lodges from 1766 to 1778; he was a relative, possibly the son, of Benjamin Cole, who in 1729 engraved and published the book known as "Cole's Constitutions." The other interesting names are Alexander, Lord Colville (1710–1770), who was initiated in Halifax, Nova Scotia, in 1750, and was Master of the Second Lodge in

Boston from 1750 to 1752; James Boswell (1740–1795), the biographer of Dr Samuel Johnson; and the historian Edward Gibbon, Jr (1737–1794), whose *Decline and Fall of the Roman Empire* began to appear in 1776.

Three years after the London edition, Calcott's book was published in Boston. It appeared there in two issues. The first lists 415 subscribers, and the second adds another 23 ("received too late to be inserted in their proper Places"). In order to sell 438 copies in America (263 in Massachusetts, 78 in New York, 73 in Nova Scotia, and 24 in Connecticut), Calcott must have spoken to audiences in the New World, as he had in Britain.

He will be one of the earliest in a long line of English brethren who have enjoyed American hospitality while on the Masonic speaking circuit. William R. Denslow says he came to America twice, and from the details of the lists, it certainly looks as if he was here in 1772. In fact, it is possible that he stayed for an extended period, because on 7 October 1774 he wrote to the Grand Secretary stating that he was back in England suffering from ill-health after a period abroad.

His list of American subscribers, which gives the Masonic rank and title of many of the officers of the Provincial Grand Lodges and the constituent lodges, has several familiar names. Calcott's visit took place on the very eve of the American Revolution, and his list includes people whose names are associated with the struggle in one way or another. A few remained on the British side, such as Jonathan Belcher (1710–1776), Chief Justice of Nova Scotia, and Sir John Johnson (1742–1830), the commander of the New York Loyalist regiment known as the Royal Greens.

At least one of Calcott's subscribers refused to take either side, the Past Warden of New York, the Quaker grammarian Lindley Murray (1745–1826). And a whole array of luminaries was on the victorious side: from New York, Robert R. Livingston, Jr, (1746–1813), the first chancellor of the state, and Dr Samuel Bard (1742–1821), who became Washington's personal physician after the war; from North Carolina, John Simpson, Brigadier General of Militia; and from Massachusetts, Richard Gridley (1711–1796), wounded at Bunker Hill; William Palfrey (1741–1780), Washington's Aide-de-Camp and Paymaster-General; Paul Revere (1735–1818), immortalized in Longfellow's poem; John Rowe (died 1787), who according to one story suggested the idea of the Boston tea-party; and Joseph Warren (1741–1775), who lost his life at Bunker Hill. . . .

CONCLUSION. HIS EFFECT ON THE RITUAL

Ever since modern Masonry was established, notable Freemasons have spoken to their Brethren about the nature of the Craft, its history, and its ideals. From the first twenty years of the Premier Grand Lodge, we have several such speeches; one delivered by the antiquary Francis Drake at York in 1726; one by Edward Oakley at London in 1728; another by Martin Clare at London in 1735; and yet another by the Chevalier Andrew Ramsay in Paris in 1736. But splendid and inspiring though they may have been, they had no particular effect on the practices, beliefs, or wording of the Craft in subsequent years. This is where the three great expounders broke new ground. They included a number of addresses, and even phrases, that were taken up by later Masons.

Wellins Calcott published his book, as we have seen, in 1769. It is particularly exciting to read for anybody who has had some experience of the Masonic ritual. Quite regularly, as he goes through it, he will find a group of words, or a sentence, or an episode, that still belongs to the Craft. Sometimes Calcott borrowed the words we know so well; thus, he takes over from French sources an allusion to the Biblical story of the Ephraimites at the passages of the river Jordan.

Again, from William Smith's *Pocket Companion* of 1735 he quotes the charge to the newly initiated Brother (the one containing the words, "ancient, as having subsisted from time immemorial"). He has those two groups of three, wisdom, strength, and beauty, and freedom, fervency, and zeal, which go back at least as far as Samuel Prichard's *Masonry Dissected* of 1730. He refers to that other trio, brotherly love, relief, and truth, which is found in Masonic catechisms as early as 1724.

He speaks of God as the Great Architect of the Universe, a phrase that has been a part of Masonry at least since Anderson's first book of *Constitutions* in 1723, and which Anderson apparently took over from the theologian John Calvin. Calcott more than once refers to Masonry as the royal art, another phrase from Anderson. He alludes several times to the liberal arts and sciences, which were mentioned even in the Old Charges of the operative stone masons.

Sometimes however it appears that Calcott was the first one to print the text that now sounds so familiar. More than once he refers to "moral and social virtue," words which are still heard in the benediction at closing. He speaks, as the Masonic ritual does even today in some parts of the world, of Pythagoras and the Egyptian philosophers, who concealed their ideas under the cover of hieroglyphics, and who taught their principles through allegory and symbol.

He juxtaposes, as some Masons still do, Abraham's readiness to sacrifice Isaac, David's prayers to appease the wrath of God, and Solomon's building of the temple—three grand offerings that all took place, according to tradition, on Mount Moriah. Calcott knows why it is that the two brazen pillars at the porch of the temple were cast hollow—though he regards the reason as a Masonic secret, and refuses to disclose it. He says, as it is still said in the charge to the Fellowcraft, that "the *internal,* and not the *external,* qualifications of a man, are what *masonry* regards," and he notes further that it is needless to enlarge on the duties required of a Mason, because "your own experience will soon evince the real value and utility of this *science.*" He observes that in the lodge-room a Freemason will find "no other contention but *who can work best, who can agree best*," and his words, slightly altered, are still used when a lecturer ponders the symbolism of the trowel.

He is the first one to publish the justification for having lodge-officers: "Such is the nature of our constitution, that as some must of necessity, *rule* and *teach,* so others must of course learn to *obey;*" this explanation is still given, almost unaltered, in the charge to the Brethren at installation.

As Stokes says, "Whether these expressions are due to Calcott or whether he took them out of some old working is immaterial; at any rate Calcott put them into print, and so ensured their continued existence in exact phraseology; for this service alone he merits our thanks and our remembrance."

If we have guessed right about the way in which advance sales of books were generated, it seems to follow that Wellins Calcott may well have attended Masonic gatherings with a number of distinguished brethren. Just imagine, sitting in lodge with Boswell, or Gibbon, or Paul Revere, or Chancellor Livingston! It makes one realize how much smaller the world was then! And add to this the fact that Calcott devised some of the phrases that we still use today. Despite so many years of neglect, perhaps his name deserves to be remembered after all.

LOYALIST MASONS DURING THE AMERICAN REVOLUTION

[As you read this piece, I ask you to remember that I come from another country, and that my land, and my ancestors, have not always been on cordial terms with the United States of America.]

INTRODUCTION

This is an important week (July 11, 1987), and an important year, in history, and in Masonry. Everyone in the free world is acquainted with the ringing phrases of the Declaration of Independence, adopted 211 years ago last week. "We hold these truths to be self-evident, that all men are created equal, that they are endowed by their Creator with certain unalienable Rights, that among these are Life, Liberty, and the Pursuit of Happiness." And some of us know that, of the fifty-six who signed that Declaration, nine were Freemasons.

All those who value responsible government must be aware as well that just 200 years ago, in Philadelphia, the duly accredited delegates from the separate states met together for four months, hammering out a Constitution for their country, "in Order to form a more perfect Union, establish Justice, ensure domestic Tranquility, provide for the common Defence, promote the general Welfare, and secure the blessings of Liberty. . . ."

Thirty-nine delegates signed the document, and thirteen of them, exactly one-third, were Masons. They included Bro. Gunning Bedford Jr, the First Grand Master of Masons in Delaware; his country home, Lombardy Hall, located just outside Wilmington, is once more in Masonic hands, and is being restored. Others who signed were Bro. David Brearley, the first Grand Master of New Jersey; Bro. John Blair, Grand Master of Virginia; Bro. Benjamin Franklin, Provincial Grand Master for Pennsylvania; and of course Bro. George Washington, Charter Master of Alexandria Lodge in Virginia. Truly a record to be proud of! And in this connection, I must pause for a moment to pay tribute to the memory of the student who documented all these facts, the late Bro. Ronald E. Heaton of Pennsylvania; he died just three months ago (31 March 1987), at the age of eighty-eight.

CANADA AND THE U.S.A.

I am however conscious of the fact that I'm an alien, a foreigner here. The relationship between Canada and the United States is a strange one. You

149

don't think about us very much; but we have to be aware of you all the time. Our population is tiny—only about one-tenth of yours—and nearly all of us are right along the border, where we are constantly exposed to intensive cultural brain-washing from your television stations. It's like being in bed with an elephant, a never-ending struggle to keep our share of the blankets, to preserve our cultural identity, and some measure of our political and economic integrity.

Recently a Canadian author, writing in an American magazine, put it rather well. She said, in part:

> The noses of a great many Canadians resemble Porky Pig's. This comes from spending so much time pressing them against the longest undefended one-way mirror in the world. The Canadians looking through this mirror behave the way people on the hidden side of such mirrors usually do: they observe, analyze, ponder, snoop and wonder what all the activity on the other side means in decipherable human terms. The Americans, bless their innocent little hearts, are rarely aware that they are even being watched, much less by the Canadians. . . . If they think about Canada at all, it's only when things get a bit snowy or the water goes off or the Canadians start fussing over some piddly detail, such as fish. Then they regard them as unpatriotic; for Americans don't really see Canadians as foreigners, not unless they do something weird like speak French or beat the New York Yankees at baseball. Really, think the Americans, the Canadians are just like us, or would be if they could (Margaret Atwood, quoted in the (Toronto) *Globe and Mail,* 5 April 1986).

Patriotism is a splendid virtue, justly admired by Freemasons. To love your country and to be proud of its origins is a fine thing. Now, as they say, I don't want to break anyone's rice bowl, but it often seems to me that Americans are patriotic to such an extent that it interferes with their sense of realism. As Stephen Decatur said, "My country right or wrong, but my country." I live in a small country which (it goes without saying) could not continue to exist without the benign acquiescence of our powerful neighbor. We speak proudly of "the longest undefended frontier in the world." The situation in Hungary, Czechoslovakia, and Afghanistan serves to remind us that not all small countries are so blessed in their neighbors. But that doesn't mean that all Canadians are therefore obliged to think only American thoughts, to worship at American shrines, and to admire only American heroes.

THE AMERICAN REVOLUTION

Over the past ten years your country has celebrated the bicentenary of the American Revolution, with a tremendous outpouring of patriotism. Freemasons, as is only proper, have joined in this celebration; and the Masonic press has published all sorts of things about the role of the Craft in those great days. It has doubtless been a wonderful experience for those three million Masons who happen to be American citizens. For the rest of us, all this literature has been not quite so fascinating. It is proper to remind ourselves that there may be more than one way of looking at things.

The "enemy" during the Revolution did not consist entirely of red-coated British regulars or mitred Hessian mercenaries. There were Americans, native-born Americans, on the losing side, and some of them fought for their cause in militia regiments composed entirely of colonials. In general they get pretty short shrift in your history books. I mean, have you ever read anything nice about Benedict Arnold, or Walter Butler? If they're mentioned at all, it's only as traitors and bloodthirsty villains.

Over the last year or so, in an effort to redress the balance, I've been writing a series on these people for *The Philalethes* magazine. In general it has been well-received; but one American brother got upset, and published a two-page attack on me, calling me a yo-yo, a knee-jerk liberal, and a low-grade mentality, and accused me of rewriting history. So if I seem a little nervous at being with you today, this may be the reason.

Now, let me return to the Loyalists in the Revolution. These Loyalist Masons were not all scoundrels or villains, but they did look at things in a different light. Some of their attitudes are not extinct even today.

In 1775 the Continental Congress sent an army of liberation into Quebec in order to make it into "the fourteenth colony." At least, that is the American view. A recent Canadian newspaper sees it otherwise: America, the protector of peace? "One of the first acts of the fledgling United States in 1775 was to invade another country. . . . Hardly a [peaceful] beginning."

According to a new book the ringing proclamation that "all men are created equal, that they are endowed by their Creator with certain unalienable rights. . . ." applied only to "white, male, adult, Protestant heads of property-owning families." In a review of this same book the man whom you call "the Father of his country" is cited as "a Virginia slave-owning traitor." These quotations are not intended to be offensive, but should serve to remind you that some of our patriotic posturings are based not on the simple facts, but on a subjective interpretation of historical events.

In Canada we have a different history, and the facts we learn in school don't always coincide with yours. For example, you may know that the first white men to cross America and reach the Pacific north of Mexico were two Freemasons, Meriwether Lewis and William Clark, in 1805. Actually twelve years earlier, in 1793, Alexander Mackenzie had got to the Western Sea by travelling through Canada.

Again, every American schoolchild knows how the Emancipation Proclamation of January 1, 1863, abolished slavery. He may not realize that the hated British tyrants had already freed the slaves thirty years earlier (7 August 1833), and the contemptible Loyalist refugees in Canada had done the same thing forty years before that (9 July 1793).

War at the best of times is hideous, even when waged in a distant land against people who speak another language or look different. How much worse when it pits neighbor against neighbor, brother against brother, friend against friend! The American Revolution, do not forget, was a civil war. Those who wanted to remain loyal to the authority of the crown "were regarded as traitors and were treated as such. In many of the colonies their property was confiscated, they were fined and heavily taxed, large numbers of them were imprisoned, others were banished, and several were put to death. A favorite method of dealing with them consisted in 'tarring and feathering. . . .' " It seems like a harsh way for people who pay lip service to the rights of the individual to deal with those who happen to hold political views that differ from theirs.

After the war some 50,000 of the "Loyalists" came north to Canada, where they could remain under the British flag. In due course they founded the provinces of New Brunswick and Ontario. Their number, like the ranks of the rebels, included some Freemasons.

A civil war poses ethical problems for all concerned. For Masons, one in particular is raised by the second of "The Charges of a Free-Mason," which has appeared in virtually every book of Masonic *Constitutions* printed since 1723. "A Mason is a peaceable Subject to the Civil Powers, wherever he resides or works, and is never to be concern'd in Plots or Conspiracies against the Peace and Welfare of the Nation, nor to behave himself undutifully. . . . If a Brother should be a Rebel against the State, he is not to be countenanc'd in his Rebellion, however he may be pitied as an unhappy man. . . ."

One wonders what Bro. George Washington was thinking as he violated this charge, or Bro. Benjamin Franklin, or Bro. Joseph Warren, or (before he saw the error of his ways) Bro. Benedict Arnold. The Loyalist brethren, whatever other worries they may have had, at least had clear consciences in this regard. Perhaps it is fitting for us to look at a few of them from time to time.

REV. JOHN BEARDSLEY.

Let me give an example or two. Let me cite a family named Vanderburgh, a Dutch family that had settled in New Amsterdam in 1653. About sixty years later they moved up the Hudson to Poughkeepsie. In 1776 there were two brothers. James (1729–1794) was 47 at the outbreak. A good man, he was Colonel of the 5th Regiment Dutchess County militia; and he served as a

Deputy to the Third Provincial Congress in 1776. George Washington's diary mentions that he stayed at Colonel Vanderburgh's home twice in 1781. His gravestone carries the square and compasses. Here was a Mason who did his bit for the cause of justice.

His older Brother Henry (1717–1792) was known as Judge Vanderburgh. He was a Justice of the Inferior Court and a Warden of Christ Church, Poughkeepsie. The minister of his church, the Rev. John Beardsley, was a native of Connecticut, educated at Yale and Columbia. The minutes of the Masonic lodge at Poughkeepsie record that he preached the St John's Day Sermon in 1771, 1772, and 1774, and on one occasion the brethren formally passed a vote of thanks and presented him with a large folio Bible.

Rev. Mr Beardsley was opposed to the Revolution, and received "repeated insults" from those who supported it. His church services were suspended from 13 July 1776. When he persisted in his refusal to take the Oath of Allegiance to the State, he was confined to his farm, being permitted only "to go and Visit the sick & Baptize Infants where requested."

In his troubles, Beardsley was associated with Judge Henry Vanderburgh, whom we mentioned a minute ago. Early in December 1777 the Commission for Detecting and Defeating Conspiracies in New York reported that the more radical revolutionaries might actually inflict physical harm on Mr Beardsley and Mr Vanderburgh, and they therefore requested permission to send them through the lines to New York, which was in British hands.

Finally on 13 December the Governor of New York granted permission for the Reverend John Beardsley and his family, and Mr Henry Vanderburgh and his family, "with their Wearing Apparel & necessary Bedding for the Familly & Provission for their Passage," to go down the Hudson to the city in a sloop-of-war under a flag of truce.

In June 1778 in New York Beardsley became Chaplain of the newly organized Loyal American Regiment. Soon afterwards he was initiated into a Masonic lodge in New York. In 1781, when a new Provincial Grand Lodge was formed, Bro. Beardsley was unanimously chosen Junior Grand Warden, an office which he filled until the Loyalists left the city in 1783. Before the departure, he and seventeen other clergymen met together and signed a "Plan of Religious and Literary Institution for the Province of Nova Scotia." This eventually led to the foundation of the University of King's College, Halifax.

Together with many other Loyalists Rev. John Beardsley (aged 51) and Judge Henry Vanderburgh (aged 66) gave up everything; they lost their homes and property, and went into exile, settling in the unoccupied part of what is now New Brunswick. Beardsley was "the first clergyman of any denomination to minister to the spiritual needs of the exiles." On 9 March 1784 the Masons invited him to become the first Master of the earliest lodge formed under local authority in this part of the province.

He built the first church to be consecrated in the province. He continued active in Masonic affairs until as late as 1803, when he preached a St John's Day Sermon on the text Hebrews 13:1, "Let brotherly love continue." He died in 1809.

Beardsley is regarded as the Founder of Freemasonry in the Province of New Brunswick. In 1916 the Grand Lodge of New Brunswick unveiled a brass memorial tablet to his memory in the church where he is buried, and in 1968 it instituted the Rev. John Beardsley Medallion, awarded every year for outstanding contributions to the Grand Lodge and to the advancement of Freemasonry.

Now, stand back and look at the picture. After the War, Bro. James Vanderburgh, who had the good fortune to be on the winning side, prospered, and lived in his mansion, beloved and respected of all, until his death at an advanced age. His brother Henry Vanderburgh, an old man for those days, and his minister, the Rev. John Beardsley, lost all they had, and were sent to carve new homes for themselves in the wilderness of Canada. Who was right? Colonel James Vanderburgh, or Judge Henry Vanderburgh? Henry was my ancestor six generations back.

JOHN BUTLER.

Not only families were torn apart. So were lodges. St Patrick's Lodge, at Johnstown, the first Masonic body in upstate New York, was chartered in 1763. By the outbreak of hostilities it had enrolled forty-seven members. Nine of them fought in the battle of Oriskany (6 August 1777): three on the rebel side, including the commander, General Nicholas Herkimer, and his adjutant, Major John Frey. Six were on the loyal side, including Major John Frey's blood brother, Major Hendrick Frey. Another was Captain John Butler; and let us look at him a bit more closely.

John Butler was baptized in New London, Connecticut, on 25 April 1728, the son of Lieutenant Walter Butler, who had come out from Ireland as a soldier in 1711. About 1733 Walter Butler moved to the Mohawk Valley, and his family followed him a few years later. They settled at Butlersbury, not too far from Johnstown. Young John learned enough of the Indian languages to become an interpreter, and served in the French and Indian War as a Lieutenant in the Indian Department. In fact he was present at the capture of Fort Niagara (1759). He was named a Justice of the Peace, and was commissioned a Lieutenant Colonel of militia. He continued to work with the Indians, and they clearly trusted him.

At the very beginning of the Revolution, in 1775, Butler declared for the king, and left his home. He was posted to Niagara and arrived there on 17 November 1775. His wife and younger children were imprisoned as hostages in Albany until an exchange could be arranged. (Actually the man responsible for their care was another member of the lodge, Christopher Yates, Chairman of the Committee of Safety. He must have carried out his duties with compassion and understanding. After the War, Butler's son William came back to Albany to claim Yates's daughter Eve as his bride.) Anyway, during the Revolution, Butler persuaded the Indians to fight actively for the British. In 1777 he raised a regiment of Loyalists called Butler's Rangers, who became well known for their ability as woodsmen and skirmishers. They followed to the letter the Plan of Discipline laid down by Robert Rogers during the French and Indian War: traveling light, walking in single file with scouts on all sides, never camping before dark, and so on. This made them awesomely effective in the woods.

Just one example: in 1782, in the Ohio country, Butler's Rangers ambushed and killed or captured three-quarters of a force of Kentuckians sent after them under Colonel Daniel Boone, who was himself no slouch as a frontiersman.

Butler stayed in Niagara after the war, and was given the responsibility of finding suitable settlers from among the Loyalist refugees. He founded a village there which is now called Niagara-on-the-Lake; parts of it have been maintained as of old or restored to their former condition. In some ways it evokes, on a smaller scale, the spirit of Williamsburg, and is worth a visit. He was a Judge in the District Court, Deputy Superintendent of Indian Affairs, and a colonel of militia. In 1785 he submitted to the government a full account of his services during the revolution. His commanding officer gave him a testimonial asserting that "the decided part which the Six . . . Indian Nations took in favor of the King's Government was in a great measures effected by the laborious and unremitting Exertions of His Influence with that People." He died 13 May 1796.

He became a member of Union Lodge, No 1, Albany, apparently on 10 April 1766. Then in the Charter of St Patrick's Lodge, in 1766, he is named as the Charter Secretary. After the Revolution, when there came a time of relative ease, he petitioned for a lodge to be formed at Niagara—the second in the settlement—and a Provincial Warrant was duly issued from Quebec in 1787 to St John's Lodge, Niagara; the Charter Master was John Butler.

Its descendant is still working today, as Niagara Lodge, No 2, G.R.C. The first lodge room erected in Ontario for Masonic purposes was Freemasons' Hall at Niagara, built by the Land Board in 1791. Until the local church was completed, the Masonic hall was used for divine services; it was also the meeting place for the first elected representative government of the colony in September 1792. When the Provincial Grand Lodge became active, in August of that year, Butler was installed as Provincial Senior Grand Warden.

Woodsman, loyal officer of the king for over thirty years, a trusted friend of the Indian people, a skilful warrior and administrator, who obviously found scope for his talents in Freemasonry—John Butler. Not a bad man to remember. Now let us look at another one.

JOSEPH BRANT.

Brant was an Indian, the first Indian to become a Mason. During the American Revolution the Indians, particularly the Iroquois, had a bad press. There were two reasons: they were not white, and they had the misfortune, for the most part, to be on the losing side. One of them was called by the poet Thomas Campbell "the Mammoth, the foe, the Monster Brandt, with all his howling desolating band."

Thayendanegea, a Mohawk, known also as Joseph, was born near what is now Akron, Ohio, in 1742. When he was about ten his widowed mother brought him back to her old home in the Mohawk Valley of upstate New York. She married a new husband, whose name was Barnet or Brant, and the child came to be called Brant's Joseph, or eventually Joseph Brant.

As a mere boy he served with the British Forces in the French and Indian War. His abilities impressed Bro. Sir William Johnson, who in 1761 arranged to have him sent to Moor's Indian Charity School, in Lebanon, Connecticut. (This was no run-of-the-mill elementary school, but was intended to train missionaries; nine years later it moved to Hanover, N.H., and received a charter as Dartmouth College.)

Joseph became fluent in English, and is said also to have learned Latin and Greek. He helped to translate Mark's Gospel into Mohawk. When hostilities broke out in 1775, he went to England as part of a delegation to ascertain, and perhaps influence, official policy on Indian affairs. He returned home convinced that the fortunes of his people were bound up with loyalty to the king.

He persuaded many of the Iroquois to support the British forces, and himself led a contingent throughout the contest. This is not the place to retrace his campaigns, but it is worth noting that he played a significant role in the victories at Oriskany in 1777, and Cherry Valley in 1778. The latter is enshrined in American history-books as the Cherry Valley "Massacre." But an American historian has pointed out that any decisive Indian victory is generally labeled a "massacre;" in this one thirty-one non-combatants were killed.

We of course know, with the wisdom of hindsight, what **real** massacres are—Gnadenhuetten (1782, 96 Delawares), Sand Creek (1864, 133 Cheyennes), Wounded Knee (1890, 300 Sioux), Mount Dajo (1906, 600 Moros), My Lai (1968, 200 Vietnamese)—and Cherry Valley hardly qualifies. To be sure, civilians were killed, but apparently the Senecas were responsible. In the words of an American historian, "Brant and his followers tried desperately, and with some success, to save numbers of white non-combatants."

Civil war is a bloody business, and the atrocities in this one were not all on one side. In 1776 New Hampshire offered a bounty on Indian scalps. In October of 1778 the rebels wiped out the Mohawk settlements at Unadilla. "The finest Indian town I ever saw," wrote the commander; "about 40 good houses, Square logs, Shingles & stone Chimneys, good Floors, glass windows, &c."—leveled to the ground. Such savagery was official policy at the highest level.

On 31 May 1779 Bro. George Washington wrote to Bro. John Sullivan (later to become the first Grand Master of Masons in New Hampshire), "This expedition you are appointed to command is to be directed against the hostile tribes of the Six Nations of Indians with their associates and adherents. The immediate objects are the total destruction and devastation of their settlements and the capture of as many prisoners of every sex and age as possible. It will be essential to ruin their crops in the ground and prevent their planting more. Parties should be detached to lay waste all the settlements around, with instructions to do it in the most effectual manner, that the country not be merely over-run, but destroyed." **That** is why the Iroquois named Washington "Town Destroyer."

After the War Brant led his people to what is now Ontario, Canada, where a great tract of land along the Grand River, amounting to 600,000 acres, was given to them, "which them & their Posterity are to enjoy for ever." They brought with them a silver communion service that had been presented to their ancestors in 1712 by Queen Anne, and had been buried for safekeeping during the war. In the new land they built a village near what is now the city of Brantford. In 1785 they erected a Church there, called Her Majesty's Chapel of the Mohawks—the first Protestant Church in the Canadas, the oldest surviving place of worship in Ontario, and the only Royal Chapel outside Britain. It has recently been restored, and is worth a visit the next time you are in the vicinity.

Brant spent much of the rest of his life trying to mobilize a confederacy of Indians to resist the American push westward, but his efforts were frustrated. He died at Burlington, Upper Canada, 24 November 1807.

During his first visit to England Brant was initiated into Masonry in Lodge No 417, which met at the Falcon, in Princes Street, Leicester Field, London. His certificate is dated 26 April 1776. He brought it home to America with him and kept it carefully, as if he intended to be a keen Mason.

During the rebellion and its immediate aftermath, there cannot have been much opportunity for fraternal sociability on the frontier, though there are several apocryphal stories of Masonic prisoners being spared by Brant when they gave a Masonic sign. More than a decade after the war, in July of 1795, the first Provincial Grand Lodge of Upper Canada was organized, and Brant was able to become more active.

On 31 January 1796 he attended the organizational meeting of the Barton Lodge, at the western end of Lake Ontario (it is still working, as No 6 on the Grand Register of Canada). About this time or earlier, others of his people must have joined the Craft, for in 1797 a lodge is reported in the Mohawk Village; it received Provincial Warrant No 11 in 1798, with Joseph Brant as the first Master. The lodge ceased to work within a few years, but records show that Brant's affection for Masonry continued unimpaired.

Brant is now recognized as "a noble figure who devoted his whole life to the advancement of his people." His initiation into the Craft was a milestone in Masonry Universal, and he clearly found something congenial in this society that advocated the brotherhood of man.

SIR JOHN JOHNSON.

Sir John Johnson was born in 1742, at Johnstown, New York, the son of Sir William Johnson, who came out from Ireland in 1737 and became master of a vast estate in the Mohawk Valley. At the age of thirteen, in 1755, John served as a volunteer under his father's command at the Battle of Lake George, when the French Army under Baron Dieskau was defeated and its General taken prisoner. (For this service his father was created a Baronet, and received the sum of £5000 Sterling). After the French and Indian War, young John proceeded to England to polish his manners and enlarge his circle of acquaintance. In 1765 he was himself knighted. On his father's death in 1774 he became the 2nd Baronet Johnson of New York.

When the Revolution began he was unalterably loyal to the king. He escaped from his home with about 700 followers, and in 1776 succeeded in reaching Montreal. There he was granted a commission to raise a regiment from among his Tory friends, to be called the King's Royal Regiment of New York. Known as the Royal Yorkers, or the Royal Greens, it served throughout the war, particularly in upstate New York.

(Let me pause here to tip my hat, because three of my wife's ancestors served in the First Battalion, Sergeant Jesse Wright, Private Evan Roys, and Drummer Alexander Rose.)

After the war Sir John settled in Montreal; the government awarded him £45,000 Sterling in compensation for his losses. He was named Superintendent of Indian Affaira for British North America, and kept the office as long as he lived. The Iroquois called him "He who Made the House to Tremble," and said that he was a good father to the red children. He died 4 January 1830, in his 88th year.

About 1767, while he was in England, he was initiated into Masonry in Royal Lodge, No 313, which met at The Thatched House, St James' Street, London. The same year he was named Provincial Grand Master of New York by the Grand Master; he soon returned to America, and probably affiliated with the lodge that his father had founded a year earlier. He was not particularly active as Provincial Grand Master, but he or his deputy warranted three lodges between 1774 and 1776.

After the War, in 1788, he was named Provincial Grand Master for Canada. In 1790 and 1791 he warranted three lodges, one of them being Dorchester Lodge, at Vergennes, Vermont, which is still working.

There was of course another Masonic Grand Lodge, the Ancients, violently opposed to the Grand Lodge represented by Johnson. In 1792 the Ancients named His Royal Highness, Prince Edward, Queen Victoria's father, as Provincial Grand Master for Lower Canada. The Prince's supporters were militant, and adopted some unbrotherly proceedings against their rivals. On one occasion a member of a Moderns lodge in Montreal presented himself as a visitor to an Ancients lodge in the City of Quebec. Not only was the visitor rejected, but his certificate was burnt in open lodge. When Sir John heard of this, he declared "that he would not continue to exercise any Masonic function which could possibly bring him into collision with the son of his Sovereign." In consequence, he never again convened his Provincial Grand Lodge, and his patent in fact became dormant. Most of his lodges died out, or went over to the Ancients.

Many years later, after the two rival Grand Lodges amalgamated, Sir John did lay the foundation stone for the Montreal General Hospital, with Masonic ceremony, in 1821. At his death in 1830 he was buried with military and Masonic honors. According to the report in the *Montreal Gazette*:

> The procession was led by the 24th Regiment, attended by their fine band, playing tunes most suited to the solemn occasion; then followed the hearse drawn by four black horses, in which rested the coffin, covered with the Military insignia of the departed Brigadier General. The relatives, and the numerous friends of the deceased, were next in the order of procession—the remainder of which consisted of the Provincial Grand Lodge for this District and the Officers of the Private Lodges of the city, over which Sir John Johnson had long presided as Provincial Grand Master, till his bodily infirmities required his retirement from his honorable station in the craft. After the Freemasons, followed a body of Indians, about 300 in number, with about 100 females, from the Missions of Caughnawaga, St Regis, and the Lake of Two Mountains. The procession proceeded to the Episcopal Church of this city, where the funeral service was read.

Sir John Johnson's Regiment played a major role in the revolution; and its members were important in the settlement of Ontario, some seven townships being reserved for them. Sir John himself was "regarded as the most outstanding of the United Empire Loyalists in Canada," and he was certainly the most distinguished Mason to come north after the Revolution.

JOHN WALDEN MEYERS.

In the first part of the eighteenth century a number of German immigrants settled in the colony of New York, near the junction of the Mohawk and Hudson Rivers. Among them was a man named Waeldermeier, who came from the Kingdom of Prussia to find a new home in Albany County. There in 1745 his son Johannes was born, and baptized in the local German Reformed Church. As time passed, Johannes (or Hans) Waltermyer, grew up, married a neighbor's daughter, and began to raise a family. At the outbreak of the American Revolution, he was a farmer, with a perpetual lease of 200 acres a few miles south of Albany. He had cleared 100 acres, built a house and a barn, and planted an orchard.

When the troubles came, at first he took no part. In 1777 Hans left his farm and moved north to join the British under General John Burgoyne. He was attached to Jessup's Corps, and at once returned behind enemy lines to enlist more Loyalist recruits. Waltermyer continued in British service, but without ever meeting the enemy in the open field. He served as a courier and collector of intelligence, repeatedly traveling up and down the Hudson River from New York to the St Lawrence valley. He held the rank of Captain. In due course he took the name of John Walden Meyers instead of Hans Waltermyer.

Not long after he left home his farm was declared forfeit, and his livestock and possessions were seized by the rebels. He tells us that he lost seven horses, four cows, five young cattle, thirty hogs, utensils, furniture, and 140 bushels of wheat. In October 1778 the Board of Commissioners for Detecting and Defeating Conspiracies gave his wife and children leave to pass through the lines to New York City, where they spent the rest of the War, while he continued on special assignment.

The fact that he was able to move almost at will through hostile territory without getting caught suggests, in the first place, that there were enough Loyalist sympathizers to help him along the way, and, in the second place, that he was a pretty fair woodsman himself. Meyers was the ringleader in two spectacular escapades. In 1781 with a few followers he carried out the raid on the tiny hamlet of Ballstown, six miles north of Schenectady. They managed to capture the four rebel officers there and carry them behind British lines.

Two months later he tried to kidnap General Philip Schuyler from his palatial mansion, "The Pastures," just outside Albany. But the intended victim was tipped off. In the words of an American historian, "The party entered the dwelling, commenced packing up the plate, and a search for the General. But that gentleman opened a window, and, as if speaking to an armed force of his own, called out,—'Come on, my brave fellows; surround the house, and secure the villains who are plundering.' This happy strategem caused Waltermyer and his followers to betake themselves to flight."

During one trip past his old home near Albany John Walden Meyers dropped in on an old friend. Somehow the rebel militia got wind of it, and rode up the house. He saw them coming, sprang out the back window, and raced for the nearby woods. The enemy caught sight of him, and several of them set out in pursuit. Tying up their steeds at the edge of the forest, they continued on foot. He doubled back, picked out the best horse, and galloped off.

Mothers around Albany used to tell their children that Hans Waltermyer would eat them if they didn't behave. He did not deserve this unsavory reputation, and even the American historian says that Meyers "was noted for enterprise and daring, but not for cruelty or ferocity." If he had been on the other side, he would have been immortalized in song and story, on radio and television, as a hero, a sort of Scarlet Pimpernel. As it is, if he is remembered at all, it is in a more sinister light. Perhaps nothing else could be expected; as a great man once said, "History is the propaganda of the victors."

After the war he was reunited with his wife and children. They settled south of Montreal; then, briefly, in the vicinity of Kingston, further west. Finally in 1786 he moved to the frontier of habitation, and within a few years he had built a mill near the mouth of a river, where he knew that colonists would soon arrive. The settlement took the name of Meyers Creek, and here in 1796 Meyers built the first brick house in Ontario. His mill prospered, his farm-land blossomed, and he died, well-to-do and full of years, in 1821.

Meyers became a Mason in Quebec city, in St Andrew's Lodge, No 2 on the Provincial Register, No 221 on the English Register. His certificate is dated 28 February 1780. (His biographer suggests that the Masonic belief in the brotherhood of man moved him so deeply that he determined to free his slaves as soon as the family was together again. It's a nice thought, but personally I doubt whether Masonry ever persuaded a man to do something that he wouldn't have done anyway; certainly the ideals of the Craft never prompted other slave-holding Masons, Bro. George Washington for example, to take any such heroic steps.)

The next year, in 1781, the Provincial Grand Lodge of Quebec issued a warrant to a group of officers in the King's Rangers to meet as St James's Lodge, No 24, at what is now Kingston. The first Senior Warden was Captain John Walden Meyers. He soon moved on. Within a few years a Provincial Grand Lodge was formed in Upper Canada; and under its authority in 1801 Lodge No 17 was formed in Meyers Creek. The first Master, naturally, was the patriarch of the settlement, John Walden Meyers. The lodge is still working today.

A picturesque figure, this frontier farmer-turned-spy; a soldier who was more effective on his own, perhaps, than he would have been in the serried ranks of a regiment; a man who displayed the endurance and resourcefulness, so typical of the American colonist, in fighting for a lost cause, and then in hacking out a home in the wilderness; a brother who found something to admire in the gentle Craft; in short, a forgotten hero who has a just claim on our attention as a pioneer settler, and a pioneer Freemason, in the Province of Ontario.

That will perhaps be sufficient. I hope that I have succeeded in doing two things—in making you look perhaps a bit more critically at your own history, and in persuading you that some of these early Masons on the losing side are worth a bit of our attention.

SIMON McGILLIVRAY (ca 1785–1840): FUR TRADER AND FREEMASON

[During the year 1982–83 I served as Master of the Premier Lodge of Research, Quatuor Coronati, No 2076, London. After being placed in the Chair of King Solomon, I delivered my inaugural address, which ran like this.]

INTRODUCTION: THE NORTH WEST COMPANY

The topic for this year's Inaugural Address is appropriate for a speaker who comes from Canada. It concerns a man who was born two hundred years ago. Not quite a century ago, Bro. John Ross Robertson—a name known to some of you in other connections—was in Britain, collecting material for his gigantic *History of Freemasonry in Canada*. In the course of his researches, he met the daughter of this man, and cross-examined her about her father.

Later, she wrote to her son about John Ross Robertson in these terms: "He is entirely different from my previous idea—a big man with that awful accent which Lizzie says all Scotch Canadians have. . . ."

The British people are so tactful when they speak to us face-to-face, that we tend to forget just how colonials sound to them. So it is well to have it on record. Your speaker today will address you for a few minutes in his own dialect, "that awful accent, which . . . all Scotch Canadians have."

The Dominion of Canada is a land of spectacular beauty, where pines and maples grow, great prairies spread, and lordly rivers flow. It is filled with breath-taking natural wonders: the tidal bore of the Petitcodiac River; the Percé Rock at the tip of the Gaspé Peninsula; the thundering Horseshoe Falls of Niagara, which every minute carry thirty-four million gallons of water over a cliff 176 feet high; the Ouimet Canyon, so deep and dark and airless that Arctic plants grow on the floor; Mount Assiniboine, "the Matterhorn of the Rockies;" the emerald waters of Lake Louise; the vast Columbia icefields; the Hell's Gate narrows in the Fraser Gorge; the list is endless.

It is also a harsh land. In the southernmost part of it, the thermometer often hits a humid 100 degrees on the Fahrenheit scale (that's 38 degrees Centigrade) for several days on end. In winter it sometimes stays at 0 degrees Fahrenheit (minus 18 degrees Centigrade) for as much as a week at a time. This is the land that Voltaire dismissed as "quelques arpents de neige" ("a few acres of snow").

In the early days no European ever settled there by choice. They went first in search of the spice-route to the Orient. They thought they had found it, and so they called the people they met, "Indians," and one part of the country they reached, "Lachine," or "China." But they were mistaken. Then one explorer reported the cod and herring so thick on the Grand Banks of the New Found Land that they sometimes stayed his ships. So they came for the fish. Then someone else found the foxes and the muskrats and the martens and the beaver. There were fortunes to be made in furs and they came for the furs.

We easily forget how immense the land is. It stretches one-fifth of the way around the world. A thousand miles up the St Lawrence from the Atlantic lies Montreal. From there west to the Pacific is another three thousand miles—roughly the distance from London to Jerusalem. Most of this vast tract was explored by the fur-traders in their canoes, and in the years around 1800 the most active of them belonged to the North West Company of Montreal. Alexander Mackenzie of "the concern" (as it was known) went down the river that bears his name to the Frozen or Polar Sea in 1789. Four years later he crossed the Rocky Mountains and found the Western Ocean—more than a decade before Lewis and Clark, who are sometimes alleged to have been "the first explorers to reach the Pacific by crossing the continent north of Mexico." In 1808 Simon Fraser of the concern fought his way down the tumultuous Fraser River to the Sea. In the years 1807–1811 David Thompson of the concern, "the greatest land geographer who ever lived," surveyed the entire Columbia River system, and in 1813 and 1814 he drew, for the concern, the first map of the great Canadian northwest.

LIFE OF SIMON McGILLIVRAY

Our interest today is with Simon McGillivray, another member of the concern. He was born about 1785, in the Scottish Highlands not too far from Loch Ness, the youngest son of a poor cousin of the Chief of Clan MacGillivray. His mother was a sister of Simon McTavish, known as "The Marquis," the fabulously rich chief Director of the North West Company. At the age of twenty young Simon joined the concern, as a partner in the London house that ran the English end of the business. His affairs prospered, and he became quite well-to-do, and cut a respectable swath in London society. His residences, at No 2, Suffolk Lane, and then at No 7, Lancaster Place, were filled with oil paintings and *objets d'art*.

Then in 1813 he became a partner in the Montreal house that practically controlled the North West Company, and for most of the next decade he would spend his summers in the New World. He tells us that during the years from 1815 to 1818 he travelled in Canada a total of 4400 miles—by canoe.

Now, to speak personally for a minute, I like canoes, and have paddled a bit. This past summer my wife and I went with our two younger sons into the interior of Algonquin Park. We took it very slowly, as befits our advanced years. We carried all our provisions, and spent a week in the wilderness paddling and portaging, swimming and tenting. We saw hardly another human for the whole time, but lots of beaver and chipmunks and loons, a few moose, and one dead bear. It was a wonderful trip; we calculated that the four of us, in our two canoes, paddled about thirty miles in all. Simon, remember, covered 4400 miles.

Of course the canoes were different. **Ours** was made of fibreglass; it was sixteen feet long and weighed about fifty pounds, had a crew of two, and carried a pay-load of maybe 200 pounds. Simon didn't have to paddle. **He** traveled as a privileged passenger, in a trading canoe, the *canot de maître*, made of cedar strip and birch bark; it was 35 feet long, weighed 600 pounds, had a crew of ten, and carried a pay-load of three tons. Not a bad way to see the country!

Every year the North West Company held a rendezvous at its wilderness capital, Fort William—named after Simon's brother William McGillivray, the director of the concern. The "wintering partners," who lived in the distant trapping country of Athabaska, would bring their harvest of furs east, and the "agents," the business partners from Montreal, would bring their supplies and trade-goods west. They would converge at the Fort, close to the midpoint between them. The two groups would hold a meeting to decide company affairs; then they exchanged their cargoes, and made their way back to their respective homes. We know that Simon attended the rendezvous at Fort William on several occasions, and in 1815 he conducted the meeting.

Perhaps it is appropriate to mention that during the years 1971 to 1976 the Government of Ontario restored Old Fort William as it was in 1816, and it is now a public heritage park. We were privileged to go there this past summer, and it was (in the vivid jargon of the young) mind-blowing. You can arrive by boat, and are welcomed at the wharf by a North West Company piper. All the guides are in period costume and are in fact playing the rôles of particular people. There's a palisade around the site, enclosing some thirty-five buildings, and ten more stand outside the fortifications. You go into the Great Hall, and there at one end is a painted portrait of the Chief Director, William McGillivray. Not too far away is an oil painting of his brother Simon McGillivray, wearing his Masonic regalia. You could easily spend half a day in the Fort, and I seriously recommend it to you. It's located in the City of Thunder Bay, which is in my own Province of Ontario, so it's quite close to Toronto. I think my road map said it was only 900 miles away.

But we must return to the past. There were troubles in the fur-trade. The details do not concern us, but the outcome was important for our hero's life.

In 1821 Simon negotiated an amalgamation between the North West Company and its rival, the Hudson's Bay Company. It looks as if he was out-manoeuvred in the bargaining. Within a few years he was shut out from the management, and the profits, of the new house. By this time, his Montreal firm, which was supposed to wind up the affairs of the old North West Company, had three partners. In 1825 one of them went mad, another (his brother William) died, and Simon was left in sole charge. When he came to inspect the books, he found that the company had insufficient assets to meet its debts. He declared it insolvent; and in order to discharge his responsibilities as he saw them, he assigned to trustees the whole of his own estate (valued at upwards of £100,000) as well as the whole of his brother's estate. By this stroke of a pen he was transformed from a wealthy merchant to an unemployed executive of very moderate means.

He passed through a difficult ten years, hiring himself out as a salaried administrator, first to the Canada Land Company, and then to the United Mexican Mining Association. He spent five years in Mexico, and I could tell you many interesting things that happened there, but it would not be to our immediate purpose. Finally in 1834 he returned home to London, was welcomed as a partner in a stock-brokerage house, purchased a part interest in a major London newspaper, and reestablished himself. It was too late; he had strained his health in Mexico, and on 9 June 1840 he died in London at the age of 55.

HIS MASONIC CAREER

Our main concern here however is with Simon's Masonic career, so now let us turn to that. He was initiated on 23 April 1807 (St George's Day) in Shakespear Lodge, No 131, London. He was only twenty-two years of age, and it would be interesting to know who sponsored him into Masonry. The information no doubt still exists in the records of Shakespear Lodge, No 99. Unfortunately the Secretary seems to be too concerned about the present to answer letters about the past. At all events, Simon was Master of his lodge on three occasions. He also belonged to several other lodges, including some quite prestigious ones. In 1813 he joined the Lodge of Antiquity, No 2, of which the Grand Master, H.R.H. the Duke of Sussex, was permanent Master. In 1814 he was the moving spirit behind the formation of the Royal Inverness Lodge, No 648, the first lodge to be warranted after the Union. It was formed by the Officers of the Loyal North Briton Volunteer Corps, of which the Duke of Sussex was Commanding Officer, and in which McGillivray was a Captain. The Duke installed McGillivray as Master in 1816. He also belonged to the Duke's personal lodge, Alpha, No 43. The recurrent connection with the Duke is striking.

In Grand Lodge, McGillivray filled various senior posts, and was named Provincial Grand Master for Upper Canada in 1822, when he was on the point of making a business trip to the colony.

PROVINCIAL GRAND MASTER OF UPPER CANADA

He reached Canada in July 1822. He was an able man, and an experienced Mason, but a grim set of problems confronted him. His predecessor as Provincial Grand Master, William Jarvis, had been empowered to grant one-year dispensations for the holding of lodges, but not to issue warrants. Not only had he, in defiance of the terms of his patent, granted warrants, but he neglected to enter his lodges on the register of Grand Lodge. After Jarvis had ceased to act, a group of brethren in the Niagara region behaved as if his patent were transferable, elected their own officers, and continued to issue warrants to new lodges. After Jarvis's death, the Grand Masonic Convention met in Kingston, proceeded to give its own dispensations to new lodges, and even selected its own nominee for the office of Provincial Grand Master. As all these actions were irregular from the point of view of strict Masonic jurisprudence, hardly one of the English lodges in the province was working under proper authority. Both the Convention and the Niagara Grand Lodge moreover were convinced that the other group in the province was irregular and was likely to prove intractable.

A firm hand was needed, but in a velvet glove. McGillivray had the necessary qualities. Within four months, he had brought order out of chaos, and restored brotherly love across the province. Before his arrival in Canada he had been briefed on the difficulties ahead of him. On 13 August, he left Montreal for the Upper Province. *En route* he stopped at Brockville, to talk with the chief members of the Convention. Then he went directly to Niagara, and talked with the leading brethren of that district. He found both parties to be, as he put it, "respectable and reasonable Men." He would not talk with either group in its corporate capacity, but insisted on dealing with them as individual Masons. He refused to take sides, since he saw that neither group was without fault.

Early in September he sent notice to the lodges calling a meeting of the Provincial Grand Lodge. Each lodge was instructed to enter a petition for a new dispensation, signed by at least seven members, together with a copy of its previous authority to meet, a full list of its members, a copy of its by-laws, and the fees required for registration in Grand Lodge. If everything was in order, the Provincial Grand Master would issue a new dispensation, "upon receiving which, and not before, the Master, Wardens and Past Masters of such Lodge will be qualified to be admitted and to vote, in the Provincial Grand Lodge."

The representatives of three lodges in Western Ontario banded together, protested the fact that the new Provincial Grand Master had been appointed in England rather than in Canada, complained that it was unjust to be asked for further fees, and said that their lodges did not have enough time to prepare the documents. McGillivray was not to be taken in. He would not meet them as a committee of delegates, but only as private individuals. In his report to the Grand Master he recounted his response. "I requested them to understand," he said, "that they were not to expect concessions, as if I were negotiating with them, or had any point to gain by persuading them. . . . They were at present not within the pale of legitimate Masonry, and . . . I was authorized to receive them into fraternity on very liberal terms. . . . If they neglected or refused to follow these instructions, . . . they would be excluded from communication with the lodges forming the regular establishment." There was no further trouble.

The Provincial Grand Lodge met at York (that is, Toronto) on September 23 1822, with representatives from sixteen lodges. Members of two others which had not yet received dispensations were later admitted as visitors. The Provincial Grand Master refused to let the delegates consider the actions of either the Convention or the Niagara Grand Lodge, or even to let their names appear in the minutes. Confirmation of the proceedings of the one would have implied censure of the other. In his appointments to office he continued to soothe old wounds. As his Deputy he named Colonel James FitzGibbon, an authentic military hero of the War of 1812. He conferred the rank of Past Deputy Provincial Grand Master on the President of the Convention, and on two brethren who had successively headed the Niagara brethren. The Junior Grand Warden, the Grand Chaplain, and the Junior Grand Deacon were from lodges of the Convention. The Senior Grand Warden and the Senior Grand Deacon came from the Niagara region. The Grand Treasurer was H.M.'s Receiver-General for the Province. And to facilitate communications, he named two Grand Secretaries, one from the capital at York, and one from a provincial town 150 miles to the east.

On his return to England he presented a full report to the Grand Master, H.R.H. the Duke of Sussex. He also forwarded petitions for twenty-one lodges. The warrants were duly issued, backdated to 23 September 1822. Grand Lodge conferred on him the rare distinction of moving a vote of thanks, duly engrossed on vellum and presented to him.

This was the only time that McGillivray was able to attend the communication of his Provincial Grand Lodge. It met annually with his Deputy in the chair—first Colonel James FitzGibbon, and then from 1825 John Beikie, the Clerk of the Executive Council of the Province. Most of the proceedings were routine.

The meeting of 1825, with the best of intentions, attempted to introduce some wide-ranging reforms. It proposed to build a residential school for the children of poor and deceased Masons, soliciting funds for this purpose, if need be, from the British public. It also canvassed the possibility of having an itinerant lecturer called the Grand Visitor, who would inculcate uniform working.

R.W.Bro. McGillivray had intended to be there, but he was detained by adverse weather, and arrived two days late. After consultation with the officers, he issued a circular for distribution with the minutes. In it he commented at length on the proceedings, and demonstrated how the two projects were ill-conceived and impracticable. He tempered his criticism with words of praise, and offered some suggestions. He recommended that, for the convenience of the brethren in the eastern part of the province, the delegates should hold a meeting each year in Kingston in addition to the one in York. He confessed to a startling innovation of his own. According to the *Constitutions*, the Provincial Grand Lodge "ceases to exist on the death, resignation, suspension or removal of the Provincial Grand Master." He had petitioned the Grand Master that this rule should be waived for the Canadian brethren, and that they should be empowered to meet under the Deputy Provincial Grand Master, until a successor was appointed.

THE CRISIS OVER THE IRISH LODGE IN CANADA

As well as the twenty-one lodges with English warrants, there was also one Irish Lodge in the Province—Duke of Leinster, No 283, which had been warranted in 1821 as the second Irish civilian lodge abroad. There was a certain amount of friction between it and its English neighbors, but more complications were to follow. In 1823 the British Parliament passed an act "for preventing the administering and taking of unlawful Oaths in Ireland." It was not directed specifically at the Freemasons, but they fell victims to it. All Irish lodges ceased to meet for a year or more, and the lodge in Canada did not know where it stood.

Finally on 22 December 1825 the Irish brethren submitted a petition to McGillivray requesting a warrant. The members of the lodge were clearly of two minds; some were disposed to accept local authority; others preferred to maintain their affiliation with Ireland. A group of brethren haled the Master-elect before the magistrates, and charged him with absconding with the warrant and *Constitutions*. After the evidence was heard, the charges were dismissed, and the documents were returned to the Master. The complainants thereupon threatened to seize them by force, and they were left for safe-keeping in the magistrate's hands.

On 4 February McGillivray issued a dispensation empowering Leinster Lodge to meet under the authority of the United Grand Lodge of England. The problem seemed solved. Soon afterwards he returned to England, and again presented a full report on the whole business. He suggested that the

Grand Master might contact the Grand Master of Ireland in this connection, and the Duke of Sussex duly wrote to the Duke of Leinster on 7 July 1826, pointing out that it would be advantageous, during the current time of troubles, for Irish lodges to place themselves under the immediate protection and guidance of the United Grand Lodge of England. This was "a view hardly likely to commend itself to the Irish Craft generally." The Grand Lodge of Ireland drafted a crisp reply, and issued a new warrant to the Irish Lodge in Kingston, which continued to work until 1850. This episode must count as one of McGillivray's failures.

GRAND SUPERINTENDENT FOR UPPER CANADA

Now in the printed version of the text we go on to talk about Royal Arch Masonry. At the same time that he was named Provincial Grand Master of Upper Canada, Simon McGillivray was appointed Grand Superintendent of the same province. He never convoked his Provincial Grand Chapter, and we attempt to explain why. This involves a full account of early Royal Arch Masonry in Ontario, which has never been properly surveyed before. In brief, the reason is that pioneer Royal Arch Masonry was in the American tradition, asserting control over four degrees, and with the presiding officer being called the High Priest. McGillivray did not succeed in reforming the Royal Arch in Ontario, and so today it still works the American system.

JOHN AULDJO (1805–1886), DEPUTY PROVINCIAL GRAND MASTER

Then we go on to talk about John Auldjo. Towards the end of his life McGillivray appointed a Deputy Provincial Grand Master for Upper Canada. He went out to the New World and sent back an interesting report on Masonry in Ontario in 1837. Auldjo is a fascinating minor figure of history and we've learned a bit more about him than was ever known before. He was born in Montreal, to another Scottish family there that was engaged in the trade. In his youth, after his mother died in childbirth, his father took him back to England. He did a certain amount for Masonry, but we don't have time to discuss it in full.

LORD DURHAM: ALMOST PROVINCIAL GRAND MASTER

Then we talk about the Earl of Durham. He was sent out to Canada as Governor in 1838, and in due course presented what is called Lord Durham's report, which set the pattern for granting responsible representative government to the overseas colonies. Durham was also a notable Mason, and the powers-that-be contemplated giving him extraordinary Masonic authority. The prospect was considered of having McGillivray resign to make room for him, and the archives actually have a draft of a patent of authority to Durham, but it was never issued.

For fuller details on all these subjects, you'll have to consult the full version of this address. For the time being, all I can do is attempt to whet your appetites.

DEATH AND ASSESSMENT OF SIMON McGILLIVRAY

Simon McGillivray died at about eleven o'clock on Tuesday night, 9 June 1840, at his residence, Dartmouth Row, Blackheath, aged fifty-six. I can tell you exactly what he died of, and thereby hangs an interesting story. During his last illness he was attended by a Quaker girl, a practical nurse who was a close friend of his wife. Every day she wrote to her sister, describing the progressive symptoms that Simon was displaying; her account is preserved. Dr Robert J. Burns, a heart specialist in Toronto, rather enjoyed diagnosing a patient that couldn't talk back. He says that Simon died of congestive heart failure, most likely arising from underlined coronary artery disease, with *angina pectoris*, and probably several episodes of myocardial infarction, that is, heart attacks, and complicated by kidney failure and infection (probably pneumonia). It sounds like magic, but there you are.

He was buried in the family vault of his father-in-law Sir John Easthope, in Norwood Cemetery near London. He left one daughter, and another was born after his death. His grandchildren included a Professor of Greek at the University of Oxford.

Now we must attempt to assess McGillivray's significance. Comments made by friend and foe alike reveal Simon as an honorable and attractive man, scrupulous almost to the point of eccentricity, and with an unusually facile pen. The turncoat Colin Robertson, a Nor' Wester engaged by the Hudson's Bay Company against his erstwhile associates, writes: "I like Simon . . .; there is a sort of highland pride and frankness about the little fellow. . . . He has no blarney about him." The sharpest gibe that a representative of the rival company could devise for him was "Simon pure."

A fellow officer in his regiment, the Loyal North Briton Volunteer Corps, recalls that he was "most uncompromising in what he thought right; nothing would make him swerve from the course of that which he considered a duty; his persevering and untiring zeal was the theme of constant praise; get him to any cause and you had him for life." A diplomat who had been on the staff of the British legation in Mexico during McGillivray's time there pronounces him to be "the ablest, most talented and indefatigable man he ever met with." The man who was his director in the Canada Company, the United Mexican

Mining Association, and the *Morning Chronicle* pays tribute to his "high gentlemanly qualities, Stern Sense of honor, sound judgment, and practical common sense, together with the unflinching honesty which [he has] maintained in a season of severe Trial." That prickly controversialist Dr Robert Crucefix characterises him as "in disposition amiable, in character highminded, in honor untainted." The obituary notice in his own newspaper, to be sure, is laudatory, but hardly at variance with the facts:

> Few men so extensively engaged in important business have passed through with a higher reputation, for unsullied integrity and rigid adherence to principles than Mr M'Gillivray. No man ever hesitated to place the most implicit reliance on his honor. His word was sacred. His intentions were always pure, and his conduct open and straightforward. . . . But if he was inflexibly just, he was, at the same time, kind and generous almost to a fault. His confidence once bestowed was not lightly withdrawn, and he was a firm and unshaken friend in the hour of trial.
>
> His natural abilities were strong, and he had carefully cultivated them. . . . His taste in the fine arts was generally admitted. He was a close reasoner, and whatever he wrote was remarkable for a lucid arrangement. Having arrived carefully and methodically at his conclusions, he was with difficulty driven from the opinions he had once embraced. He never pronounced an opinion till he had carefully examined the subject.

We may permit ourselves to enlarge on several of these observations. Mc-Gillivray's correspondence reveals him as a remorseless disputant, who systematically demolished every argument advanced by his antagonists. He had a conciliatory technique that served him well in Canada. When the point that he wished to establish had been fully admitted, he would make a minor concession in order to give the other party some cause for satisfaction. We have examples of his generosity. He paid off the debts of one of his English lodges, amounting to £150; and he advanced the same amount to his Province for initial expenses; he was never repaid. The Niagara brethren were so injudicious as to suggest that the notorious Christopher Danby in his dotage had some claim on the resources of the Provincial Grand Lodge. After he had cut away the ground from beneath their feet, McGillivray concluded his response with the words, "So much, in the public Situation in which I am placed, I have felt it necessary to say. As an individual, I inclose my mite for the relief of a Br. in distress. . . ."

Fashions in history change, and it is now the style to deny the rôle of the hero, and to ascribe all great results to the effects of social and economic factors. Yet it can be argued that Simon McGillivray did leave a permanent legacy.

In the profane world, if he had any effect it came from his negotiations for the union of the two rival fur-trading companies in British North America.

Their hostility was profitless, and harmony in the wilderness was essential. After amalgamation the new company had a trade monopoly of the whole West. It was also granted the authority to administer justice and local government, and because of its activity the region remained British rather than being taken over by the Americans or the Russians. Yet the result of the negotiations of 1821 turned out to be not so much an amalgamation as an absorption. The old Nor' Westers were soon locked out of the administration, and, as if by design, their achievements were consigned to oblivion for a century. As well, the economic progress of the colony of Canada was temporarily set back by the merger. The fur trade brought tremendous wealth to Montreal. The office of "the concern" had paid out to its employees no less than forty thousand pounds Sterling annually. With the change of management this cash-flow was diverted to Hudson Bay. A loss so important could not fail to be speedily and severely felt.

For Simon himself the amalgamation was catastrophic. By the failure of his Montreal house he was reduced from a rich businessman to a salaried hireling. In a wry little anecdote Marjorie Wilkins Campbell recounts how his brother's descendants were always introduced ceremoniously to the portraits of William and Simon McGillivray. Their guide would say (pointing at William), "That one made the fortune," and (pointing at Simon), "That one lost it!'

In the field of Freemasonry however Simon's achievements are clear and lasting. His effect on the evolution of Canadian Masonry was decisive, simply because he was the most skilled brother ever sent out to head the craft in the colony. Usually the Provincial Grand Master was selected for his local eminence in civil or business affairs, without regard to the depth of his Masonic knowledge. No doubt the system worked well in provinces where Masonry stood on a solid basis. There were enough experienced brethren to maintain regularity, the area was free from disruptive alien interference, and the public distinction of the Provincial Grand Master served to enhance the lustre of the order. In the remote and undeveloped colony of Upper Canada in 1792, the situation was different. William Jarvis, the Provincial Grand Master, was Provincial Secretary and Registrar of Records—and a Mason of one month's standing. The results were calamitous, for there were but few Masons in the province, and they ill-trained; they lay open to the strong Masonic influence of the United States.

Simon McGillivray single-handedly altered the direction in which the Craft was evolving in Canada. Without his intervention modern Masonry there would be entirely different. He unified the warring factions and stopped them from dissipating their energies in pointless rivalry. He regularised the irregular lodges, and caused twenty-one warrants to be issued; thirteen of his lodges are still active.

But the chief consequence of his work lay in the area of ritual, and can the more readily be seen if we look at those rites and regions where he was not active. He had no effect for example on the independent Grand Royal Arch Chapter of Upper Canada. Its practice, of conferring other degrees in addition to the Holy Royal Arch, has been perpetuated all across the country. Again, today in the rest of Canada many craft lodges follow what is called the "Ancient York Rite," which is really an American working derived from pre-Union rituals.

Upper Canada was moving in the same direction until McGillivray arrived. In his report to the Grand Master he speaks of new immigrants who, being "more practised in Masonry than those whom they thus joined, became Instructors, or in other words introduced innovations, which were received the more readily in consequence of the disorganized state of the ruling powers. . . ."

This development was halted, and today virtually all the lodges in Ontario follow the "Canadian Working," derived from the post-Union ritual which was brought to Canada in 1825. Its introduction and diffusion are almost certainly due to McGillivray.

Simon McGillivray was a good man. Even if his achievements hardly match his promise, we may still assume that he was content. In his own sphere he hewed rigidly to the advice that he offered for the Prime Minister in 1832:

> Stick to your principle throughout, and let your administration stand or fall with it. Let others if they like truckle or temporise, but be you firm, and you will either carry your principle through, or retire from the arena with a higher name than that of any who has filled your place before you. And is not that after all the most noble object of ambition?

He retired from the Canadian arena prematurely, but certain memorials of his steadfastness are still with us.

MacLEOD MOORE AND PIKE: TWO SCOTTISH RITE MASONS

[It can't be very often that someone who is not a member of the Ancient and Accepted Scottish Rite is allowed to address one of their assemblies. I had the good fortune to be invited to do so.]

MacLEOD MOORE

An outsider can hardly be expected to know what sort of remarks are best suited for an occasion such as this. Certainly it is proper to congratulate those who have seen new truths and received new degrees today. I'm stronger on facts than I am on inspirational oratory, and as well, perhaps, a word of history is never amiss.

As the philosopher George Santayana once said, "Those who cannot remember the past are condemned to repeat it." And so I propose to speak to you about two men, incredibly important to the Scottish Rite, two men who lived at the same time, and died nearly a century ago.

First is Colonel William James Bury MacLeod Moore—quite a mouthful; MacLeod Moore we shall call him. The name MacLeod was inherited from his great grandmother, and so he should be a distant relative of mine. As nearly as I can tell, he was a seventh cousin of my father.

He belonged to the landed gentry of Ireland, and was born in County Kildare on 4 January 1810. He went to Scotland for his education, and received all three Masonic degrees in Glenkindel Lodge, No 333, Aberdeen on a single evening, 17 August 1827. As he was only seventeen years old at the time, presumably he was a Lewis, the son of a Mason, since in Scotland they could be initiated before they turned twenty-one. He went to Sandhurst Military Academy, and on graduation was commissioned in the British regular forces in the 69th Regiment of Foot. This was his career, and he served in various parts of the world, including the West Indies and Malta.

During these years he joined the Royal Arch and the Knights Templar. He was pensioned out after twenty-one years, and came to North America in 1852, with the title Staff Officer of Out-Pensioners, and the rank of Lieutenant-Colonel. He was still relatively young, just 42, and he spent the rest of his life in Canada.

Whether it was by inheritance or from his military pension, he was a gentleman of leisure, and he turned to Masonry to keep himself occupied. In Kingston, the very year of his arrival, he affiliated with The Ancient St John's Lodge, and The Ancient Frontenac Chapter, and within a few years he was Charter Master of Corinthian Lodge in Ottawa, and Charter First Principal of Carleton Chapter in the same place. At the time that he became active, Masonry in Canada consisted of only the three Craft degrees and the four degrees of the Royal Arch.

The population of Canada was increasing rapidly, and MacLeod Moore recognized the need for more Masonic bodies. He was what I should call a pot-hunter, who joined many concordant orders; some of them he introduced to Canada, such as the Red Cross of Constantine, the Royal Ark Mariners, the Masonic Rosicrucian Society, the Swedenborgian Rite, and the Royal Order of Scotland.

As well, he was active and held high office in others, such as the Cryptic Rite, the Knight Templar Priests, the Novices and Knights of St John the Evangelist in Palestine, the Masonic Order of St Lawrence, and the Ancient and Primitive Rite.

In Kingston MacLeod Moore also found that there had once been a preceptory of Knights Templar, but it had been dormant since 1826, in the aftermath of the Morgan affair. He revived it, under English authority, in 1854, and the same year he received from England the title of Provincial Grand Commander for Canada.

For the next thirty-six years he was the senior presiding officer of Knight Templary here, under various titles as the jurisdiction expanded, and when the independent Sovereign Great Priory was formed in 1884, he was elected Supreme Grand Master for life. This was clearly his main love in Masonry. He wrote and spoke extensively about the background of the order, and about its philosophy. In both England and the United States he was recognized as an authority, and when Henry Leonard Stillson and William James Hughan were putting together their great new *History of the Ancient and Honorable Fraternity of Free and Accepted Masons and Concordant Orders* (1890) they invited MacLeod Moore to contribute a section on the Knights Templar.

In 1863, during the War between the States, he went to New York, and there he received all the Scottish Rite degrees, including even the 33rd.

Not everyone makes it to the top in one trip, and this must testify to the respect in which he was held. At all events, here was a new Order to bring home, and so, in 1867, he applied to the Supreme Council, Northern Masonic Jurisdiction, in the United States, for authority to proceed in introducing the Rite to Canada. His request was properly referred to the Supreme Council for England and Wales, and on 6 May 1868, just 120 years ago today, a dispensation was issued, authorizing him to establish chapters and consistories at London, Hamilton, and Toronto. Later that year he was made an Active Member of the Supreme Council, and Deputy for Ontario and Quebec.

He organized the Moore Sovereign Consistory, named of course for himself, on 10 July 1868, and the Hamilton and London Chapters of the Rose

Croix four days later. After five more months, when he saw the Rite properly established in Canada, he resigned as local Deputy.

He continued to be active in the Rite, and to devote attention as well to other concordant orders. He died in Prescott, Ontario, on 1 September 1890, at the age of eighty. The distinguished historian Reginald Vanderbilt Harris rightly calls him the "Founder of the [Scottish] Rite in Canada."

ALBERT PIKE

We turn now to our other hero. Albert Pike was born in Boston, on 29 December 1809, just 6 days before MacLeod Moore. At the age of 14 he entered Harvard, but had to withdraw, because he ran short of money. He was well trained, literate and articulate, and started out as a school-teacher; he was quite successful and soon became principal of a school near Boston. **First career, educator.**

In 1831, because of problems with the school board, and perhaps also because of a broken heart, Pike left New England for ever. He travelled by stagecoach, steamer, keel-boat, wagon-train, horseback, and finally on foot, through Cincinnati, Nashville, and St Louis, nearly 3000 miles in a round-about route, to the wild lands of the far west. **Second career, explorer.**

Towards year-end he reached Santa Fe, which was still a city in Mexico, and stayed for nine months. Then he joined a party of adventurers heading back east to New Orleans. On the way they met bands of natives, and Pike came to have a great respect for the American Indian. Somehow his party managed to take a wrong turn, and ended up in Arkansas. He decided to stay, and began to write for the local paper. His contributions were so good that, at the age of 23, he was invited to become associate editor of *The Arkansas Advocate*, of Little Rock; a year later he was able to purchase it. **Third career, newspaperman.**

Then Pike took up the study of law by reading legal texts on his own, and when he was 24, he applied to a Justice of the Superior Court for admission to the bar. Judge Lacey recognized his qualities and immediately granted his request, without too searching an examination. Actually, the judge noted ironically that, while someone with a medical diploma could make mistakes and kill people, he'd never heard of anybody being killed by the practice of law. **Fourth career, lawyer.**

According to Harris Elwood Starr, "he became one of the best informed and most capable lawyers of the [American] Southwest," and at the age of 32 he was admitted to practise before the Supreme Court of the United States. He served as advocate for the Indian tribes, the Creeks, Choctaws, and Chickasaws, in their lawsuits against the government over land claims; he finally won them awards totalling four and a half million dollars, which still does not sound bad.

In 1839 he got some poetry published in *Blackwood's Magazine*, a British literary journal; and the editor said that he ought to "take his place in the highest order of his country's poets." **Fifth career, literary man.**

In the Mexican War of 1848 he was commissioned captain of cavalry, and was cited for gallantry at Buena Vista. **Sixth career, soldier.**

He managed to quarrel with his commander, and fought a duel with him, but no blood was shed.

When the American Civil War broke out in April 1861, he was in Southern territory, and was named Brigadier General for the Indian country. According to their treaties, the tribes were not required to fight outside their own territory, but Pike's superior officer ordered him to lead them against the enemy, and so he commanded them at the battle of Pea Ridge, in Arkansas (March 1862). Because he felt that the Indians had been treated unfairly, he resigned his commission in November of 1862, and took no further part in the hostilities, beyond publishing some scathing denunciations of his superiors.

A year and a half later he was named a Justice of the Arkansas Supreme Court. **Seventh career, judge.**

When the Northern troops regained Arkansas in 1864, the commander of the occupation forces was Colonel Thomas Hart Benton, a Past Grand Master of Iowa; he knew that General Pike had a superb Masonic library, and he realized that, with feelings still running high, there was a risk of violence. He therefore placed a cordon of Union troops around Pike's house, to save it from destruction. This was one of the great examples of brotherhood in action during the conflict.

When the war came to an end, in 1865, Pike was indicted in a Federal court, on a charge of inciting Indians to wage war against the government. He fled to Canada, and remained here for several months, until he was granted a presidential amnesty. He moved to Washington in 1868, and spent the rest of his life there, mostly working full time on behalf of Masonry. **Eighth career, professional Mason.**

He died on 2 April 1891, at the age of 81, seven months after MacLeod Moore.

PIKE THE MASON

Next, let us summarize Albert Pike's Masonic activities. He was raised to the Sublime Degree of a Master Mason in Western Star Lodge, No 2, Little Rock, Arkansas, in August 1850, when he was 40. Three months later he was exalted in a Royal Arch Chapter. Within three years he was installed as Master of his lodge, received the Cryptic Degrees, became a Knight Templar, and was chosen Grand High Priest of the Grand Chapter of Arkansas.

On three days in March 1853, he received the 4th to the 32nd Degrees from Dr Albert Mackey, the author of *Mackey's Masonic Encyclopedia*. In

1859 he became Sovereign Grand Commander of the Southern Jurisdiction—eight and a half years after becoming a Mason! Talk about swift progress! He remained Sovereign Grand Commander for over thirty-two years, ruling the Rite with an iron hand, promoting it, and propagating it, and seeing it grow in strength.

He is buried in that magnificent museum and library known as The House of the Temple, in Washington, D.C. In the words of the great Carl Claudy, "He found the Scottish Rite in a cabin and left it in a Temple."

Pike's most lasting services to the Order were in his writings. Two projects were particularly influential. First, soon after joining the Rite he was named to a committee to revise the ceremonies. When he found the ritual, all the parts of it, except for the Rose Croix, were, in his words, "incoherent gabble," "chaotic nonsense," "unintelligible jargon," "worthless trash." "They taught a Mason nothing that he did not know before. Not impressive in any way. No man of intellect and knowledge could regard them, as literary productions, with any respect." In the name of the committee, Pike single-handedly wrote the rituals for the Scottish Rite, Southern Jurisdiction.

His other great work was *Morals and Dogma of The Ancient and Accepted Scottish Rite*, which was first published in 1871. It is an immense volume, of some 860 pages, and consists of lectures and a commentary on the first thirty-two degrees.

PIKE'S LEGACY

Several years ago, some non-Masons contacted the Grand Secretary of every Grand Lodge in the United States, and asked for the names of the most authoritative books on Masonry. Over half of the responses mentioned Pike's *Morals and Dogma*. This has done us great harm, because the people who had asked the question were religious fanatics, and they now had a specific authorized text to show how wicked the Masons were. They have obviously gone through it carefully, and have found much that, when taken out of context, or slightly abbreviated, is damning. A number of such passages were quoted for example in a sermon preached in Toronto by Pastor Ron Carlson of Milwaukee sixteen months ago, and they appear as well in various anti-Masonic pamphlets.

Consider the impact on fundamentalist evangelical Christians of the following quotations from *Morals and Dogma*:

page 219: "Masonry is a *worship* . . ., a . . . religion . . . planted in the heart of universal humanity. . . . The ministers of this religion are all Masons."

and again, page 525: "Masonry . . . sees in Moses, . . . in Confucius and Zoroaster, in Jesus of Nazareth, and in the Arabian Iconoclast [Mohammed], Great Teachers . . ., and . . . no more."

and again, page 745: "The Bible . . . [is] a collection . . . of monstrous absurdities."

Of course it is wrong to treat any book in such a fashion. You cannot approach *Morals and Dogma* in this arbitrary way, any more than you can take Biblical statements out of their context.

Consider the words of Jesus in *Matthew* 10:35: "I am come to set a man at variance against his father, and the daughter against her mother." What would an outsider make of that as an expression of the sanctity of the Christian family? But even apart from this difficulty, there are other problems in citing Pike as the final authority.

The interpretation of almost everything in Masonry is left up to the individual. The symbols mean different things to different people. The experienced craftsman can suggest his own particular view of things to new members, but he cannot, he should not, he must not, tell initiates what they shall believe. It is therefore important for us to say, to all who will listen, that Albert Pike was a great and learned man, who had read much and thought much, but that he does not speak for us as Freemasons.

Because Pike's figure is so much larger than life, and because he did so much for Masonry, there is a tendency to put him on a pedestal. Official publications are effusive and one-sided, and tend to treat his big book as the last word. My own feelings are ambivalent.

Obviously he was endowed with a superb and wide-ranging mind. He was a pretty fair linguist, and could study law-codes in French, Latin, and Spanish; and as well he had picked up a smattering of Greek, Hebrew, and Sanskrit. Beyond this, he was a tireless worker, who read everything and remembered everything he read.

He did not take orders gracefully, and this caused him difficulties both as a teacher and as a soldier; you will recall that he fought with his school board, and he fought with his superior officers in the army. He had a clear sense of his own worth, and had to travel far to get the recognition that he felt was his due.

In my books, anyone who tries out eight different occupations by the time he is fifty, even if he succeeds in all of them, has personal problems. He realized the enduring importance of appearances, and he was an image builder, a *poseur*, in the days before that was fashionable. Many portraits survive, both photographs and paintings, and none of them can be called a candid camera snapshot.

Let me remind you of two of the most familiar images: smouldering black eyes over a black beard, beneath a hood or cowl, like a monk or an Arctic explorer (1850); and musing on the terrestrial globe, like some Biblical patriarch, with a full white beard and long white hair, longer than the fashion, artfully arranged over his shoulders.

In Masonry he moved ahead too quickly, and entered the Rite less than three years after joining the Craft, without ever understanding or appreciating the first three grades. Pike never accepted the fact that the Scottish Rite Degrees were devised in France after 1737, but he continued to imagine that in some way they were descended from primitive Masonry, and preserved the mystical truths of the ancients. In fact, because of his wilder fantasies he is one of those Masons whom I in my more intolerant moments regard as "mystical nuts."

PIKE THE ORATOR

But despite this taint of mysticism, the man was clear sighted. He had a sound instinct for right and wrong, and (in Coil's words) "a profound belief in an all-wise, moral, and beneficent God." And, oh, he could write! He could recognize essential truths on which all good men agree, and express them clearly in such a way they they sound fresh, compelling, and even inspiring; you find yourself listening, and inwardly nodding your head. Denys Page, one of my other heroes, has described this as the ability to add "a glitter of rhetoric round the fringes of the self-evident." Let me give you an example. The Craft ritual tells us "to make a daily advancement in knowledge," "to be careful to perform our allotted task while it is yet day," and "to relieve the distresses and soothe the afflictions of our neighbour." But hear what Pike makes of these obvious injunctions!

We think, at the age of twenty, that life is much too long for that which we have to learn and do; and that there is an almost fabulous distance between our age and that of our Grandfather. But when, at the age of sixty, if we are fortunate enough to reach it, or unfortunate enough, as the case may be, and we halt and look back along the way that we have come, and cast up and try to balance our accounts with Time, we find that we have made Life much too short. We then in our minds deduct from the sum total of our years, the hours that we unnecessarily have spent in sleep; the waking hours each day, during which the surface of the mind's pool has not been stirred or ruffled by a single thought; the days that we have got rid of as we could, to attain some real or fancied object that lay beyond; and the hours misspent in folly and dissipation; and we acknowledge with many a sigh, that we could have learned and done, in half a score of years well spent, more than we *have* learned and done in our forty years of manhood.

To learn and to do! This is the soul's work here below. The soul *grows*, as surely as an oak grows. As the tree takes the air and the particles that float in the air, the dew and the rain, and the food that in the earth lies piled around its roots; and by its mysterious chemistry transmutes them into sap and fibre, into wood and leaf, and flower and fruit, and taste and color and perfume; so the soul drinks in knowledge, and by a divine alchemy changes what it learns into its own substance, and *grows*, with an inherent Force and Power like those which lie hid in the small germ of the acorn.

To sleep little, and to study much; to say little, and to hear and think much; to learn, that we may be able to do; and then to do, earnestly and vigorously, whatever is required by Duty, by the interests of our fellows, our country, and mankind,—these are the duties which Masonry prescribes to its initiates.

These stirring words come from a lecture that Pike gave before the Grand Lodge of Louisiana in 1858, and later incorporated into his commentary on the Fifth Degree, the Perfect Master.

I hear you ask, why is this American Mason important for us here today? Fair question! The original sanction for the Scottish Rite in Canada came from England, true. But the Moore Sovereign Consistory conferred no degrees for almost four years, and then only after our own people were able to obtain copies of the ritual from Albert Pike. That is, the earliest degrees here were given in Pike's words! And with regard to the situation today, I have taken the liberty of consulting Dr Charles Sankey, who knows more about the evolution of the Scottish Rite liturgy than anyone else in Canada. He tells me that substantial amounts of the Ritual as it is used here are still derived from Albert Pike; in particular many of the lectures in the various degrees. He mentions especially the lecture of the 19th Degree, which some of you had the opportunity to hear this morning. Of course I am not entitled to know what is in it, but I am told by those whose judgment I trust that it is magnificent and inspiring, and that it is by Albert Pike.

William James Bury MacLeod Moore, the founder of the Rite in Canada; and Albert Pike, the real founder of the modern Scottish Rite, and the author of much of its ritual. Two names for you to remember. Two men of outstanding ability, who were by no means perfect, but who never stopped working for Masonry, two men (in the words of John Edmund Barss)

> Whose lives were built in wisdom, strength, and beauty,
> Stone upon stone, square-hewn and founded well,
> Who loved the light—who trod the path of duty.
> Greet you well, brethren! Brethren, greet you well!

HIRAMIC MONOLOGUE

[My friend Frederick John Cooper, a distinguished English Mason, Deputy Provincial Grand Master of Devon, full member of Quatuor Coronati Lodge, had a wonderful sense of humor. He wrote the following monologue, and presented it from time to time in English lodges, always with great success. The problem was that it was composed in colloquial English, which is a little bit different from what we're used to on this side of the Atlantic. So Tony Richards and I undertook to translate it into Canadian dialect. I hope it is still intelligible for those who live south of the border. In my judgment it counts as Masonic education. It will make those who listen to it think a bit.]

(A man is sitting at a large table covered with plans and drawings. He has a pair of compasses in his hand, and he is describing an arc on a design. The telephone rings. He takes no notice except to frown. It rings again. Exasperated, he lifts the receiver.)

Hello! Hiram here! **(pause)** Hello, hello! Hiram of Tyre speaking!

No, no, not His Majesty! His Nibs is up in the hills, where it's cool. This is Hiram Abif. Who is this calling?

Adoniram! Great to hear from you! Where are you? What are you up to?

Lebanon! You lucky son of a camel! And in charge of the saw-mill operation too! That's great! No wonder we're getting all the wood-products up to specification! Wish I could say the same about the quarry stuff! No labor problems, I hope?

How many thousand? I know there's a policy of full employment in Lebanon, but that's ridiculous! What are you doing with them all?

One working and ten looking on? Well, that system isn't unique, you know, Adda.

We're moving along all right, I suppose, but I'm getting a lot of trouble over the rationing. I said at the start that this system of giving these young boys a weekly allowance of corn, wine and oil would never work. We supplied them with little hand-mills for the corn, and field ovens for the baking—but they just wouldn't use them. As soon as they got their ration each week, they flogged the corn for the wine—with the predictable result. We got some pretty funny looking ashlars! However, things are better now. We do our own baking, and issue the rations already cooked—but still there's a lot of fiddling going on.

I'm worried to death really. We have this deadline for the opening, but it will be a miracle if everything is ready in time for the Dedication. The trouble is that YOU KNOW WHO can never make up his mind on detail. He's continually changing the plans. Now, after we thought that we had everything under control, he has this brilliant idea about the Memorial Pillars.

That's right, MEMORIAL PILLARS! (pause) You know—the Fire and Cloud and all that jazz!

Well, it was too late to incorporate them into the actual building, and so they'll have to be placed outside the Porchway or Entrance. His idea is to make them out of METAL, as if stone wasn't good enough. There's only one place I know of to cast something that big, and that's down there between Succoth and Zeredatha; you know, in the claygrounds on the bottom land of the Jordan. Transportation is going to be a nightmare, uphill all the way; and just one jolt, and the wretched things'll crack.

No, I haven't a clue who he thinks he's going to get to supervise the casting. Oh, and I forgot to tell you, he wants them formed hollow, with only a hand's breadth of material. And he wants to put Archives in them. (pause) Yes, Archives; scrolls of vellum and parchment and so on. Can you imagine keeping the files in there? Once these young clerks and secretaries get in there and start messing about, they'll be in there all day!

We tried to get the names of the Pillars out of him, so that we could include them in the casting, but he'll only give us the name of one. That's to be named after his great great grandfather. But he's being very coy about the other one. I think he's going to announce it on the day. Probably going to honor one of the officials who take part in the Ceremony. You know how it is, Adda. It's always the fellow who can do a good piece of ritual that gets the honor, not the one who's been doing all the background work. Gawd, I hate this masonic politics!

But my main trouble here is the unreliability of the overseers. Some of them can't even read a blueprint! Do you know, every morning when I get into the office (and that's about the sixth hour), there's a line-up of Fellow-crafts, supposedly overseers, asking me to explain detail that should be obvious to anyone competent. I spend half my time doing work that should be done by the overseers. I tell you, Adda, I'm convinced that if I ever took a day off, the whole Project would be plunged into utter confusion.

Apart from that, the overseers are quite incapable of carrying out the trade-testing. This means that a lot of fair workmen who should be getting trade pay are not receiving any differential—and it's causing a bit of bad feeling. And when the work ends here, and they move on to other jobs, they won't have any evidence of their grade.

As a matter of fact, I had three of them in my office the other day who were very rude to me about the delay in their trade-testing. I promised them faithfully that I would carry out their test today, after the midday break. So we'll have to see about that!

Now, is there anything else on your mind? (**pause**) I don't want to appear rude, but it's almost time for the noon whistle. I like to make a bit of an inspection during the lunch break. Also, Phase One is completed now, you know, and it's cool and peaceful and quiet in there; great view over the valley from the gateways. Not a soul in sight, and it gives me a chance to collect my thoughts. Only moment of quiet I have all day! Then, after a few minutes there, I'll come back here, have a bit of bread and cheese, and maybe a pomegranate, and then I'll be all set for the afternoon.

Oh, yeah, sure! I'm okay. It's just the pressure, the constant pressure. It gets to me! I sometimes feel I don't have much time. . . . I don't have much time. But it'll soon be over with!

Well, it's been nice talking to you! We must get together when you're in town again. Take care now! Good bye!

INDEX